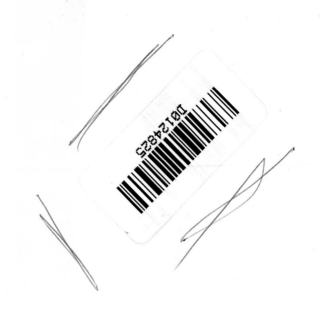

*Giovanni di Paolo, Adoration of the Magi.* c. 1450. National Gallery of Art, Washington, D.C.

# NEW ESSAYS ON THE
# PSYCHOLOGY OF ART

# RUDOLF ARNHEIM

# New Essays

## ON THE

# Psychology of Art

UNIVERSITY OF CALIFORNIA PRESS

Berkeley    Los Angeles    London

University of California Press
Berkeley and Los Angeles, California

University of California Press, Ltd.
London, England

Library of Congress Cataloging in Publication Data

Arnheim, Rudolf.
NEW ESSAYS ON THE PSYCHOLOGY OF ART.

Includes index.
1. Art—Psychology. 2. Visual perception. I. Title.
N71.A675  1986      701'.1'5      85–1062
ISBN 0–520–05553–5
ISBN 0–520–05554–3 (pbk.)

Printed in the United States of America
1  2  3  4  5  6  7  8  9

*To John and Marie Gay*
*Artists and Loyal Companions*

# CONTENTS

# FOREWORD

AFTER THEIR scattered and sometimes inconspicuous first appearances in various periodicals, the essays that follow have returned for a family reunion. This gives them a new lease on life, but it also makes for substantial changes.

Articles in professional journals profit from a permanence of their own, albeit one tied to the time of publication. A discipline grows like a tree, one on which the nature and function of every new twig is determined by its place in the whole. Each contribution justifies itself by addressing a question that the profession has put on the agenda at that time. Later workers along the same line dutifully cite their forerunners by name and date, with the implication that the passage of time equals progress, and that the pioneers of today stand on the shoulders of yesterday's dwarfs. Everybody profits from the safety of the totem pole.

The advantages for organized research are obvious, but the system also imposes constrictions that are not everybody's dish. It has not been mine, partly by temperament and partly because for a lifetime I have barked up more than one tree. Nobody can hope to make sense of a field of study without being aware in a general way of current questions and answers; but I have always drawn my references from wherever I happened to find them, from the wise men of antiquity as readily as from last year's crop of publications; and I have picked my questions from the puzzles I encountered on my own road. In consequence, my papers tend to look like mavericks in the company in which they first appear and reveal their *raison d'être* only when they are allowed to come home and complement one another.

This is particularly true because these papers stand on an expanse of ground that has been parceled out among the professions. It is only natural that at a time when in each field the quantity of facts and theories to be known is increasing fearfully, the psychologists, the art historians, the educators, the therapists, and even the free-wheeling philosophers are driven to cultivating their own gardens. Not that what I have been growing in mine is less particular; it's just that I have tried to breed a specialty from what looks like a bunch of hybrids.

Two decades ago, my faithful and patient publishers issued a first collection of my essays, *Toward a Psychology of Art*. What was then a new specialty is now more nearly established. But rather than attempt to survey the field of the psychology of art systematically, I have continued my forays into particular problematic regions that have stirred my curiosity. Intent simply on clarifying in each case what the topic required, I found myself sharpening certain basic principles and exploring the range of their application. It is in the nature of the present collection of articles, however, that instead of dominating the book as conspicuous headings, these principles are everywhere implied. Their omnipresence surprised me when I gathered the material and looked at it as a whole. It is my hope that these pervasive reappearances of guiding themes will not be seen as so many repetitions, bound to annoy the reader, but as the ties by which the various observations would be fastened together were they given their place in the edifice of thought in which they belong.

What would such an edifice look like? It may be worthwhile here to give a brief sketch of it if the reader will tolerate the abstract formulations that are inevitable in condensed accounts of theory. My main concern continues to be epistemological; that is, I study the mind's cognitive dealings with the world of reality. From the beginning I have been convinced that the dominant instrument of those dealings is sensory perception, especially visual perception. Perception turns out to be not a mechanical recording of the stimuli imposed by the physical world upon the receptor organs of man and animal, but the eminently active and creative grasping of structure. This grasping of structure is accomplished by the kind of field process that has been analyzed in gestalt psychology. It serves to provide the organism not only with an inventory of objects, but primarily with the dynamic expression of shapes, of colors, and of musical tones. Pervasive perceptual expression makes the arts possible.

Cognition through perceptual field processes—that is my way of defining intuition, which functions with the secondary but indispensable help of the intellect. The intellect complements intuitive synopsis with networks of linear chains of concepts. Consequently, its principal tool is verbal language, consisting of chains of signs that stand for abstractions. One can fully acknowledge the importance of language, yet refuse to share the currently fashionable infatuation that burdens words with unreasonable responsibilities. Together, intuition and the intellect produce thinking, which is inseparable from perception in the sciences as well as the arts.

The organizational principles that govern perception in the nervous system and its reflections in consciousness are one of the three constituents of human cognition. The second is the objective structure of physical reality as conveyed to the mind through the senses. To this objective structure art, science, and the common sense of practical life strive to do justice. In emphasizing the objective conditions of reality, I try to counteract the destructive effect of philosophical relativism. In particular I have explored the properties of space and time experiences in their relevance to the arts.

The third constituent of cognitive activity is especially pertinent to the arts. It has to do with the properties of the media through which cognitive experience takes shape. In my analyses of the media I point to the many misunderstandings that arise, especially in the interpretation of nonrealistic artforms, when, for example, traits of pictures deriving from the character of two-dimensional representation are attributed to phenomena observed in natural space. Visual representations are not manipulations of nature but equivalents furnished with the facilities of the medium.

These and other guiding ideas continue to develop as they come and go in the essays of this book. In reviewing the text of the selections, I have kept them as independent of one another as they were in their original conceptions. Yet simply as a result of my dealing with them together, I began to look differently at some of their aspects. This led to many changes, some minor, some substantial. I have never considered my writings immutable, but thought of them more nearly as records of an ongoing struggle for more light. Perhaps instead of being caught in the finality of printed books, such records should be kept on one of those newfangled screens that permit an author to change his mind and his words for the better as long as he is around.

R.A.

*Ann Arbor, Michigan*
*1984*

# Part I

# CONCERNING AN
# ADORATION

No ONE to whom a work of art has truly spoken talks back to it in analytical prose without apprehension. One may feel that art alone has a right to respond to art. If, however, one looks at an actual example—for instance, Rilke's "Fifth Duino Elegy," inspired by Picasso's *Saltimbanques* of 1905—one realizes that a poet or perhaps a musician can indeed evoke some aspects of the experience conveyed by a painting or sculpture, but only in terms of his own poetry or music, not by direct reference to the medium of the original work itself. A poem can pay homage to a picture; but only obliquely can it help the picture speak its own language.

Historians and critics can say many useful things about a painting without any reference to it as a work of art. They can analyze its symbolism, derive its topic from philosophical or theological sources and its form from models of the past; they can also use it as a social document or as the manifestation of a mental attitude. All this, however, can be limited to the picture as a conveyor of factual information and need not relate to its power of transmitting the artist's statement through the expression of form and subject matter. Therefore, many sensitive historians or critics would agree with Hans Sedlmayr when he asserts that such approaches fail to account for factors that can be explained only as artistic qualities (3, p. 37). This amounts to saying that unless the analyst

First published in *Art Education*, vol. 23, no. 8 (November 1970).

has intuitively grasped the aesthetic message of a painting, he cannot hope to deal with it intellectually as a work of art.

We all know those occasional melancholy hours in a museum or gallery when the exhibits hang and stand around, absurdly silent like the discarded costumes of last night's performance. The viewer is not disposed to respond to the "dynamic" qualities of shape and color, and therefore the physical object is duly present and observable, but the work of art is not. Or, to use another example, we know the frustration of trying to convey a painting's perfection and richness so evident to our eyes to a companion who does not see them.

The old-style art teacher who limits himself to pointing out the subject matter; his new-style successor who asks the children how many round shapes or red spots they can find in the picture—neither does much more than encourage the child to look. To make the work come alive is another matter. In order to do so, one must become aware, systematically but intuitively, of the factors of shape and color that carry the visual forces of direction, relation, expression, because these visual forces provide the principal access to the symbolic meaning of art.

What does such a demand amount to in practice? As an illustration I will select one of those paintings to which the average visitor pays little attention, a small *Adoration of the Magi* by Giovanni di Paolo in the National Gallery in Washington (frontispiece). It is the sort of work that connoisseurs of an earlier generation used to discuss with a condescending smile and an easy flourish of language. A critic in 1914 referred to its creator as a "good-natured painter whose pleasant, homely chatter is interspersed at times with delightful song" (1, p. 177).[1] Giovanni di Paolo had passed him by.

Any valid introduction to one work of art is a revelation of art in general, but only when it conveys the shock of greatness. Different works will do this for different people, and therefore the interpreter must make his own choice in the hope that the principles he describes in his examples will be recognized by others in works they prefer.

In the second chapter of Matthew, we read the story as our painter knew it:

When they had heard the king, they departed; and, lo, the star, which they saw in the east, went before them, till it came and stood over where the young child was. When they saw the star, they rejoiced with exceeding great joy. And when they were come into the house, they saw the young child with Mary his

---

[1] Parenthetical references will be found at the end of each essay.

mother and fell down, and worshiped him: and when they had opened their treasures, they presented unto him gifts; gold, and frankincense, and myrrh.

Told in words, the story is full of *when*'s. One thing happens after another in a temporal sequence. In the painting, the members of the cast display the counterpoint between action and stasis: the kings travel and arrive; the star moves and stops; the kings pay their respects while the family in the stable poses at rest. The painting, being neither literature nor theater nor film, is outside time. What it represents is something better than a momentary segment of the story. The painter offers not a snapshot, but an equivalent. He synthesizes all the salient aspects: the pilgrimage, the arrival, the recognition, the homage, and the blessing; and he translates action and stillness into their pictorial counterparts.

Just as the picture does not simply compress the episodes of the story in the time dimension, it does not squeeze the spatial expanse of the story like an accordion. The kings and their retinue sprawl freely over the grounds within the frame of the picture. They are outside the grotto but also indoors. The gospel says Joseph's family was in the house, and astronomically the star must have stood all those many miles above in the sky. But the painter cannot be said to have simply reduced physical height or torn down the front wall of the house. Rather he starts afresh from the surface of the tiny panel and accords to each element the place that makes it visible and defines its function in the whole. He redeploys the total scene within the frontal plane. If our sense of the picture plane, which young children and other innocents possess spontaneously and which the painters of our century have reestablished, is at all intact, we do not experience this frontal display as a constrictive artifice but as natural behavior in two-dimensional space. We are no more aware of flatness than a fish is of water. The invariant conditions of the medium are not explicitly perceived; they are the unnoticed rules of the pictorial game.

A sense of well-being emanates from an arrangement that conforms to the medium. In such an arrangement, every component of the story is spatially free to exist and to act according to its function. Since the story is presented from a particular viewing point, it has an order of graded eminence, with the action in the foreground, the setting of grotto and building behind it, and the landscape in the distant background. This order is not the accidental result of perspective, as it might be reproduced by the camera of a news reporter, but one that is inherent in the logic of the pictorial event itself. The superpositions are not arbitrary. The human figures overlap the setting. The child covers his mother, and Mary covers

Joseph. The kneeling king covers the trough and the ass, and only the hand of the Son of God is permitted to intrude into the halo and forehead of the prostrated leader of the pageant.

The colors help to create order. Red, a strongly advancing color, is reserved for the frontal scene of action. Two main spots of blue serve to unify the broadly unfolded array of figures in a wide leap from the grooms on the left to the seated Madonna on the right. The robes of father, mother, and king hold the Christ child enclosed in the center of a triangular grouping of the three primary colors: yellow, blue, and red.

Such unification is needed because the scene comprises elements of great variety. The story evolves from left to right—the direction in which the sense of sight travels naturally—it makes us arrive with the visitors and run into the family group. The clump of heads of men and horses on the left unravels into a linear sequence, which moves up and down like the notes of a melody. It climbs upward to the standing king, who embodies the height of worldly power, then descends toward the kneeling king and the submissive king—three phases of a unitary "stroboscopic" action—and rises again steeply to the head of the Madonna.

The linear sequence is supplemented by cross-connections. The erect king and the Virgin, in the same range of height, face one another across a gaping cave as the supreme secular and ecclesiastic powers like the Ghibellines and the Guelphs. The outcome of the confrontation is depicted in the act of submission. The worthiest of the three secular rulers deposits his crown at the feet of the Madonna.

The arrangement of the figures in the frontal plane is strongly dynamic. Unlike the musical notes of a score, which signify progressions of varying tension but cannot, simply by their own appearance, generate that tension, the shapes of our Sienese painter's figures are charged with directed energy. The entrance of the horses from behind the scenes and the bunching of the figures on the left must be experienced as events. The group of the three grooms is like a gathering of power, which sends forth, first, the twin pages, then makes a long leap to the upright king. There the movement seems to be braked by sudden, reverent hesitation: the step descending to the kneeling king is shorter, as though contracted. Another long, syncopated leap reaches the head of the bearded elder. Now the sequence of figures clusters again into a group, that of the family, only to fade out in an oblique slide through the heads of the two attendant ladies. Unless this dynamic sequence comes across with musical immediacy, the picture is not working.

Our description implies that formal patterns cannot be separated from subject matter. The diagrams by which interpreters of art like to expose basic compositional patterns can be valid, but only if in the skeleton they reveal the living creature. In our particular example the arrangement of figure shapes is profoundly modified, for example, by the directions in which the persons are looking. Gazing backward at invisible latecomers, two of the grooms indicate that the story comes from beyond the frame. A chorus of faces—pages, kings, animals—is directed toward the family triad, which responds with the opposite orientation. None of this would be comprehensible to a viewer who had never seen a human head. Nor would he perceive the powerful vectors generated by the eyes of the performers. The directed glances of child and mother, which pass beyond the blessing action at their feet and address the broader event as a whole, are compositional axes of prime importance, every bit as active as if they were carried by tangible shapes; and the closed face of Joseph blocks one of the channels of interrelation between the two groups as effectively as a rolled-down shutter.

In a broader sense, every detail of information about the representational content of a picture not only adds to what we know but changes what we see. It is psychologically false to assume that nothing is seen but what stimulates the retinae of the eyes. One need only compare the visual experience of a picture telling a familiar story with, say, a Persian miniature, equally present to the eyes, yet largely elusive if one is ignorant of what is going on. The foolish notion that true art appreciation ignores the subject matter—together with equally restrictive iconological studies, discussing subject matter only—has estranged generations of students from pertinent aesthetic understanding and experience.

It is true, however, that in successful works of art the most evident overall structure tends to symbolize the fundamental theme. The arrangement of Giovanni di Paolo's figures directly conveys the action of visual forces embodying arrival, confrontation, submission. All the descriptive detail of the picture is subsumed in a highly abstract, simple pattern, which makes the work look monumental whether it is seen in a reproduction, on a large screen, or on the tiny original wood panel of 10¼ by 17¾ inches. This compositional device invests the small painting with greatness, both because it achieves complete correspondence and interrelation of content and form and because it presents the plenitude of the visual world in the light of organizing thought.

After noticing the abstractness of the guiding pattern, we are ready to consider the most spectacular compositional feature of the painting, namely, the rock formation of the cave behind the scene of the Adoration.

What matters here is not that these shapes fail to resemble real rocks, but that they contribute a decisive visual theme to the picture. The formation rises from the left in a fugue of rapid, overlapping waves toward the star of Bethlehem, which stands directly above the head of the child. This crescendo of pure form, as "abstract" as a work of modern art, tells the story once more. But here the symbolization goes even beyond that of the visual melody in the foreground figures. It dispenses with the theatrical narration, the acting-out of the intricate relations between worldly and sacred powers. It shows nothing but the onrush from the terrestrial ground to the heights of salvation, represented by the golden light of the star. This elemental and powerful reach, comparable only to an organ prelude, is after all the underlying theme of the whole teeming episode. We now see that the two renderings of the story complement each other. The rising arch of the cave is counterpoised by the dip in the sequence of principal figures; and even the tilted checkerboard of the

*Figure 1.* Giovanni di Paolo, *Adoration of the Magi.* After 1423. Cleveland Museum of Art, Holden Fund.

*Figure* 2. Gentile da Fabriano, *Adoration of the Magi*. 1423.
Uffizi Gallery, Florence.

fields in the background supports with its isometric parallels the dominant drive toward the star.

By now, if the analysis has been at all appropriate, the picture must
have begun to speak. In that case one can, if one wishes, go beyond the
confines of the single work and see it in context. Painted around the
middle of the fifteenth century, when the artist was probably in his fifties,
this mature composition can be compared with his somewhat earlier rendering of the same subject, now in the Cleveland Museum of Art (Figure
1). The Cleveland picture is essentially a copy of Gentile da Fabriano's
celebrated *Adoration of the Magi* (Figure 2), painted in 1423 for Santa
Trinità in Florence and now in the Uffizi; it shows most impressively how
a developing artist, under the impact of a prestigious master, is cramped
in the use of his own imagination. He lacks the consistency of the other
man's style and is yet unable to realize his own. After a look at the Cleveland picture, we see in the Washington *Adoration* the liberation of an
artist who has found himself and therefore can find in his own idiom a
supremely adequate form for the story he wishes to tell. From here, one
can trace the artist's progress further, to the John the Baptist series of the
Chicago Art Institute, considered by some to be Giovanni's highest accomplishment (2).

There are many other avenues, historical, aesthetic, social, one can
pursue from and to Giovanni di Paolo's *Adoration*. But, to emphasize it
again, none of these extensions is truly justified unless the painting has
revealed itself as a work of art in the first place. The experience of art,
provided by one of its great examples, must be the beginning and the end
of all such explorations.

## References

1. Breck, Joseph. "Some Paintings by Giovanni di Paolo." *Art in America*, vol. 2
   (1914), pp. 177ff.
2. Francis, Henry Sayles. "A New Giovanni di Paolo." *Art Quarterly*, vol. 5
   (1942), pp. 313–22.
3. Sedlmayr, Hans. *Kunst und Wahrheit*. Hamburg: Rowohlt, 1958.

# Part II

# THE DOUBLE-EDGED MIND: INTUITION AND THE INTELLECT

I HAVE it on good authority that there are educators who neglect or even despise intuition. They are certain that the only way of acquiring solid and useful knowledge is the way of the intellect, and that the only mental arena in which the intellect can be trained and applied is that of verbal and mathematical language. Furthermore, they are convinced that the principal disciplines of learning are based exclusively on intellectual thought operations, whereas intuition is reserved for the visual and performing arts, poetry, or music. Intuition is considered a mysterious gift, bestowed on an occasional individual by the gods or by heredity and therefore hardly teachable. For the same reason, intuitive work is not expected to require serious mental effort. In consequence, in the planning of school curricula, "solid" programs are distinguished from the light-weight ones, which give undue space to the arts (5).

On the following pages I shall attempt to demonstrate why, to the best of my understanding, this view of learning is psychologically incorrect and educationally harmful. I will show that intuition is not a freakish specialty of clairvoyants and artists but one of the two fundamental and indispensable branches of cognition. The two sustain all operations of productive learning in all fields of knowledge, and they are crippled

First published in Elliot W. Eisner, ed., *Learning the Ways of Knowing*, 85th Yearbook of the National Society for the Study of Education, Chicago, 1985.

without each other's help. Those readers who feel more assured when they can assign a habitat in the physical world to a mental ability may want to locate intuition in the right hemisphere of the brain, installed in quarters as roomy and respectable as those of the intellect in the left brain.

Intuition and the intellect are the two cognitive procedures. By cognition I shall mean here the acquisition of knowledge in the most comprehensive sense of the term. Cognition, thus understood, reaches from the most elementary recording of sensations to the most refined accounting for human experience—from the mere awareness of a fragrance in the air or the flash of a passing bird to a historical study of the causes of the French Revolution or a physiological analysis of the endocrine system in the mammalian body, or perhaps a painter's or musician's conception of discord striving toward harmony.

Traditionally, the acquisition of knowledge was believed to come about through the cooperation of two mental powers: the gathering of raw information by the senses and the processing of that information by the more central mechanisms of the brain. In this view, perceiving was limited to doing the lowly spadework for the more august executives of thought. Even so, it was clear from the beginning that the gathering of perceptual material could not be entirely mechanical. Thinking did not possess the kind of monopoly attributed to it. In my book *Visual Thinking* I showed that perception and thinking cannot function separately (2). The capacities commonly credited to thinking—distinguishing, comparing, singling out, etc.—operate in elementary perception; at the same time all thinking requires a sensory basis. Thus I shall work in what follows with a continuum of cognition that reaches from direct perception to the most theoretical constructs. Once this is agreed upon, I can take the step to which this essay is devoted. I can specify the two procedures that are available to the mind for the acquisition of knowledge, and I can indicate how intimately they depend upon each other.

Intuition and intellect are somewhat complexly related to perception and thinking. Intuition is best defined as one particular property of perception, namely its ability to apprehend directly the effect of an interaction taking place in a field or gestalt situation. Intuition is also limited to perception because in cognition, perception alone operates by field processes. Since, however, perception is nowhere separate from thinking, intuition has a share in every cognitive act, be it more typically perceptual or more like reasoning. And the intellect, too, operates at all levels of cognition.

Our two concepts are by no means new. They pervade the entire history of philosophical psychology and have been variously defined and evaluated. Intuition, in particular, has served as the name of just about every mental ability that was not considered intellectual. It is a sobering experience to read the thirty-one definitions of intuition given by K. W. Wild (24, chap. 12). Even so, a basic distinction has tended to prevail. In the seventeenth century, René Descartes, in his *Rules for the Direction of the Mind*, states that we arrive at an understanding of things by means of two kinds of operation, which he calls intuition and deduction, or, in less technical words, perspicacity and sagacity. "By *intuition* I understand not the fluctuating testimony of the senses nor the misleading judgment that proceeds from the blundering constructions of imagination but the conception which an unclouded and attentive mind gives us so readily and distinctly that we are wholly freed from doubt about that which we understand." Thus, Descartes thinks of intuition not as the less reliable but as the more reliable faculty of the mind. He calls intuition simpler than deduction and therefore more certain. "Thus each individual can mentally have intuition of the fact that he exists and that he thinks; that the triangle is bounded by three lines only, the sphere by a single surface, and so on. Facts of such a kind are far more numerous than many people think, disdaining as they do to direct their attention upon such simple matters." By *deduction*, on the other hand, "we understand all necessary inference from other facts that are known with certainty," i.e., acquired by intuitively gained knowledge (4, Rule III, p. 7).

In our direct experience we are better acquainted with the intellect, for the good reason that intellectual operations tend to consist of chains of logical inferences whose links are often observable in the light of consciousness and clearly distinguishable from one another. The steps of a mathematical proof are an obvious example. Intellectual skill is clearly teachable. Its services can be obtained somewhat like those of a machine; in fact, intellectual operations of high complexity are carried out nowadays by digital computers.[1]

Intuition is much less easily understood because we know it mostly by its achievements, whereas its mode of operation tends to elude awareness. It is like a gift from nowhere and therefore has sometimes been attributed to superhuman inspiration or, more recently, to inborn in-

---

[1] The controversy over whether or not machines can think intelligently would profit from the realization that our present computers can perform the kind of operation needed for intellectual cognition, but not those required for intuition. Hence the limitation of their services for the thinking mind.

stinct. For Plato intuition was the highest level of human wisdom, since it afforded a direct view of the transcendental essences to which all the things of our experience owe their presence. Again in our own century the direct vision of essences (*Wesensschau*) was proclaimed by the phenomenologists of the Husserl School as the royal road to truth (19).

Depending on the style of the times, intellect and intuition were considered collaborators, in need of each other, or rivals, who interfered with each other's effectiveness. This latter conviction, a child of Romanticism, was forcefully proclaimed by Giambattista Vico, whose views are lucidly summarized in Benedetto Croce's history of aesthetics (3). Identifying the intellect with philosophy and intuition with poetry, Vico stated that "metaphysics and poetry are naturally opposed to each other." The former resists the judgment of the senses, the latter makes it its principal directive—a view that leads to the characteristic statement: "La Fantasia tanto è più robusta, quanto è più debole il Raziocinio"; the weaker reasoning, the stronger the power of poetry (21, Book 1, Elements 36).

In the nineteenth century the Romantic split between intuition and intellect led to a conflict between the worshipers of intuition, who viewed the intellectual disciplines of the scientists and logicians with contempt, and the adherents of reason, who deprecated the nonrational character of intuition as "irrational." This harmful controversy between two one-sided conceptions of human cognition is still fully with us. In educational practice, as I mentioned at the outset, intuition has been considered an untrainable specialty of the arts, a luxury, and a recreational respite from the useful skills, which are considered purely intellectual.

It is high time to rescue intuition from its mysterious aura of "poetical" inspiration and to assign it to a precise psychological phenomenon that is badly in need of a name. As I mentioned earlier, intuition is a cognitive capacity reserved to the activity of the senses because it operates by means of field processes, and only sensory perception can supply knowledge through field processes. Consider ordinary vision as an example. Vision starts physiologically with optical stimuli projected upon the many millions of retinal receptors. Those many dot-sized recordings have to be organized in a unified image, which ultimately consists of visual objects of various shape, size, and color, differentially located in space.[2] The rules that control such organization have been extensively

---

[2] There is no need here to discuss the form detectors, those hereditary shortcuts that simplify certain basic types of form perception at the retinal or cerebral level. The fundamental task of visual organization cannot be performed by those special mechanisms.

studied by gestalt psychologists, with the principal finding that vision operates as a field process, meaning that the place and function of each component is determined by the structure as a whole (11, 12). Within this overall structure, which extends across space and time, all components depend upon one another, so that, for example, the color we perceive a certain object to be depends on the colors of its neighbors. By intuition, then, I mean the field or gestalt aspect of perception.

As a rule, the articulation of a perceptual image comes about rapidly and below the level of consciousness. We open our eyes and find the world already given. Only special circumstances make us realize that it takes an intricate process to form an image. When the stimulus situation is complex, unclear, or ambiguous, we consciously struggle for a stable organization, one that defines each part and each relation and so establishes a state of finality. The need for such stable organization is less obvious in daily, practical orientation, for which we commonly need little more than a rough inventory of the relevant features of the environment: Where is the door, and is it open or closed? A much better defined image is needed when we try to see a painting as a work of art. This requires a thorough examination of all the relations constituting the whole, because the components of a work of art do not just label for identification ("This is a horse!"), but through all their visual properties convey the work's meaning. Faced with such a task, the viewer, whether the artist or a beholder, explores the perceptual qualities of weight and directed tension that characterize the various components of the work. The viewer thereby experiences the image as a system of forces, which behave like the constituents of any field of forces, namely, they strive toward a state of equilibrium (1, chap. 9). What concerns us here is that this state of equilibrium is tested, evaluated, and corrected entirely by direct perceptual experience, the way one keeps one's balance on a bicycle by responding to the kinesthetic sensations in one's body.

Needless to say, aesthetic perception is a very special case. I am referring here to the arts only because they offer us the experience of watching intuition at work. In musical composition and performance, too, a striving for balanced order is directly perceived, and the kinesthetic control of the bicycle rider repeats itself in the ways dancers, actors, and acrobats direct the action of their bodies. For that matter, the infant's struggle in learning to stay upright and walk is an early, impressive demonstration of intuitive motor control.

The more elementary visual product of intuitive cognition is the world of defined objects, the distinction between figure and background, the relations between components, and other aspects of perceptual organization. The world as given to us, the world we take for granted, is not simply a ready-made gift, delivered by courtesy of the physical environment. It is the product of complex operations that take place in the nervous system of the observer below the threshold of awareness.

In every individual's development, then, knowledge of the environment and orientation within the environment begin with the intuitive exploration of the perceptually given. This is true for what happens at the beginning of life, and it repeats itself in every act of cognition that takes off from the apprehension of the facts delivered by the senses. To do justice to the complexity of this task, we must add that mental activity is not limited to processing the information received from outside. Cognition comes about biologically as the means by which the organism pursues its goals. Cognition distinguishes desirable from hostile targets and focuses on what is vitally relevant. It singles out what is important and thereby restructures the image in the service of the perceiver's needs. A hunter's world looks different from that of a botanist or poet. The input of these various determining forces, cognitive as well as motivational, is forged into a unified perceptual image by the mental power we call intuition. Thus intuition is the basis of it all; and it therefore deserves all the respect we can offer.

Intuition alone, however, would not get us far enough. It supplies us with the overall structure of a situation and determines the place and function of every component within the whole. But this fundamental gain is achieved at a price. If every given entity risks looking different every time it appears in a different context, generalization becomes difficult or even impossible. Generalization, however, is a mainstay of cognition. It lets us recognize what we have perceived in the past and therefore enables us to apply to the present what we have learned before. It allows for classification, that is, for the grouping of variations under a common heading. It creates generalized concepts; and without these concepts there can be no fruitful cognition. Such operations, based on standardized mental contents, are the domain of the intellect.[3]

There exists, then, a permanent tug-of-war between two basic tendencies in cognition, namely, that of seeing every given situation as a unified whole of interacting forces and that of constituting a world of stable entities whose properties can be known and recognized over time.

[3] At the most elementary biological level these invariant cognitive entities are represented by the sensory stimuli that act as releasers for the reflex reactions of animals. Konrad Lorenz (14) describes them as "simplified diagrams of the adequate situation."

Each of the two tendencies would be hopelessly one-sided without the other. If, for example, we considered the "personality" of some individual as a constant, unaffected by the forces acting upon him or her in a given setting, we would operate with an impoverished template that would not account for the actual behavior of the person in a given situation. If, on the other hand, we could not extricate a constant image of the person from the context of any particular situation, we would be left with repeated samplings of characteristics, each different from the other and none supplying us with the underlying identity of what we are trying to grasp. We all know the experience of children who do not recognize their teachers when they meet them in the grocery store.

In consequence, the two approaches to cognition must cooperate from the beginning and forever. What is primarily given is the totality of the perceptual field, in which interaction is maximal. This field is by no means homogeneous. Normally it is made up of variously connected units, constituting an organization, which in turn modifies the role and character of each unit whenever the context changes. Projected upon this field is the need to identify relevant elements, to isolate them from the context and give them the stability that will let them persist through kaleidoscopic changes of setting. To repeat our example: the figure of the teacher, which in the mind of the younger child is inextricably tied to a particular setting, namely the schoolroom, is eventually conceived as a self-contained entity, defined by certain enduring properties and detachable from any particular setting. This segregation allows the child not only to identify the figure of the teacher independent of the context but also to group various teachers variously met under the common conceptual heading "teacher." Solidified conceptual units of this kind are the material needed for the operations of the intellect.

The foregoing description of the cognitive process is easily misunderstood. It calls for a few explanatory notes. First, the stabilized entities I say are needed for generalization may be confused with the "schemata" that, according to some psychologists, are the necessary premise for the perception of visual objects. I am talking here *not* of primary schemata that make perception possible but of a secondary hardening by which perceptual entities are detached from their intuitive context (16, pp. 20, 23, 63). Second, I am *not* saying that the intellect supplies operations of a higher rank, which in the development of the mind supersedes the more elementary intuitive perception. Rather, in order to avoid the one-sidedness to which I referred before, the parts of the total field must be perceived both as inseparable components of the whole context and as persistent standardized elements. Third, I am *not* saying that the hardening of field components into segregated units removes the cognitive process from the realm of intuition and makes knowledge exclusively a matter of the intellect. On the contrary, the formation of such self-contained units is in itself quite typically an intuitive process, by which various aspects and appearances of an entity and various examples of one and the same class of things are forged into one representative structure. The generalized concept *cat* can come about through the intuitive conformation of many aspects of one cat and of a multitude of cats met in the course of experience. Such intuitive concept formation, which reorganizes and compounds the overall structure of individual instances, differs in principle from the intellectual procedure of traditional logic, which classifies by extirpating common elements.[4]

We are now in a position to clarify the distinction between intuitive and intellectual cognition. The intellect handles connections between standardized units. It is therefore limited to linear relationships. Intellectually, the statement a + b = c is a linear chain of three elements connected by two relations, of which one is a summation, the other an equation. It can be read in either direction, as a statement about the parts or as one about the whole, but in both cases it is sequential. Nor can more than one of the two statements be dealt with at one and the same time.[5] Of course, all pertinent statements can be assembled and arranged in a diagram as to their relative locations, crossings, successions, etc. Such an assembly represents what I have called an intellectual network (2, pp. 233ff.). Although the relations making up such a network can be shown together, the intellect cannot deal with them together but only with one after the other. Hence the basically insoluble problem of describing a field process intellectually: how is one to account in sequence (diachronically) for the components of a totality (gestalt) that operate simultaneously (synchronically)? How, for example, can a historian manage to describe the constellation of events that led to World War II? How can an art theorist describe intellectually the way the components of a painting interact to create the composition of the whole? Propositional language, which consists of linear chains of standardized units, has come

---

[4] The psychologist Max Wertheimer gave much thought to a gestalt logic in which he intended, for example, to develop a theory of concept formation based on structural organization rather than shared elements.

[5] I am referring here not to the ability to perform two or more unrelated activities at the same time, but to carrying out two or more mutually exclusive intellectual activities simultaneously. See Neisser (17).

about as a product of the intellect; but while language suits the needs of the intellect perfectly, it has a desperate time dealing with field processes, with images, with physical or social constellations, with the weather or a human personality, with works of art, poetry, and music.

How does verbal language tackle the problem of dealing with synoptic structures in a linear medium? The problem can be solved because language, though verbally linear, evokes referents that can be images and are therefore subject to intuitive synthesis. A line of poetry, picked at random, will make the point: "Though the names of their weed-grown stones are rained away" (20). As the mind of the reader or listener is led along the chain of words, the words evoke their referents, which organize the unitary image of the mossy gravestones with their eroded names. Through the translation of words into images, the intellectual chain of items is returned to the intuitive conception that inspired the verbal statement in the first place. Needless to say, this translation of words into images is no privilege of poetry, but is equally indispensable when someone wishes to understand, by means of a verbal description, the flow chart of a business organization or the endocrine system of the human body. The words do their best to supply the pieces of an appropriate image, and the image supplies an intuitive synopsis of the overall structure.

Synopsis is not the only indispensable condition for the understanding of an organized whole. Equally important is structural hierarchy. We must be able to see where in such a whole any particular component is located. Does it stand on top or at the bottom, in the center or on the periphery? Is it unique or coordinated with many others? (22). The intellect can arrive at the answer to such questions by ascertaining the linear relations between single items, adding them up, patching all the connections together into a comprehensive network, and finally drawing a conclusion. Intuition complements this process by grasping the whole structure in simultaneity and seeing each component in its place in the total hierarchy. A simple example will illustrate the difference. A quick glance at Figure 3 reveals the hierarchy of the row of squares synoptically: one of the squares is at the top, another at the bottom, while the others dwell, each in its place, in between. The unaided intellect would have to proceed link by link, defining the height of each element with regard to that of its neighbors. From the sum of these linear connections the intellect could derive the pattern as a whole, the way a blind man explores the shape of an object with a stick. That would be the price to be paid if productive thinking were to forgo the help of intuition.

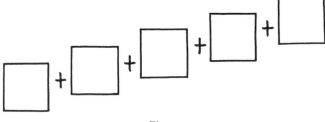

*Figure 3.*

At this point in our study, some practical examples will serve to illustrate the indispensable cooperation of intuition and intellect. Let us assume that a high school class is studying the geography and history of Sicily. The teacher and the textbook furnish a number of solid facts. Sicily, an island in the Mediterranean, belongs to the Republic of Italy, from whose mainland it is separated by the Straits of Messina. A map shows where the island can be found. The pupils learn about its size, its population, its agriculture, its volcanoes. They are given a list of the political powers that occupied it in succession: the Greeks, the Romans, the Saracens, the Normans, the Germans, the French. These facts, interesting or not, are unlikely to stay in the students' memory unless they are linked to a guiding theme that unites and organizes them and yields the live experience of a dynamic presence. Such a theme is best provided by an image, in our example by the puzzling contradiction between two images. One of them derives from a map of Italy, showing the sturdy boot of the long promontory, to whose toe the island of Sicily is lightly attached like an appendix, a mere afterthought. It does not seem to belong. The part of Italy farthest from Central Europe, to which Italy is tied culturally, politically, and economically, the island on this map provides the students' intuition with an unforgettable image, readily related to the neglect and isolation to which Sicily has been subjected by the "real" Italy and its government.

But there is another image. This one focuses on the Mediterranean, the breeding ground of Western culture, the busy basin formed by the East and the West, Islam and Christendom, the European North and the African South. This second map, too, shows Sicily, but this time not as a negligible appendix. Rather it is now located close to the center of the cultural context. When the students turn from the first map to the second, they experience what in the psychology of problem solving is called the restructuring of a visual situation. The island moves from its inferior position at the outskirts of the European continent to the very center of the entire Western world, geographically suited to being the seat of its ruler. And under the impact of this intuitive revelation, teacher and students can now remember that for a few momentous years around 1200, Palermo was in fact the capital of the West, the throne of Emperor Frederick II, that cosmopolitan genius who spoke all the languages and united in his mind the spirit of the North and the South, Christianity and Islam. No reasonably sensitive learner will fail to realize the tragic contrast in Sicily's history between what the island seemed predestined to be and what it became when the center of the Western world shifted from the Mediterranean to Northern Europe. This intuitive apprehension of geographic structure will make history come alive with an immediacy that could hardly be matched by a mere combinative listing of individual facts and relations.[6]

Not all geographical maps are so accommodating as to reflect striking political or cultural situations through visual symbolism; but in any field of study and for any purpose, images are available that offer an intuitive grasp of the cognitive situation, be they diagrams or metaphors, photographs, cartoons, or rituals; and it is easy to show in every practical case that such intuitive apprehension of the total situation is not just an enjoyable illustration but an essential foundation for the total cognitive process.

I will now cite an example from a field that is considered the very prototype of knowledge acquired through the intellectual method of sequential progression, namely, the mathematical proof. The mathematician starts from a problem and proceeds by uncovering partial relationships, each one accredited by intuitive evidence or by a previously supplied proof and each one leading logically to the next link in the chain, until the last one provides the *demonstrandum*. Every proof traces its authority directly or indirectly back to the axioms, and at least in the original Euclidian sense axioms are facts of self-evident intuition. We are reminded of Descartes's assertion that "mankind has no road towards certain knowledge open to us, save those of self-evident intuition and necessary deduction" (4, Rule XII). Descartes also maintained that any intuited proposition "must be grasped in its totality at the same time and not successively." This points to a serious difficulty arising in sequential

---

[6]Allan K. Henrikson (9) has shown in important papers that the visual organization of world maps in the minds of policy makers can have a fundamental influence on political strategy. It makes all the difference, for example, whether the North Atlantic is viewed as a lake that unifies America and Europe or as a divider that confines the Western Hemisphere to a map of its own, separate from the map of Europe.

demonstration. Each link of the chain, although it may be intuitively evident in itself, is self-contained and structurally separate from its neighbors, so that the sequence looks more like a freight train than a melody. The student manages to understand each single fact in and by itself but finds it connected to the next by a mere coupler. The rationale of the sequence passes him by, and it is for this reason that Schopenhauer compared Euclidian proofs to conjurers' tricks. "Almost always truth enters by the backdoor in deriving *per accidens* from some secondary circumstance." He refers specifically to the auxiliary lines commonly used to prove the Pythagorean theorem (18, Book 1, sec. 15).

The familiar Pythagorean figure is beautiful in the sense that it clearly presents to the eyes the relation to be explored: the triangle in the center, with the three squares attached to its sides (Figure 4a). This figure, which represents the problem-solving situation, must be present in the student's mind and must remain directly related to each step of the operation if the student is to stay in touch with what is going on. Instead the very opposite takes place. The three commonly used auxiliary lines smash the structure of the problem situation like a brick thrown through a window; or perhaps it would be more appropriate to say that they scratch out the pattern on which the student is supposed to work (Figure 4b). Through the introduction of the auxiliary lines, each side of the right-angled triangle is perversely united with one side of a square to form the roof of a new triangle, which works against the grain of the Pythagorean pattern. Under the influence of these new, paradoxical shapes the original pattern vanishes from the scene, only to reemerge from the conjurer's bag unexpectedly at the end of the demonstration. The proof is ingenious but ugly.

This violation of the conditions that favor intuition may be unavoidable, but the teacher should be aware of the educational price exacted by a one-sided reliance on intellectual sequence. Actually there are ways of demonstrating the Pythagorean theorem by means of a single, coherent switch of the configuration. Let us arrange four equal triangles in the square of Figure 5a. The large square thereby created in the center is the one described on the hypotenuse. If we cut the four triangles out of cardboard, we can easily rearrange them as shown in Figure 5b. The two squares that are now created by our four triangles are obviously the ones described on the other two sides of the triangle; and it is also clear that the space occupied by the two smaller squares is equivalent to that of the larger square. The Pythagorean theorem has been made directly plausible to the eyes.

Here, too, a restructuring has transformed the initial problem situation, but the rearrangement refers to the structure as a whole and keeps

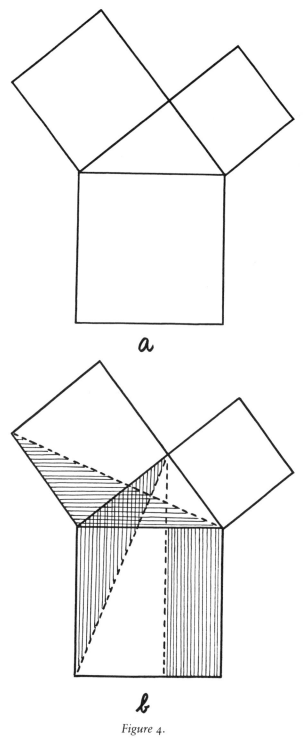

*a*

*b*

Figure 4.

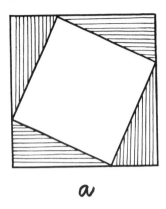
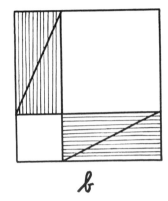

*a*                    *b*

*Figure 5.*

the original pattern directly discernible in the new one so that the comparison between them can be accomplished by direct intuition. This is what mathematicians call a "beautiful" proof. ("The mathematician's patterns, like the painter's or the poet's, must be *beautiful*," writes G. H. Hardy; "the ideas, like the colors or the words, must fit together in a harmonious way. Beauty is the first test; there is no permanent place in the world for ugly mathematics"; 8, p. 85.)

One reason why intuition has been treated with suspicion by those who believe that knowledge should be acquired only by intellectual means is, as I observed earlier, the way in which the results of intuition seem to fall from the skies like a gift of the gods or of inspiration. Now add to this the misleading belief that when a situation is apprehended as a whole it comes across as an indivisible unity, a holistic totality, an all-or-nothing like a flash of light or a mere feeling. According to this belief, intuitive insight is not accessible to analysis, nor does it require it. Thus, Leibniz in his *Nouveaux Essais* offers the example of a polygon with 1,000 edges (13, Book 2, chap. 29). Intellectually one can discover in such a figure all sorts of properties; but intuitively one cannot distinguish it from a polygon with 999 edges. Leibniz calls this sort of image *confused*, in the original Latin sense of the term; that is, all elements are fused and mingled together in an indivisible whole. Even so, he refers to porters or carriers who can tell the weight of a load to the exact pound. This ability is practically useful, and it is based on a *clear* image. But such an image, says Leibniz, although clear, is *confused* rather than *distinct* because it reveals "neither the nature nor the properties" of the object. Obviously, intuition would be of little cognitive value if it did suffer from this limitation.

But does it? Kant, in his *Anthropology*, objected to Leibniz's assertion that perception (*Sinnlichkeit*) is distinguished from intellect merely by a deficiency, namely a lack of distinctness in the apprehension of the parts (10, Book 1, chap. 1). He retorts that perception "is something thoroughly positive and an indispensable addition to the intellect, if insight is to be obtained." To be sure, certain acts of recognition or description are based on nothing but the most generic characteristics of the object. We tell from a distance, This is a helicopter, a goldfinch, a painting by Matisse! And an artist can render a human figure by the simplest of shapes. In such cases the lack of detailed structure is not due to a deficiency of intuitive cognition but to the benign principle of parsimony that governs recognition and representation. It is a virtue rather than a fault that cognition refuses to record a perceptual situation with the mechanical completeness of a photograph. Rather, the structural level of the image is geared intelligently to the purpose of the cognitive act. For the mere distinction between two objects it is helpful to limit the observation to the most pertinent characteristics—a principle that, needless to say, holds for the intellect as much as for intuition. When the task requires it, however, intuitive perception can be every bit as detailed and rigorous as that of the intellect.

No unprejudiced observer will overlook the articulate structure of intuited images if he as much as looks at the world around him. What could be richer and more precise, what more clearly distinct, than the array of visual objects that faces us at any moment? The psychologist W. R. Garner is easily misunderstood when in his article "The Analysis of Unanalyzed Perceptions" he writes:

Thus I want to accept the fact that a great deal of perception involves a complete lack of analysis by the perceiving organism, that forms are perceived as unitary wholes, that attributes may be perceived as integral under some circumstances, and that such stimulus properties as good figure, symmetry, rhythm, and even motion are perceived in a totally nonanalytic way. At the same time I want to argue that for us as scienti‑s, each of these holistic or unanalyzed phenomena is capable of the kind of careful and constructive analysis that allows us to come to understand the true nature of the phenomena under study. (6, p. 120)

When Garner describes intuitive images as unanalyzable, he may seem to be committing the traditional error of denying that integrated wholes possess structure, whereas all he wants to do is to distinguish the intuitive perception of structural organization from the specifically intellectual procedure of isolating the components of a whole and the relations between them.

The distinction is clear and useful, but it seems to me most important to avoid the suggestion that the perceptions of what Garner calls the "ordinary person" are entirely intuitive whereas the scientist's procedure relies solely on intellectual analysis. If this were true, the configural factors, which determine the character of any field situation, would be ignored by the scientist when he constructs his network of conceptual elements—a procedure whose inadequacy has been so strikingly demonstrated by the gestalt psychologists. Actually, every successful scientific investigation of a field process begins with an intuitive grasp of the configuration to be accounted for, and the intellectual network of elements and relations must endeavor, by constant matching, to approach as closely as possible the structure of that configuration. On the other hand, ordinary perception is so thoroughly composed of well-defined parts that one can hardly indicate the moment at which some such elements are segregated from the context and subjected to intellectual analysis. As a simple example take our conception of causality. "When we infer effects from causes," writes David Hume in his *Treatise of Human Nature*, "we must establish the existence of these causes; which we have only two ways of doing, either by an immediate perception of our memory or senses, or by an inference from other causes" (part 1, sec. 4). Take a red billiard ball hitting a white one and setting it in motion. Intuitively we observe two clearly distinct units, inseparably conjoined by a transfer of power from the red component of the process to the white (15). When this phenomenon is accounted for by intellectual analysis, it is reduced to two units in temporal conjunction; and perhaps a force transferring energy is added as a connecting link, a third element, to take care of the intuitively perceived act of causation.[7]

What are we to make of all this? We recognize that practically all the mental and physical topics we wish to study, to teach, to learn about, are field or gestalt processes. This is true for biology, physiology, psychology, and the arts, for the social sciences and a good deal of natural science as well. These processes range all the way from the theoretical extreme of total interaction to the opposite limiting case of totally independent sums of parts. Typically the configural context is interspersed with "petrified" elements, which act as constraints because they are not influenced by the structure of the whole. Examples of such "one-way causation," as Kon-

---

[7]I cannot concern myself here with the truth value of propositions and perceptions. Intuitive perception can tell the truth about the physical situations on which it reports, or, as in optical illusions, it can be unreliable. Similarly, intellectual analysis may do more or less justice to the psychological or physical facts to which it refers.

rad Lorenz calls it, would be, within limits, the effect of skeletal bones upon the dynamics of muscles and tendons or the constraints of the Articles of the Constitution upon the pushes and pulls of our nation's history (14, p. 158). A game of chess is understood as an intuitive configuration within which the properties of each piece are invariable. Similarly, relations between subwholes range from the extreme of total absence of subdivision in the whole to almost total lack of interaction between the parts.

To accommodate this variety of structures the human mind is equipped with two cognitive procedures, intuitive perception and intellectual analysis. These two abilities are equally valuable and equally indispensable. Neither is unique to particular human activities; they are both common to all of them. Intuition is privileged to perceive the overall structure of configurations. Intellectual analysis serves to abstract the character of entities and events from individual contexts and defines them "as such." Intuition and intellect do not operate separately but in almost every case require each other's cooperation. In education, to neglect the one in favor of the other or to keep them apart cannot but cripple the minds we are trying to nurture.

## References

1. Arnheim, Rudolf. *Art and Visual Perception.* New version. Berkeley and Los Angeles: University of California Press, 1974.
2. ———. *Visual Thinking.* Berkeley and Los Angeles: University of California Press, 1967.
3. Croce, Benedetto. *Aesthetic as Science of Expression and General Linguistic.* New York: Noonday, 1953.
4. Descartes, René. "Rules for the Direction of the Mind." In *Philosophical Works of Descartes.* New York: Dover, 1955.
5. Eisner, Elliot W. *Cognition and Curriculum.* New York: Longman, 1982.
6. Garner, W. R. "The Analysis of Unanalyzed Perceptions." In Kubovy and Pomerantz (12).
7. Gottmann, Jean, ed. *Center and Periphery: Spatial Variation in Politics.* Beverly Hills, Calif.: Sage Publications, 1980.
8. Hardy, G. H. *A Mathematician's Apology.* Cambridge: Cambridge University Press, 1967.
9. Henrikson, Allan K. "America's Changing Place in the World: From Periphery to Center." In Gottman (7).
10. Kant, Immanuel. *Anthropology from a Pragmatic Point of View.*
11. Köhler, Wolfgang. *Gestalt Psychology.* New York: Liveright, 1947.
12. Kubovy, Michael, and James B. Pomerantz, eds. *Perceptual Organization.* Hillsdale, N.J.: Erlbaum, 1981.

13. Leibniz, Gottfried Wilhelm. *New Essays Concerning Human Understanding*.
14. Lorenz, Konrad. *The Role of Gestalt Perception in Animal and Human Behavior*. In Whyte (23).
15. Michotte, Albert. *The Perception of Causality*. New York: Basic Books, 1963.
16. Neisser, Ulric. *Cognition and Reality*. San Francisco: Freeman, 1976.
17. ———. "The Multiplicity of Thought." *British Journal of Psychology*, vol. 54 (1963).
18. Schopenhauer, Arthur. *Die Welt als Wille und Vorstellung*.
19. Thévenaz, Pierre. *What Is Phenomenology?* Chicago: Quadrangle, 1962.
20. Thomas, Dylan. "In the White Giant's Thigh." In *In Country Sleep*. New York: New Directions, 1952.
21. Vico, Giambattista. *The New Science*. Ithaca, N.Y.: Cornell University Press, 1948.
22. Wertheimer, Max. "A Girl Describes Her Office." In *Productive Thinking*. Chicago: University of Chicago Press, 1982.
23. Whyte, Lancelot L., ed. *Aspects of Form*. Bloomington: Indiana University Press, 1951.
24. Wild, K. W. *Intuition*. Cambridge: Cambridge University Press, 1938.

# MAX WERTHEIMER AND
# GESTALT PSYCHOLOGY

MAX WERTHEIMER arrived on the scene of American psychology in the early 1930s as a conspicuous and disquieting figure. It was a time when a fundamental change in attitude and outlook had become apparent in a new generation of psychologists. Reassured by the precision of their equipment, their measurements, and their formulae, many of these new scientific practitioners seemed unimpressed by the apparent endlessness of their task, the complexity of nature, the delicacy of organic functioning, the awe-inspiring recesses of the mind. Businesslike and matter-of-fact, they were trained to go about their work by asking some particular question, selected in such a way as to fit the measurable dimensions of controllable situations; they did the experiments, calculated the results, published them, and proceeded to the next job. Not that they were insensitive to the charm and fascination of the oldtimers among their colleagues, whose faces were etched with the haunting awareness of the unfathomable. They saw the quiet smile that greeted their confident assertions, and they listened, as children will to fairy tales, when the head of the department quoted from the classics. They sensed that here was something strangely beautiful, but related to their own work in only a quaint, outdated fashion, something they were lacking but that had to be saved for retirement musings.

Developed from its first publication in *Salmagundi* 1969/70, which was reprinted in *The Legacy of the German Refugee Intellectuals*, ed. Robert Boyers (New York: Schocken, 1972).

*Figure 6.* Max Wertheimer at the New School,
May 1942. Drawing by R.A.

Hence the powerful effect of Max Wertheimer on the few hundred students and colleagues who, during his decade in America, came in direct contact with him. Here was a man who called for a fuller vision and less mechanical procedure not as a dream but as a technical research requirement, to be applied immediately and in practice. Romantic and frail, with the nonconformist's Nietzsche moustache, Wertheimer lectured in his improvised English at the Graduate Faculty of the New School for Social Research in New York City. He described aspects of the mind that induced a shock of recognition in his listeners but seemed beyond the grasp of accepted procedure. And while the vision was humane and gentle, its application demanded an unexpected discipline, a stringency of argument and proof for which the students were not trained. Hence their devotion, irritation, despair.

Wertheimer was one of the three principal proponents of gestalt psychology who had come to the United States. Owing to their presence in this country, the strange-sounding name of the new doctrine became familiar to American psychologists; but to what extent were theory and practice influenced by the new ideas? Wolfgang Köhler, who went to

Swarthmore, was well known for his experiments on the intelligence of chimpanzees. But while his results were recognized as substantial, his explanatory concepts—"insight," for example—sounded uncomfortable, and there was little realization that his special study of the psychology of problem solving was part of a totally new and comprehensive approach to psychology in general. Köhler's early book on gestalten in physics has never been translated, and his later experiments on the figural aftereffect in visual perception were again received as an interesting specialty without broader implications. The third man of the gestalt triumvirate, Kurt Koffka of Smith College, wrote the standard treatise on gestalt psychology, a book densely packed with valuable facts and ideas but so hard on the reader that it served philosophers better than psychologists.

What do psychology textbooks say about gestalt psychology, about Wertheimer? Students learn that, according to gestalt theory, a whole is more than or different from the sum of its parts—an innocuous-sounding statement, unlikely to impress them as revolutionary or practically relevant. Of Wertheimer they read that he performed early experiments on illusory movement and on the perception of visual shape. But again, as in the case of Köhler, the connection of these studies to the basic gestalt thesis is not spelled out.

The textbooks describe Wertheimer's rules of perceptual grouping: when a person looks at an assortment of shapes, they will be seen as related to one another if they are similar in size or shape or color or some other perceptual trait. Such an assemblage of elements does not seem to exemplify a gestalt process, and in fact the rules of grouping constitute only the first part of a paper in which Wertheimer moved from a more traditional approach to the revolutionary switch, showing that a perceptual pattern cannot be accounted for merely *from below*, that is, by tracing the relations between elements, as the rules of grouping do. Such an account requires an approach *from above*: only by describing the overall structure of the pattern can one determine the place and function of each part and the nature of its relations to other parts. This reversal of the customary scientific approach, calling for totally different methods, is generally omitted from what students are told about Wertheimer's study of shape perception.

However piecemeal and preliminary the rules of perceptual grouping are, they can be shown to involve the basic characteristic of the gestalt attitude, namely, a respect for the inherent nature of the situation confronting the observer. In Wertheimer's view, the rules of grouping are not arbitrarily imposed by the perceiver upon an incoherent collection of shapes. Rather, the constellation of the elements themselves, their own objective properties, influence the groupings made by the observer's mind.

This respect for the structure of the physical world as it impinges upon the nervous system has been stressed by gestalt psychologists in conscious opposition to the subjectivism of British empiricist philosophy, on which the training of most American psychologists is based. According to that tradition, the sensory stimulus material by which a human being or animal is informed about the outer world is in itself amorphous, an accumulation of elements. It is the recipient mind that ties them together by connections established in the past. In consequence, association by frequent coincidence in subjective time and space became the dominant explanatory principle of experimental psychology in this country.

Needless to say, the two antagonistic theories were based on opposite world views: the one, proudly asserting the dominion of the individual's views and judgments over the environment; the other, distinctly irritated by such egocentrism, affirming that it was man's task to find his own humble place in the world and to take the cues for his conduct and comprehension from the order of that world. In the social realm, gestalt theory demanded of the citizen that he derive his rights and duties from the objectively ascertained functions and needs of society. Here, then, the deeply ingrained individualism of the Anglo-Saxon tradition, the suspicion of central power and planning from above, was implicitly challenged by a scientific approach that, in moments of bad temper, was even accused of being totalitarian.

One of Wertheimer's favorite epithets of defiance was the word "blind." It referred to self-centered, prejudiced, insensitive behavior, a lack of openness to the "requirements" of the situation—another key term of gestalt theory. This is the common theme of Wertheimer's seemingly disparate interests, his own explorations of perceptual structure and productive thinking, and the research problems his disciples worked on at the New School. Of these, I will give three examples. One of his assistants, Solomon E. Asch, developed a social psychology intended to replace the dichotomy of individual and group with an integrated view of social interaction and its intrinsic dynamics. A Chinese student, Gwan-Yuen Li, explored the Taoist concept of non-willing (*wu-wei*) as a philosophical doctrine to show how man may bring himself into accord with the powers inherent in the cosmos and society. A third disciple, Abraham S. Luchins, demonstrated in an experimental study on rigidity how a pre-established mental set prevents a person from freely searching a problem situation for a solution suggested by the particular conditions of that situation.

Wertheimer himself devoted several of his last papers to philosophical discussions of ethics, values, freedom, and democracy, pointing in each case to the difference between willful, personal preference and the objective requirements of the situation. These objective components, however, are not to be sought only outside, in the physical world, but also in the physiological and mental functioning within each person. The nervous system and consciousness, as a part of man's world, make their own contributions and have their own requirements—not to be confused with the merely subjective inclinations of the individual. For example, the way in which a certain visual pattern is seen depends (a) on the stimulus configuration and (b) on the formative tendencies of the nervous system, as distinguished from the effects of the particular observer's interests, past experience, or capricious choice.

One senses here an impatience with individual differences, which is indeed characteristic of gestalt psychologists. This elicited no protest from behaviorists, but it tended to disappoint those American psychologists who concentrated on the genetic, social, and clinical aspects of human personality, with a strong practical emphasis on the character and needs of the individual person. Gestalt psychology was largely concerned with "human nature"—man as he perceives, man as he grows, man as he comprehends. Wertheimer approached psychology as a pure scientist, interested in the laws of general functioning, and at the same time like a poet, who speaks of mankind.

It will be seen that the primary impulse of Wertheimer's psychology was a respect for nature, human as well as organic and inanimate. From this respect derived his protest against the "atomistic" method, that is, the dissection of integrated entities, and against the pretension of constructing a whole from the summation of its parts. Only when these neat, convenient methods of analysis were put aside did the entities of nature reveal that they were not amorphous, but possessed a structure of their own, inherent dynamic tendencies, and indeed an objective beauty. Thus the "law of the good gestalt" was formulated by Wertheimer in opposition to the doctrine of subjective association.

The basic gestalt law describes a striving, inherent in physical and psychical entities, toward the simplest, most regular, most symmetrical structure attainable in a given situation. This tendency has been demonstrated most clearly in visual perception, but it also shows up as the drive toward tension reduction in motivation. In the thinking of gestalt psychologists, this fundamental bent of the mind reflects a tendency equally operative in the nervous system. It also holds for the field processes of physics, as Köhler has pointed out. Historically it relates to the law of entropy in thermodynamics, although this affinity is not apparent when the gestalt law is described as a tendency toward order and the entropy principle as one toward disorder.

As a law of nature, the striving toward a "good gestalt" was first of all a matter of observed fact; but there were also distinct advantages to the state of maximum order in a system. For example, in visual perception, once the simplest available version of a pattern was apprehended, it appeared more stable, made more sense, could be handled more readily. Similarly, a state of balanced order made for better functioning in a human mind, a team, a society. It was this sort of value to which Max Wertheimer as a person was passionately attached. He found in nature the tendency toward balance, order, goodness. He found it in the basic impulses of man, wherever they were not disturbed by culturally inflicted distortions and by unproductive cerebral complications. Man was basically well organized and therefore good (i.e., in proper shape for adequate functioning) because good organization was the state to which all natural systems aspired. For this reason, Wertheimer disliked persons who relished the trickeries and intricacies of sophisticated brains, and he bitterly inveighed against those philosophers and psychologists who proclaimed that selfish indulgence and destructiveness were the mainsprings of human nature. His aversion to psychoanalysis was clearly imbued with personal feelings, although it may be said that in some ways Freud and Wertheimer pursued similar goals, the one wishing to straighten out the deflections of instinctual resources in order to impose a realm of reason, the other endeavoring to restore in his fellow men their innate but badly mismanaged sense of harmonious functioning.

Wertheimer's pronouncements as a psychologist, then, were inspired by an attitude of optimism and trust, adopted as a creed and constantly expressed in his teaching. He insisted that the things of this world are basically the way they appear, that outside and inside, surface and core, correspond to each other, and that therefore the senses can be relied upon to report the truth, if only the weeds of secondary complication and distortion are cleared away. Hence his love for music and art, where the wisdom of the senses rules by definition.

I remember witnessing, in the 1940s at Wertheimer's home in New Rochelle, New York, a heated altercation between him and one of his old friends, the art historian Paul Frankl. Frankl had maintained, quite correctly, that to understand the composition of a typical Western painting one has to consider its projection upon the frontal plane. This assertion enraged Wertheimer, who needed to believe that nothing but the natural perception of three-dimensional depth occurs in unspoiled human beings. To pretend that instead of seeing the world naively as it is, people paid attention also to an unnatural optical projection was something approaching a slur on human nature. This angry response resembled Goethe's attack on Newton's discovery that white light, in contradiction to what the eyes perceive, comprises the colors of the spectrum.

There was implicit in Wertheimer's thinking the image of an ideal human being, a type familiar to us from the European literary tradition of Parsifal, Simplicissimus, Candide, Prince Myshkin, the good soldier Schweik—an unassuming hero whose childlike and spontaneous innocence penetrates the crust, reveals the core, embarrasses, amuses, and appeals to a hidden decency. In an essay on the nature of freedom ("A Story of Three Days"), Wertheimer wrote:

What differences! In the way a man faces a counterargument, faces new facts! There are men who face them freely, openmindedly, frankly, dealing honestly with them, taking them duly into account. Others are not able to do so at all: they somehow remain blind, rigid; they stick to their axioms, unable to face the arguments, the facts; or, if they do, it is to avoid or to get rid of them by some means—they are incapable of looking them squarely in the face. They cannot deal with them as free men; they are narrowed and enslaved by their position.

Inevitably there were those who reacted to his message as did Dostoevsky's Aglaia Ivanovna when she filed Prince Myshkin's letter in her copy of *Don Quixote*.

And yet, Max Wertheimer was anything but a dreamer. His spiritual ancestors were Spinoza and Goethe. Spinozistic was the notion that order and wisdom are not imposed upon nature from without but are inherent in nature itself; of great influence also was Spinoza's idea that mental and physical existence are aspects of one and the same reality and therefore reflections of each other. With Goethe, Wertheimer shared the belief in the unity of percept and concept, of observation and idea, of poetical insight and scientific scrutiny, and like Goethe he prided himself on his devotion to untiring experimentation.

He often developed his argument *more geometrico*, in Spinoza's geometrical manner; he liked algebraic formulae, and he filled his study with piles of notes that he intended to reduce to the sparest expression. Responsibility for the final wording kept him in agony, and the one comprehensive book he published, *Productive Thinking*, was finished after some twenty years of preparation in a sudden burst of determination during the few weeks before his death in 1943. Although his constant references to the richness and beauty of the things of nature seemed to promise the lazy a respite from scientific rigor, he was severe to the point of cruelty with those among his professional colleagues who glossed over problems and sacrificed verification to a soft-minded, pseudopoetical eloquence. He drove himself hard and settled for nothing less in his students.

Wertheimer loved America. A son of ancient Prague, he found in the young culture of the new world the creative freshness he preached. He liked the spontaneous ingenuity of the young men and the unspoiled imagination of the women. And he was forever indignant at selfish politics and social injustice, because these flaws tarnished not only the country that had given him a home but also the image to which he was committed as a scientist and a man.

# THE OTHER GUSTAV
# THEODOR FECHNER

GUSTAV THEODOR FECHNER is one of those great figures of the past whose names are attached, in the mind of the average student, to a few items of idea or fact. These items float in empty space, labeled but not interpreted by those authoritative names. The context in which the ideas were conceived and the facts discovered has vanished, and with it the true meaning of those ideas and facts as well. Gone, too, is the powerful figure to whom we owe them, a man with the richness and originality of a true thinker, one whose example we can ill afford to do without.

Fechner is known from psychology textbooks as the man who founded the science of psychophysics by generalizing Weber's law to state that an arithmetical increase in a perceptual response requires a geometrical increase in the physical stimulus. In addition, the student may be told that Fechner investigated people's preferences for certain proportions of rectangles and thereby not only initiated experimental aesthetics but also explored, as a trained mathematician, various ways of measuring statistical distributions in general. The awkward connection of the two fields in the minds of psychologists was prominently illustrated when Robert S. Woodworth in the 1938 edition of his *Experimental Psychology* used the chapter on aesthetics to accommodate the material on statistics.

First published in *A Century of Psychology as Science*, ed. Sigmund Koch and David E. Leary (New York: McGraw-Hill, 1985).

As long as one has nothing else to go by, it remains unclear whether Fechner's two noteworthy accomplishments have anything to do with each other and why they should have come from the same person. My attempt to describe the matrix from which they sprang will have to be somewhat skewed because I wish to deal with Fechner mainly in his relation to the psychology of art. But Fechner's concern with aesthetics derived so directly from the core of his basic conceptions that my particular perspective may not distort the view unduly. It will be necessary, however, to take a look at those conceptions before their application to aesthetics can be traced.

Fechner's experimental investigations have been selected by the textbook writers for survival because they fit the standards of what is considered relevant and respectable in much psychology. And in fact Fechner was very much the empiricist. He proposed to supplement the philosophical aesthetics that proceeded "from above" with an aesthetics "from below" and thereby to furnish its missing factual base. In his 1871 paper *Zur experimentalen Aesthetik*, he praised his precursor Ernst Heinrich Weber for having been the first man since Galileo to extend the range of exact research beyond its supposed limits, and this in a direction that he, Fechner, was pursuing himself (3, p. 555). Throughout his work he insisted that large numbers of observers were needed to make experimental results reliable, and that while aesthetics would never be as exact a science as physics, it shared this imperfection with physiology. "Man tut, was man kann," he said. You do what you can.

It is all the more remarkable that the same man was a mystic visionary of compelling power and a playful satirist as well. As a young man he published, under a pseudonym, a humorous essay on the comparative anatomy of the angels. A treatise of 1851, called by the Zoroastrian name *Zend-Avesta*, asserted that everything organic and inorganic in the universe possesses a soul, including the earth itself and the other planets. The spirit of these and other similar works is inseparable from that of the *Elements of Psychophysics*. The same deeply religious pantheist to whom we owe the most poetical ecology ever written collected the measurements of some 20,000 paintings from twenty-two art museums to study their proportions statistically.

Two principal ideas guided Fechner in his thinking. (1) The things and experiences that constitute our world are not merely coordinated and subordinated in separate categories but fit into sliding evolutionary scales, leading from the lowest levels of existence to the highest. (2) The companionship of body and mind pervades the entire universe so that nothing mental is without its physical substratum while, conversely, a good deal of what happens physically is reflected in a corresponding mental experience.

The first of these principles places Fechner with the evolutionists of the nineteenth century. Although he strongly objected to the Darwinist notion of blind selection, he preferred evolution to the premise of the traditional taxonomists, who held since the days of Plato and Aristotle that "each higher species was created anew, as it were, from the primordial ooze" (4, p. iii). What distinguishes Fechner from his contemporaries is the sweeping grandeur of his cosmological conception, which "basically is only the completion and higher conclusion of what starts from below as psychophysics." He believed that these cosmological visions constitute "the flower and fruit growing above the root for which psychophysics searches in the immediacy of knowledge" (5, p. 101). In fact, it was those visions that gave the impulse to the empirical research about the scales of thresholds. The modest scale of perceptual responses explorable in experimentation is seen as a tiny token of the giant scale reaching from the infusoria to the solar system within the all-embracing consciousness of God. We are as close to the idealism of the Bishop Berkeley as to the laboratories of Wilhelm Wundt in Leipzig.

Fechner's second principle derives directly from Spinoza, who stated that body and mind are two aspects of the same unknowable infinite substance. That hypothetical substance appears as mind under the finite attribute of thought and as body under the finite attribute of spatial extension. Fechner gave this view a more psychological turn by insisting that the double aspect was due to different standpoints. He used the perceptual example of a person looking at a cylinder (actually he called it a circle) from the inside and then again from the outside. The concavity of the first view and the convexity of the second are incompatible; they cannot be held at the same time. He also referred to the solar system as seen from the earth and from the sun. In fact, Fechner's insistence on standpoints places him in the relativistic tradition that reaches from Copernicus to Einstein and the complementarity principle of Niels Bohr. He proceeded to reason that since the standpoint that offers direct experience of mind is available only to a person's own self, and since therefore our assumption that other human beings (and perhaps animals) possess minds like our own must remain conjectural, there was no valid objection to extending the hypothesis and assuming that everything in the material world was endowed with mind. He went so far as to speculate on the soul of plants and to explain in meticulous detail how the earth and the other planets could manage to function as conscious beings without the benefit of nervous systems.

In this connection it is of psychological interest that Fechner's concern with the psychophysics of thresholds was not primary but rather an expedient, one he resorted to because in his day, certainly, the physiological counterpart to conscious experience was inaccessible to research. Only the outer physical stimuli were accessible. He therefore assumed that a direct correlation existed between physical stimulus and physiological response. This assumption permitted him to substitute the one for the other. What he called his external psychophysics, namely the relationship between physical stimulus and perceptual response, had to serve as a stand-in for the inner psychophysics he was really after, namely the relationship between the mind and its direct bodily equivalent, the nervous system.

Although the inner psychophysics eluded the experimenter, Fechner could not refrain from speculating about its nature, and he did so inevitably in terms of what is now known from gestalt psychology as isomorphism. He said in the *Zend-Avesta* that a person's thoughts cannot differ from what the "motions of the brain" permit and that conversely the motions of the brain cannot deviate from the thoughts to which they are tied (6, p. 259). And in the *Psychophysics* we are told more specifically that although we cannot infer, from what we know by direct exploration, anything about the processes and nature of the physiological substratum, we can make statements about certain structural properties common to both levels of functioning. If such properties as context, sequence, similarity or dissimilarity, intensity or weakness, are experienced in the mind, they must have their counterparts in the nervous system (7, vol. II, p. 380). He called this isomorphic correspondence the *Funktionsprinzip*.

The conviction that matter is universally endowed with mind served Fechner to avoid the nightview, as he called it, namely the scientific assertion that the beauties of light and color exist only for the conscious mind, whereas the physical world in and of itself lies in ghastly darkness. Although as an astute observer he knew the difference between the positive perception of darkness and the absence of sight in physical space (7, vol. I, p. 167), he needed his mystical biology, which described the stars as superhumanly powerful spherical eyes, to assure him that the splendor of the visual world endures objectively. God's retina, he said in his late work on the dayview as against the nightview (*Die Tagesansicht gegenüber der Nachtansicht*), consists of the surfaces of all existing things, including the retinae in the eyes of humans and animals (5, p. 53). Fechner fought the nightview of science with the same deep-seated passion that impelled Goethe in his theory of color to defend the indivisible purity of white light against Newton's contention that light is composed of the darkness and partialness of the spectral hues. For Fechner as for Goethe, the ultimate truth resided in direct sensory experience.

This conviction, of course, is the credo and axiom of all art, and in my opinion Fechner's way of looking at the world in the manner of the artist constitutes his principal contribution to aesthetics. It explains his decision to devote his last major work to aesthetics more convincingly than his own reference, in the foreword to his *Vorschule der Aesthetik*, to the few minor studies dealing explicitly with art in his earlier work (8, vol. I, p. v). In fact, we must face the vexing paradox that this last extensive effort, almost six hundred pages in length, this final consummation to which all Fechner's thought led, fails to embody his guiding ideas in the congenial medium of the arts. (One need only recall the young Schopenhauer's dealing with a similar task in the third book of his *Die Welt als Wille und Vorstellung* to become aware of the difference.) There are indications that Fechner, once he had decided to embark upon a substantial work on aesthetics, felt obliged to deal with the topics that dominated other major treatises in that field. Thus he holds forth on content and form, unity and complexity, idealism vs. realism, art vs. nature; he asks whether there is more beauty in the small or in the large; and he opines that sculpture should be in color to look more real. He does all this and much more quite sensibly and with an occasional Fechnerian flash, and he offers some useful principles and methods; but there is little of the bold originality that would distinguish his book from what professors of philosophy published then and are still publishing now on those same subjects.

There is little in the *Vorschule* to compare, for example, to the inspiration Fechner drew from seeing a waterlily spread its leaves on a pond and offer its open flower to the light. He cites this experience in his book on the soul of the plants to suggest that the lily is enabled by its shape to enjoy the pleasures of the bath and the warmth of the light to the fullest (10, p. 39). The example can be generalized to imply that by the very appearance of its form and behavior, a visual object conveys those basic sensations and strivings which the artist purifies in his work. Note here that Fechner's outlook was mostly visual, although references to sounds and music do occur in his writings. His entire life and work are pervaded by a worship bordering an obsession with light and vision. When at the age of thirty-nine he was shaken by a profound spiritual crisis, during which his religious and poetical nature rebelled against the materialism and atheism of his early years as a student of medicine and professor of physics at the University of Leipzig, he became unable to tolerate light, lived for three years in almost total darkness, and was brought to the brink of death by a concomitant inability to tolerate food. The revenge of the world he felt he had betrayed was meted out by the power of light. He had defied that power by optical experiments carried out in an irreverent spirit; and he was punished by the darkness he feared more than anything else. It was after his sudden recovery from this affliction that he developed his visionary cosmology, which eventually led to the works on psychophysics and aesthetics.

Equally characteristic is Fechner's habit of identifying the geometrical symbol of perfection, the sphere, with the eye. The planets are animate beings that demonstrate their superiority by their spherical shape. Their roundness is more beautiful than the lumps and asymmetries of the human body. Since their activities have been sublimated in pure contemplation, they have become eyes. In a bit of playful persiflage, Fechner draws on what in gestalt psychology we now call the tendency to simplest structure to describe in his essay on the anatomy of the angels the transformation of the animal head into the angel body. In the course of evolution, forehead and chin move forward and the skull bulges around a center located between the eyes. As the eyes move inward and occupy the center of the spherical structure and finally fuse into a single organ, they become the core and focus of an increasingly transparent symmetrical sphere. The organism becomes a creature of pure vision. Fechner adds that the angels communicate among themselves through the highest sense known to man: they speak in colors rather than sounds by generating beautiful paintings on their surfaces (9).

This apotheosis of vision, however, is by no means the basic theme of the *Vorschule*. Rather, in a major concession to traditional aesthetics, Fechner based his presentation on a motivational approach, the creed of hedonism, which holds that human behavior is controlled by a striving for pleasure and the avoidance of unpleasantness. We remember here that in classical philosophy hedonism was conceived of as the rationale for every human activity, but that in modern times it continued to retain its role as a sufficient explanatory principle only in the philosophy of art. There was a good reason for this. With the increasing secularization of the arts during the Renaissance, their only tangible purpose obvious to the critical observer was that they provided entertainment. This led to the insipid and unfruitful aesthetic conception of art as a source of pleasure. Nevertheless, in our century this approach was gratefully adopted by psychologists who attempted to subject people's aesthetic responses to measurement under experimental conditions. It permitted them to reduce the complicated processes that take place when people perceive, organize, and comprehend works of art to a single scalable variable— the condition most favored by scientific method. Just as in perceptual psychophysics the varying intensity of, say, a sensation of light provided the means for measuring thresholds, so the pleasure or unpleasantness of responses yielded the condition for a psychophysics of aesthetics. Fechner's investigation of people's preferences for certain proportions of rectangles became the historical prototype of his work.

Thus it came to pass that practically the entire body of experimental aesthetics up to the present time was cast in the convenient format of a hedonistic psychophysics, with the consequence that the more strictly investigators adhered to the criterion of preference, the more completely their results neglected everything that distinguishes the pleasure generated by a work of art from the pleasure generated by a dish of ice cream. Just as Fechner's work does not tell us why people prefer the ratio of the golden section to others, so most of the innumerable preference studies carried out since his time tell us deplorably little about what people see when they look at an aesthetic object, what they mean by saying that they like or dislike it, and why they prefer the objects they prefer.

Add to this that every respectable experimental setup requires that the stimulus target, too, be reducible to a single variable. Accordingly such studies in aesthetics have either followed Fechner's example by limiting their stimuli to very simple patterns or dimensions, or have worked with actual art objects, whose active properties, however, remained unexplored. Therefore the results tended either to deal with objects that had little bearing on art or to report on responses to unexamined stimuli.

A less obvious consequence of the derivation from Fechnerian psychophysics is the dominant interest in what I would call the objective percept, rather than in the individuals who act as perceivers. Fechner explained with great clarity that since he possessed no means of measuring the intensity of a pleasure response directly, he had to substitute counting for measuring, or, as he himself put it, extensive measure for intensive measure (8, vol. II, p. 600). By testing a great many observers he could use the number of votes given a particular stimulus as an indicator of the intensity of the pleasure it aroused in the human species as such and in general. Since art criticism is strongly influenced nowadays by a doctrine of relativism, which holds that there is no way of assuming that a work of art possesses an objective appearance, let alone an objective value, it is of interest that Fechner considered individual differences to be "irregular chance fluctuations" (7, vol. I, p. 77). As far as the target of the investigations was concerned, Fechner aimed principally at what he called the "lawful measurement relations of collective objects (i.e., objects consisting of an indefinitely large number of specimens that vary according to laws of chance and can be found in the most different areas)" (8, vol. II, p. 273). In recent practice, experimenters have compared the reactions of subject groups distinguished by sex, education, or attitude to complex and meaningful stimuli such as works of art. But aesthetics has yet to establish the cutoff point at which aesthetic stimuli cease to be objective percepts and become the reflections of individual or social bias.

Inevitably, the use of fairly simple and neutral stimuli and the reliance on statistical averages lead to results that differ from responses to actual works of art. For example, Fechner attributes much importance to a typical finding, which continues to haunt the laboratories of scientific aesthetics. He calls it the "principle of the aesthetic middle": people "tolerate most often and for the longest time a certain medium degree of arousal, which makes them feel neither overstimulated nor dissatisfied by a lack of sufficient occupation" (8, vol. II, pp. 217, 260). This rule is certainly valid for run-of-the-mill behavior in everyday life. In the arts it would reflect at most a neoclassicist taste for moderation.

I would like to devote the rest of this paper to the aesthetic relevance of a few other of Fechner's more general ideas. I pointed out that he made aesthetic experience dependent on the pleasure it arouses. He refused to believe, however, that the intensity of pleasure corresponded simply to the quantitative strength of the physical stimulus. Instead, in a decisive passage of the *Vorschule*, he insisted that the aesthetic effect is brought about by the formal relations within the stimulus configuration, a condition he described as harmony (8, vol. II, p. 266). What did he mean by harmony? At times he spoke of it in the conventional sense of the resolution of tension as it is found in musical chord sequences. In the passage mentioned above, however, he related harmony more boldly to one of the key concepts of his work, namely to the principle of the tendency to stability. I will refer here once more to Fechner's early fantasy about the nature and behavior of angels. There he compared the dignity of the various sense modalities and suggested that higher even than the sense of sight was the sensory awareness of gravity (9, p. 234). This highest form of perception is "the feeling of the general force of gravity, which relates all bodies to one another and is sensed by their living centers." Now gravity, the physical equivalent of our perception of weight, is brought about, according to Fechner, by the tendency to stability. It is a state of equilibrium and tension reduction, envisaged in a similar manner by the Second Law of Thermodynamics and by what we call the gestalt tendency to simplest structure (1). To be sure, a direct perceptual awareness of the forces held in equilibrium in a physical system such as the universe would indeed be a privilege of the angels. But a physiological system of a similar kind can have its equivalent in perceptual experience. The prime example is the perception of composition in the arts. The multiplicity of shapes and colors in a painting or of sounds in a piece of music is held together by a configuration of forces generated in the nervous system and reflected in the awareness of the artist and of every percipient of his work. It is this crucial aesthetic experience to which Fechner referred when he spoke of harmony.

For a final example I would like to point to a conception developed by Fechner in his book *Some Ideas on the History of the Creation and Evolution of the Organisms* (4). With his usual idealistic fervor he rejected the biological doctrine that life was derived from inorganic matter. The opposite had to be the case. He asserted that the original state of all being was that of a comprehensive primordial creature, anticipating all existing things in intricate relations and movements and held together in its chaotic fertility only by the force of gravity. From this primordial matrix, articulate organic and inorganic structures were derived through a process distinguished from ordinary cell division by what Fechner called the principle of relational differentiation. It produced at each level opposite entities complementing each other—for example, male and female. Through a Lamarckian kind of mutual adaptation as well as through a gradual slowdown in variability, a state of stability was approached. If that final state were to be fully attained, "each part through the effect of its forces would contribute to bringing the other parts and thereby the whole into a durable, and that means stable, state and maintain them in that state" (4, p. 89; see also 1).

Fechner's fantastic biology was as unlikely to find favor with the exact sciences as were his other mystical visions. But while it contradicts the facts of nature as we know them, it reminds us forcefully of what we know about psychological genesis and especially of the creative process in the arts, where indeed quite typically a global primary conception leads to increasingly articulate shape by a process of differentiation.

Components of such a conception develop a shape of their own and search for their place in the whole, whose final composition is strongly influenced by the interrelation of the parts.

A particularly clear example can be found in the growth of form conception in the artwork of young children and other early art forms. Here the store of potential shapes in the developing mind takes concrete form first in simple global figures, such as circles. I have shown elsewhere (2, chap. IV) that the increasing complexity of such artwork comes about through a process of differentiation by which each conception becomes the special case of a whole range of variations. Each of these variations, in turn, can subdivide further into an ever-richer arsenal of visual expression.

The capacity of good art to forge a multiplicity of different and often divergent parts into a productive whole has implications for moral conduct that were not lost on Fechner. He viewed the work of art as a symbol of the successful handling of social and personal conflict. As he weighed in his mind the ratio of pleasure to pain in human existence, Fechner was not inclined to underestimate the impact of evil and discord; but he also believed that the life of the individual and of the world as a whole progresses from conditions of pain to ones of increasing pleasure. He saw the desirable condition of human intercourse symbolized in the work of art, for example, in a piece of music. In his late work on the *Dayview as Against the Nightview* he says: "And so I picture the whole proceeding of the world in the familiar image of a symphony, which to be sure produces more, and more severe, dissonances than the symphonies in our concert halls, but similarly moves, nevertheless, toward a resolution, for the whole as well as for each individual" (5, p. 181). In Fechner's view, human aspiration could attain no higher fulfillment than that of matching the perfection of the work of art.

## References

1. Arnheim, Rudolf. *Entropy and Art.* Berkeley and Los Angeles: University of California Press, 1971.
2. ———. *Art and Visual Perception.* New version. Berkeley and Los Angeles: University of California Press, 1974.
3. Fechner, Gustav Theodor. *Zur experimentalen Aesthetik.* Abhandlungen der Königl. Sächsischen Gesellschaft der Wissenschaften, XiV. Leipzig: Hirzel, 1871.
4. ———. *Einige Ideen zur Schöpfungs- und Entwicklungsgeschichte der Organismen.* Leipzig: Breitkopf & Härtel, 1873.

THE OTHER GUSTAV THEODOR FECHNER / 49

5. ———. *Die Tagesansicht gegenüber der Nachtansicht.* Berlin: Deutsche Bibliothek, 1918.
6. ———. *Zend-Avesta.* Leipzig: Insel, 1919.
7. ———. *Elemente der Psychophysik.* Leipzig: Breitkopf & Härtel, 1889.
8. ———. *Vorschule der Aesthetik.* Hildesheim: Georg Holms, 1978.
9. ———. "Vergleichende Anatomie der Engel." In *Kleine Schriften von Dr. Mises.* Leipzig: Breitkopf & Härtel, 1875.
10. ———. *Nanna oder Ueber das Seelenleben der Pflanzen.* Leipzig: Voss, 1848.
11. Hermann, Imre. "Gustav Theodor Fechner: Eine psychoanalytische Studie." *Imago,* vol. 11. Leipzig: Intern. Psychoanal. Verlag, 1926.

# WILHELM WORRINGER ON
# ABSTRACTION AND EMPATHY

In 1906 Wilhelm Worringer, a twenty-five-year-old student of art history, wrote a dissertation published two years later as a book under the title *Abstraktion und Einfühlung: Ein Beitrag zur Stilpsychologie* (29). This academic "contribution to the psychology of style" turned out to be one of the most influential documents in art theory of the new century. It offered an aesthetic and psychological foundation for the new approach by which modern art was about to proceed. At the same time, it proposed a striking relation between two psychological concepts: one of them, abstraction, a two-thousand-year-old tool for the understanding of human cognition; the other, empathy, a relatively recent outgrowth of Romantic philosophy. By describing the two concepts as antagonists, Worringer sharpened and restricted their meaning in a way that has remained relevant to their discussion in psychology as well as in aesthetics.[1]

In the flow of history, all segmentation is artificial, and in that sense there is no beginning of modern art. The roots of modern art reach as far back as one cares to pursue them. If, however, one does wish to establish a starting point, it would have to be the moment at which it was no longer possible to say that the intention and purpose of visual art are

---

First published in *Confinia Psychiatrica*, vol. 10, no. 1 (1967).

[1] Carl Gustav Jung, in a chapter devoted to Worringer's concepts, relates empathy to extroversion, abstraction to introversion (9, chap. VII). On empathy in the aesthetics of the nineteenth century, consult Moos (16), chap. IV.

to imitate nature. This assertion had been maintained throughout the history of Western art. However impressively artists through the ages deviated from the physical world as it is perceived by the eyes, the theorists and critics had insisted that when an artist succeeded in deceiving human viewers and even animals by making them accept his figures or landscapes as though they were reality itself, he had attained the highest peak of his art. It is true that Plato had condemned the visual arts on precisely this score, and perfecting and idealizing the human figure was considered an additional task of the artist in antiquity as well as during the Renaissance; but the embodiment of "ideas" hardly deflected the artist's loyalty from the standards of naturalism (18).

Those standards still held at the end of the nineteenth century. Paul Cézanne, for example, was rejected on the grounds that he was incapable, physically and mentally, of doing what he was trying to do, namely to imitate nature. The French writer Joris Karl Huysmans called him "un artiste aux rétines malades" (28, p. 197). Cézanne died in 1906. In that same year, Pablo Picasso painted two pictures against which the traditional accusation could no longer be made in good faith. There was no doubt that, whether or not Picasso was capable of living up to the traditional ideal of naturalism, he was not willing to do so. This shifted the problem to the very different question of whether such deviation from "nature" could be justified. In 1906 Picasso did the famous portrait of Gertrude Stein, and he began the group composition later known as "Les Demoiselles d'Avignon." Not that the extent to which these two works deviated from nature was unique: what makes them worthy of being singled out as milestones is that the deviations occurred only in limited portions of otherwise more conventionally treated figures: in the mask-like face of the American poet and the inorganic geometry of noses and eyes in two of the five "demoiselles." Clearly, here an artist was refusing to obey the traditional standards. But what was he trying to do instead?

Worringer's dissertation contains only one brief reference to the art of his time. He roams through the ages, he goes out of the ordinary way by referring to pre-Columbian and African art; but although, as Peter Selz has pointed out, he knew Kandinsky in Munich (21, 22), his book mentions only one modern artist, Ferdinand Hodler, the melodramatic Swiss realist whose decorative nudes caused some commotion in the 1890s. And yet the effect of Worringer's thesis upon the modern movement was prompt and profound. In 1911 a leading Expressionist painter, Franz Marc, referred to *Abstraction and Empathy* as a book that "deserves the most widespread attention and in which a strictly historical mind put down a train of thought that might cause some discomfort to the worried opponents of the modern movement" (22, p. 9).

What was it about Worringer's thesis that made it possible for him to write, forty-two years later, with some professional coyness: "I refuse to pretend modestly that I am unaware of the epochal effect which the dissertation of an unknown young student at its publication had on the personal life of others and on the intellectual life of a whole period" (29, p. vii). He says that his personal disposition toward certain problems coincided unexpectedly with a whole period's readiness to reorient its standards of aesthetic value fundamentally. "Theories intended only for historical interpretations were immediately transferred to the belligerent art movement of the time." What, then, was Worringer's revolutionary thesis?

As a first approximation, one can put it as follows: Throughout the centuries of Western civilization, theorists and critics had evaluated art by the standard mentioned above, namely, as an attempt to copy nature faithfully. The most successful attainments of this ideal were found in the classical era of Greece and again in the high Renaissance. Whatever varieties of art did not measure up to this model were considered deficient, and deviations from it were explained as due either to the incapacity of young or barbarous peoples or to the material impediments imposed on the artisan by the media he employed. This one-sided approach, says Worringer, made it impossible to do justice to the art of whole continents and vast periods because their art proceeded from a fundamentally different principle. Rather than trust and worship nature, the peoples who originated such art were frightened by the irrationality of nature and therefore sought refuge in a man-made world of rationally defined shapes. Thus one had to acknowledge two poles of aesthetic sensibility. By establishing this bipolarity, Worringer provided the theoretical basis for Picasso's demonstration of the same year: modern art, like the non-realistic styles of other epochs, was not naturalistic art done badly, but a different kind of art, issuing from different premises.

Worringer opposed the traditional theory of art on still another ground. He rejected the characterization of Western art as an imitation of nature. The imitation impulse, he maintains with much feeling, does exist everywhere, but it is "worlds apart" (*himmelweit verschieden*) from what he called the style of naturalism. The pleasure deriving from the playful copying of natural things has nothing to do with art. Instead, naturalism is the classical approach to art, which springs from the pleasure found in the organic and vital; it wants not to imitate the objects of nature, but "to project the lines and forms of the originally vital . . . outward in ideal independence and perfection, in order, as it were, to furnish in every creation a stage (*Schauplatz*) for the free, unimpeded activation of one's own sense of life." This projection of the sense of life upon the artistic medium is said to come about by what Worringer, in conformity with the psychological aesthetics of the nineteenth century, called *Einfühlung*, or empathy.

We note, first of all, the excessive distinction drawn between imitation of nature and naturalistic art. The difference exists, but it became noticeable and problematic only at some late stages of art; e.g., in certain aspects of Hellenism and in by-products of the centuries during and after the Renaissance. Only through a weakening of the inborn sense of form was it possible to produce painting and sculpture that conformed to the doctrine of imitation literally and mechanically and thereby created a threat to art. If one looks at the art of the nineteenth century—not as we know it from the work of the great survivors, but for the typical attitude as manifested in the average products of the time and the practices of drawing teachers—one realizes that the threat was very real. Worringer's emphasis on the distinction is not the fruit of dispassionate historical scrutiny but an act of defense. Consciously or not, in reacting to the present danger, he was fighting the battle of modern art. "Yes, that's nicely imitated!" Cézanne had snorted ironically when some friends lauded in his presence Puvis de Chavannes's painting *Le Pauvre Pêcheur* (28, p. 104). Worringer recognized organized form in so-called naturalistic art, and he insisted that form was indispensable. However, given the theoretical situation of psychology at the time, this insight became intriguingly obscured by contamination with the concept of empathy. It is necessary, therefore, to leave Worringer at this point for a while and to examine the status of the concept empathy more generally.

Empathy stands high in the favor of clinical and social psychologists today. In a recent article, Kenneth B. Clark noted that in the year 1978 alone, eighty-six articles in the psychological literature dealt with this subject; he defined empathy as "the capacity of an individual to feel the needs, the aspirations, the frustrations, the joy, the sorrows, the anxieties, the hurt, indeed, the hunger of others as if they were his own" (6). How does empathy come about? In Clark's definition empathy is described as the ability to perceive what is felt by others and to do so by reference to one's own feelings. Generally, empathic perception has not been understood as a mere intellectual analogy made between a person's own experiences and his or her observations of another person's behavior, but rather as direct perceptual openness to the characteristics of the other person's appearance and actions. If one applies the gestalt concept of isomorphism, which assumes a directly perceivable structural similarity between outer behavior and the corresponding mental processes (2, p. 58), there is nothing mysterious about the fact that the expressiveness of behavior can be perceived and understood. Nevertheless, Harry Stack Sullivan, the most clairvoyant among Freud's followers and a supporter of empathy, calls the rationale for this capacity "thoroughly obscure": "I have had a good deal of trouble at times with people of a certain type of educational history; since they cannot refer empathy to vision, hearing, or some other special sense receptor, and since they do not know whether it is transmitted by the ether waves or air waves or what not, they find it hard to accept the idea of empathy." And, after asserting that it demonstrably exists: "So although empathy may sound mysterious, remember that there is much that sounds mysterious in the universe, only you have got used to it; and perhaps you will get used to empathy" (26, p. 41). Mystery or not, the presence of such an intuitive response is a *conditio sine qua non* if one wishes to distinguish empathy from other mental processes better called by other names. Its presence is surely indispensable if one wishes to describe the aesthetic experience, for which the concept empathy was originally coined. It helps especially in distinguishing aesthetic experience from the mere examination of visual and associative facts by which a work of art may be described, and in certain ways even understood.

If empathy requires the intuitive ability to read a person's state of mind in that person's appearance and behavior, the question remains to what extent this ability depends on the mechanism of "projection," first defined by Sigmund Freud in the 1890s as "a process of ascribing one's own drives, feelings, and sentiments to other people or to the outside world as a defensive process that permits one to be unaware of these 'undesirable' phenomena in oneself" (1, p. 8). Theodor Lipps, to whom the term *Einfühlung* (translated into English as "empathy" by Edward Titchener) owes its theoretical foundation, was quite ambiguous in this respect. His writings on the subject are remarkably rich, subtle, and also full of contradictions. Often he professes the most extreme subjectivism, holding that even the facial expression of joy or boredom perceived in another person is nothing but an imposition on the part of the observer: "All this is empathy, the transfer of myself into others. The foreign individuals of whom I know are objectified multiplications of my own self" (16, p. 178). If I see a falling stone strive toward the ground, I am merely imposing, Lipps would assert, an analogous experience of my own upon the inert object. The percept itself contains no force, no activity, no causation. Here, empathy is credited entirely to projection.

The one-sidedness of such an approach becomes evident when one takes it literally and applies it to an actual case. When Goethe in 1817, thirty years after his trip to Italy, edited his *Italian Journey*, he explained jestingly in a letter to his friend Zelter why the title page of the book bears the motto "I, too, was in Arcadia." "Italy," he writes, "is such a hackneyed country that if I could not see myself in it as though in a rejuvenating mirror, I would not want to have anything to do with it." Goethe is pretending that, from his own resources, he had to provide his travel experience with the breath of life not contained in that experience itself. Would we be willing to accept a pitiful situation of this kind as a paradigm of the aesthetic attitude? Is not any genuine encounter with a work of art the exact opposite, namely, animation flowing from the work and imposing the impact of its life upon the beholder? Here again an extreme example may illustrate the point. We are told that when Catherine of Siena saw in St. Peter's in Rome Giotto's mosaic of the "Navicella," which symbolizes salvation from tribulation by showing Christ rescuing Peter from a storm-tossed sailboat, she "suddenly felt the ship transferred to her shoulders, and she collapsed on the floor, crushed by the unbearable weight" (14, p. 106). Undeniably, the substance of this encounter is not in what Catherine did to the boat, but in what the boat did to Catherine.

Psychologists are familiar with the subjectivistic approach from Hermann Rorschach's *Psychodiagnostics*, first published in 1921 and based on experiments going back to 1911. Rorschach, the son of a drawing teacher and himself an active amateur artist, interpreted "movement responses" to his inkblots in accordance with a radical version of the empathy theory. A figure seen in motion is said to acquire a direct dynamic quality only when kinesthetic affluents are aroused in the body of the beholder (19, 20; 2, pp. 74ff.). Psychologists also know that in the clinical discussions of projection, attention is focused almost exclusively on the subjective factors determining what is imposed upon the outer world. Beyond the generic and doubtful notion that the less structured and more ambiguous the stimulus, the stronger the projection, we seem to have no systematic investigation of which particular features of a perceptual field permit what kinds of projective imposition. After paying lip service to the stimulus, we often talk as though the perceiver is hallucinating in a void.

It is therefore worth noting that Lipps himself was too observant to let his favorite theories run away with what he saw. In fact, one can easily find passages in his writings in which he maintains the very opposite. Particularly in the first section of the second volume of his *Aesthetik*, published in 1906, he insists that expression is immanent in perceptual appearance and that, for example, the "strength" of a color does not consist in the strength of the apperception invested by the perceiver but is inherent in the color's own quality. The factor of expression, which he calls "the affect," is, according to Lipps, as independent of the perceiver's arbitrary control as the path of the stars (13, p. 45). He rejects Fechner's attempt to account for the immanence of expression by means of associative factors, insisting instead upon the inseparable unity of the sensory appearance of form and the content it conveys. As to kinesthetic affluents, Lipps devotes a chapter to poking fun at the "fashionable disease of organ sensations" and suggests that one should stop talking about "these supposed factors of aesthetic enjoyment, except in order to expose them to the ridicule they deserve."[2]

An object was beautiful, Lipps held, if vitality reverberated in it; otherwise it was ugly and therefore excluded from the realm of art. It is here that Worringer sensed a crucial one-sidedness. Throughout the ages, he says, large groups of human beings have been unable to approach nature with the trustful familiarity that, according to Lipps, results from the biological affinity of man and world and that was the basis of the classical naturalism of Greek and Renaissance art. In particular, during the early phases of human development the transition from the reliable, trust-inspiring sense of touch to the confusing variety of visual appearances induced primitive man to create, as a refuge, a world of geometrically lawful shapes, considered beautiful precisely because they repudiated life through the order and regularity by which they replaced the chaos of nature. It was anxiety rather than trustful surrender that was at the root of much great art. Worringer states further that at a more advanced level of development a similarly oriented approach is found among

the peoples of the Oriental cultures ... who were the only ones to see in the external appearance of the world nothing but the shimmering veil of Maya and remained conscious of the unfathomable entanglement of all the phenomena of life. ... Their spiritual dread of space, their instinctive awareness of the relativity

---

[2] A strong commitment to the kinesthetic theory of empathy can be found in Langfeld (12).

of all that is did not, as it does in primitive peoples, precede cognition but stood above cognition. (29, p. 16)

The psychological mechanism by which such anti-organic art is produced Worringer called "abstraction." The two antagonistic varieties of art products are said to correspond in the mind to two antagonistic impulses: empathy and abstraction.

Anxiety, then, was heralded by Worringer in 1906 as one of the mainsprings of art and a principal source of its greatness—anxiety, which modern psychiatry was to propose as a principal motive of human behavior and which was to become the theme of so much poetry and prose of the twentieth century. Considering that Worringer refers to *Raumscheu*, the dread of space, in order to interpret remote regions of the history of art, it is uncanny to find another art historian, Werner Haftmann, fifty years later give the following description of Picasso's group composition of circus folk, which preceded by one year the early stirrings of Cubism as well as the writing of Worringer's dissertation:

The colored ground on which Picasso paints his strolling players is like a hollow spiritual form. It is the pictorial expression of a frequent modern existential theme—life seen as helpless exposure in an indefinable void. It has been given various names—the dread of nothingness (Heidegger), the incomprehensibility of God (Barth), non-being (Valéry). Picasso's harlequins embody modern man's basic emotional and intellectual experience, his existential homelessness and melancholy freedom. (8, vol. I, p. 96)

We have been trained to think of abstraction as an operation of withdrawal. Even in simple cognition one is supposed to arrive at generalities only by detaching oneself from the immediacy of the particular given situation. This view, however, makes for a harmful theoretical split between perception and thinking, which goes far back in the Western tradition and persists in the psychological theories of our day (3). The cognitive mode of abstraction is readily related to an attitude of the person as a whole, namely, the fearful or spiteful or even sagacious withdrawal from a threatening, chaotic, or evil environment. In the Primitives and Orientals whom Worringer had in mind, abstraction was supposed to be a reaction to the strangeness of an irrational world. In the European painters and sculptors of Worringer's generation, abstraction has often been interpreted as expressing the estrangement, or alienation, from a society that was socially, economically, and culturally detrimental to the artist. One might add the more personal factors of fear and rejection, for example, of the female body, documented for Cézanne and Kandinsky

(4, 21); Mondrian kept in his studio a single artificial tulip, meant to suggest feminine presence, whose leaf he painted white to banish any recollection of the green he found intolerable (23, pp. 86, 160). From all this we get the sense of an attitude well expressed by Paul Klee in a diary entry of 1915: "One leaves the place of the here and now and builds instead into a realm of the yonder, which can afford to be a complete yes. Abstraction—the cool Romanticism of this style, free from rhetoric, is unheard of. The more terrifying this world (precisely as today), the more abstract its art, whereas a happy world brings forth an art of the here and now" (11, #951).

It seems reasonable to conclude that Worringer's theories on abstraction were not so much the result of historical investigations as a set of speculations symptomatic of a mood of the times and therefore eagerly adopted by some contemporaries as its eloquent and authoritative theoretical justification.

However, this picture is one-sided. We may want to ask whether that early generation of Abstractionists and Cubists did indeed believe they were doing the sort of thing that a sociopsychological analysis might uncover among their unconscious motives. The quotation from Klee might suggest that they did, but on the whole the answer must be No. Mondrian in his writings speaks of art as the establishment of intrinsic reality. Abstract art, he says, strives for objective, unchangeable, universal expression; it cleans the image of the world from the realistic and subjective particulars that weaken the conceptions of mimetic art. Abstraction is not practiced in order to withdraw from the world, but to penetrate to its essence (15). As to the Cubists, we are well served by a statement of Georges Braque of 1908, apparently "the only directly quoted and recorded statement by either Braque or Picasso from before 1914" (7). Braque is reported to have said, "I couldn't portray a woman in all her natural loveliness. . . . I haven't the skill. No one has. I must, therefore, create a new sort of beauty that appears to me in terms of volume, of line, of mass, of weight, and through that beauty interpret my subjective impression. . . . I want to expose the Absolute, and not merely the factitious woman." Daniel-Henry Kahnweiler, the companion and theorist of the Cubists, explains that Picasso, far from feeling impelled to withdraw from space because of any conscious dread of it, thought it his essential task to clarify, on the flat surface of the canvas, the shape and spatial position of three-dimensional things made unreadable by the illusionistic foreshortenings in the paintings of the Renaissance tradition: "In a painting by Raphael, it is not possible to verify the distance between the tip of the nose and the mouth. I would like to paint pictures in which this is possible." A passionate concern with art as the interpreter of outer reality is manifest also in Kahnweiler's own theories. In what he calls his neo-Kantian aesthetics, he says of geometrical shapes that "they furnish us with the solid armature on which we fasten the products of our imagination, consisting of retinal excitations and stored images. They are our 'visual categories.' When we look at the outer world we somehow require of it those shapes, which it never offers us in their purity." And further on: "Without the cube, we should lack any impression of the third dimension of objects in general, and of that of their variations without the sphere and the cylinder. Our *a priori* knowledge of these shapes is the very condition of our vision, of the existence that the world of bodies has for us" (10). This was written in 1914 or 1915.[3]

Worringer, too, was of the opinion that geometric shapes enter early styles of art through the action of "laws of nature" and that they are implicit not only in inorganic matter but in the human mind as well. Primitive man did not need to look at crystals to conceive of such shapes. Geometric abstraction is rather "a pure self-creation derived from the conditions of the human organism." Nevertheless, there is no room in Worringer's thought for the observation on which we would insist nowadays, namely, that an intense expression of life is evident in styles of art whose abstractness is supposed to be due to an escape from the organic, for instance, in African and Romanesque sculpture. In regard to the Orientals, who are Worringer's prime example of spiritual withdrawal from the irrational confusion of life, we shall only note that the first and most important of the six canons constituting the doctrine of Chinese painting ever since Hsieh Ho formulated them about 500 A.D. was the "Ch'i yun sheng tung," the "Spirit Resonance (or Vibration of Vitality) and Life Movement," a quality of the brushstroke by which the Breath of Heaven "stirs all of nature to life and sustains the eternal processes of movement and change. . . . If a work of art has 'Ch'i' it inevitably reflects a vitality of spirit that is the essence of life itself" (24, 27). As to modern art, we may mention that for the most geometrical of Abstractionists, Piet Mondrian, a work of art was "art" only "in so far as it establishes life in its unchangeable aspect: as pure vitality" (15).

---

[3] When these statements were published in Kahnweiler's book of 1963, I was pleasantly surprised by their resemblance to my own approach in a paper on perceptual abstraction, which appeared in 1947 (2, pp. 31ff.). For a translation of Kahnweiler's statement see Chipp (5), p. 258. A summary of the Cubists' views of "reality" is given by Nash (17).

We are indebted to Worringer for having pointed out that under certain conditions abstract form can be a symptom of withdrawal, but we can now see that primarily and typically it serves the opposite purpose. Abstraction is the indispensable means by which all visible shapes are perceived, identified, and found to have generality and symbolic significance. For, if I may rephrase Kant's pronouncement, vision without abstraction is blind; abstraction without vision is empty (3).

Worringer's attitude toward abstraction and abstract shapes is manifest also in his belief that only organic shapes are suitable for aesthetic empathy. He derived this conviction from the Lippsian notion that an aesthetic experience occurs when a person enjoys the resonance of life in an external object. But Worringer's inference is hardly tenable. Of course, we can call a particular set of curved shapes typically organic, as distinguished from inorganic straightness, angularity, etc., but this organic quality refers only to the body and at most to the kinesthetic sensations received from limbs and trunk. The human quality to be reflected in art must surely go beyond the purely physical traits of man. It must reflect the mind. And why should we assume that the specifically organic shapes are the only ones the mind can find congenial? Straightness, after all, is as much a mental trait as the curvature of adaptation, and the simple clarity of order is described by Worringer himself as a state highly desirable to the mind. We must conclude that nothing less than the whole variety of perceivable shapes, the crooked and the straight, the irrational and the orderly, reflects the complexity of the mind. In fact, a work of art based entirely on the equivalent of organic shape would tend to nauseate us, just as an assembly of purely inorganic shapes might repel us by its dryness. The narrow notion of empathy as the pleasure of finding the organic in the organic must be replaced with that of man's preeminent desire to contemplate a world in which he is at home because, with all its monsters and mysteries and its inanimate rocks and waters, it is of his own kind.

The historical merit of Worringer's manifesto consists in his having proclaimed nonrealistic form a positive creation of the human mind, intended and able to produce lawful visual order. His bipolarity of naturalistic versus nonnaturalistic art, however, promoted not only an artificial split in the history of art but also an equally precarious psychological antagonism between man's concern with nature and his capacity for creating organized form. It is a dichotomy that continues to haunt the theoretical thinking of our century in the somewhat modified guise of the distinctions between perceptual and conceptual art, schematic and realistic art, artists who depict what they see and others who cling to what they know, art of the How and art of the What. Worringer himself, less dogmatic than the later generation, was able to say that although abstraction and empathy are "opposites that exclude each other in principle, the history of art is actually a constant interactive exchange between both tendencies." Our own thinking has yet to meet the challenge of accounting for the wider range of ways in which the arts represent the world of human experience with the help of organized form.

## References

1. Abt, Lawrence Edwin, and Leonard Bellak, eds. *Projective Psychology*. New York: Grove, 1959.
2. Arnheim, Rudolf. *Toward a Psychology of Art*. Berkeley and Los Angeles: University of California Press, 1966.
3. ———. *Visual Thinking*. Berkeley and Los Angeles: University of California Press, 1969.
4. Badt, Kurt. *Die Kunst Cézannes*. Munich: Prestel, 1956. Eng.: *The Art of Cézanne*. Berkeley and Los Angeles: University of California Press, 1965.
5. Chipp, Herschel B. *Theories of Modern Art*. Berkeley and Los Angeles: University of California Press, 1968.
6. Clark, Kenneth B. "Empathy, A Neglected Topic in Psychological Research." *American Psychologist*, vol. 35, no. 2 (Feb. 1980), pp. 187–90.
7. Fry, E. F. "Cubism 1907–1908." *Art Bulletin*, vol. 48 (1966), pp. 70–73.
8. Haftmann, Werner. *Painting in the Twentieth Century*. New York: Praeger, 1960.
9. Jung, Carl Gustav. *Psychologische Typen*. Zurich: Rascher, 1921. Eng.: *Psychological Types*. New York: Harcourt Brace, 1926.
10. Kahnweiler, Daniel-Henry. *Confessions esthétiques*. Paris: Gallimard, 1963.
11. Klee, Paul. *Tagebücher*. Cologne: Dumont, 1957. Eng.: Berkeley and Los Angeles: University of California Press, 1964.
12. Langfeld, Herbert S. *The Aesthetic Attitude*. New York: Harcourt Brace, 1920.
13. Lipps, Theodor. *Aesthetik: Psychologie des Schönen in der Kunst*, part II. Hamburg: Voss, 1906.
14. Meiss, Millard. *Painting in Florence and Siena after the Black Death*. New York: Harper & Row, 1964.
15. Mondrian, Piet. *Plastic Art and Pure Plastic Art*. New York: Wittenborn, 1945.
16. Moos, Paul. *Die deutsche Aesthetik der Gegenwart*, vol. 1. Berlin: Schuster & Loeffler, 1914.
17. Nash, J. M. "The Nature of Cubism." *Art History*, vol. 3, no. 4 (Dec. 1980), pp. 435–47.
18. Panofsky, Erwin. *Idea*. Leipzig: Teubner, 1924. Eng.: *Idea: A Concept in Art Theory*. Columbia: University of South Carolina Press, 1968.

19. Rorschach, Hermann. *Psychodiagnostik*. Berne: Huber, 1932. Eng.: *Psycho-diagnostics*. New York: Grune & Stratton, 1952.
20. Schachtel, Ernest G. "Projection and Its Relation to Character Attitudes, etc." *Psychiatry*, vol. 13 (1950), pp. 69–100.
21. Selz, Peter. "The Aesthetic Theories of Wassily Kandinsky." *Art Bulletin*, vol. 39 (1957), pp. 127–36.
22. ———. *German Expressionist Painting*. Berkeley and Los Angeles: University of California Press, 1957.
23. Seuphor, Michel. *Piet Mondrian: Life and Work*. New York: Abrams, 1956.
24. Sirén, Osvald. *The Chinese on the Art of Painting*. New York: Schocken, 1963.
25. Stern, Paul. *Einfühlung und Association in der neueren Aesthetik*. Hamburg: Voss, 1898.
26. Sullivan, Harry Stack. *The Interpersonal Theory of Psychiatry*. New York: Norton, 1953.
27. Sze, Mai-mai. *The Way of Chinese Painting*. New York: Modern Library, 1959.
28. Vollard, Antoine. *Paul Cézanne*. Paris: Crès, 1924.
29. Worringer, Wilhelm. *Abstraktion und Einfühlung*. Munich: Piper, 1911. Eng.: *Abstraction and Empathy*. New York: International Universities Press, 1953.

# Part III

# UNITY AND DIVERSITY OF THE ARTS

THERE ARE those who are attracted mostly by what distinguishes one thing from the next. Others stress the unity in the diversity. The two approaches spring from deep-seated personal and cultural attitudes. Carried to their extremes, they produce on the one side people who relish atomization and alienation almost sadistically, and on the other side those who naively and indiscriminately embrace everything in the all. If they are willing to listen to each other, they will take us closer to the truth.

The intellect has a primary need to define things by distinguishing them, whereas direct sensory experience impresses us first of all by how everything hangs together. Therefore the arts, committed to immediate experience, give much prominence to the community that transcends differences of style, media, and culture. Visual images carry their messages across historical time and geographic space. A musical ear can learn to move from one modal system to another. And the basic themes of poetry recur, similar, wherever we go. Different media can carry similar styles; they can borrow from one another and combine with ease in complex works: dance goes with music, sculpture goes with architecture, illustration goes with narration, poem goes with picture scroll. As Baudelaire walks through his forest of symbols, he finds correspondences between

First published as "The Unity of the Arts: Time, Space, and Distance," *Yearbook of Comparative and General Literature*, no. 25 (1976).

perfumes, colors, and sounds. The case for resemblance and unity is eloquently made.

The unity of the media suggests itself also when, in a biological mood, we think of the arts as extensions of the senses. The unity of the senses manifests itself genetically, in that the various modalities—of sight, sound, touch, etc.—can be said to have evolved by gradual differentiation from originally much more integrated equipment. In a recent comprehensive survey of the subject, Lawrence E. Marks states:

All of the senses, it is commonly believed, trace their evolutionary history back to a single primitive sense, a simple undifferentiated responsiveness to external stimulation. It is not difficult to imagine some early form of life, a relatively simple agglutination of cells that wriggled or withdrew when bombarded with virtually any sharp stimulus, whether mechanical, radiant, or chemical. (8, p. 182)

Unity is manifest in basic structural qualities shared across the board by different sense modalities. The unity of the senses and the corresponding unity of the arts was proclaimed in the 1920s by the musicologist Erich Maria von Hornbostel in a short but influential paper, in which he wrote: "What is essential in the sensuous-perceptible is not that which separates the senses from one another, but that which unites them; unites them among themselves; unites them with the entire (even with the nonsensuous) experience in ourselves; and with all the external world that there is to be experienced" (6).

The comparison of the arts relies on certain basic dimensions, common to all modes of sensory perception and by extension also to all modes of aesthetic experience. The artistic media show their differences in their particular ways of selecting and using these dimensions. The way the dimensions are used is directly related to basic aspects of human outlook, attitude, and behavior. It would be tempting to spell out the analogies between the characteristics of an artistic medium and the kind of person who takes to it because it meets his or her particular needs. Such an analysis would not suffice to explain why a given person became a poet rather than a painter, or why someone prefers listening to music to looking at architecture. The choices made by any particular individual or kind of person are determined by powerful additional motives—cultural, social, and psychological. But the affinities among certain kinds of perceptual experience and corresponding preferences for ways of handling the tasks of human existence are surely significant and influential.

Take the difference between conceiving of our world essentially in terms of time as opposed to space. Nietzsche, for instance, states in *The Will to Power:* "Continual transitions make it impossible to talk about the 'individual,' etc.; the very 'number' of beings is itself in flux. We would know nothing of time and nothing of motion if we did not crudely believe that we see things 'at rest' next to what moves" (9, sec. 520). To the time-oriented view, Being is a weave of events, interpreted in the arts by the temporal media of the drama and narrative literature, the dance, music, and film. Although most of these media employ objects and persons for the setting and cast of their performances, they introduce them most successfully, as Lessing showed in his *Laocoön*, when they characterize them through actions and describe them in the course of events.

Most radically, all components of music are pure action. One has to resort to the auxiliary channels of the eyes to see the players and singers persist in time. A musical theme is not a thing but a happening. This is in keeping with auditory experience quite in general, which reports exclusively on what things do; it is silent about what they are otherwise. A bird, a clock, a person exist aurally only as their singing, ticking, speaking, weeping, or coughing; they are characterized only by their adverbial properties and exist only as long as these properties endure. In a study of mine on radio as an art of sound, under the heading "In Praise of Blindness" I pointed to the noble economy of a purely auditory performance, in which musical instruments, singers, or actors enter existence only when their parts call them into action (1). No orchestra sits around waiting, no confidante listens until it is her turn to respond, and no furniture or landscape stands idle. In the world of pure sound, causality is restricted to sequence: one thing follows the other in a linear dimension. In a musical composition, a novel, a dance, the audience participates in the exploring and unfolding of a situation, the building or undoing of a structure, the solving of a problem, and so on. Essentially they are pure action.

In the temporal arts, the listener or viewer can mount the vehicle of action and stay with the unfolding events. The spatial setting is either completely absent, as in a radio performance, or is traversed by the course of events, as in any well-made film. In a good film, Nietzsche's vision does become reality: all existing things are sucked into the time dimension, they arrive and leave, and their image changes from moment to moment, in keeping with their role. They are actors rather than props. Persistence in space is redefined as resistance to the flow of change, as, for example, when still photographs are inserted into a moving scene. The more complete the transformation of things into action, the more nearly film becomes visual music. Only in the inept hands of the theatrical filmmakers promoted by the talking film does the image on the screen appear loaded with inert scenery and bystanders who hamper the progress of visual action.

But instead of riding the crest of the action in a typical time-bound art, the viewer can also identify with a timeless setting. This can happen in the theater, a medium poised ambiguously between the two attitudes. The spectator may move with the action in a temporal state of mind and acknowledge the stage as a mere frame within which the events take place; or he may find himself anchored to the spatial ambiance, of which the stage is a part, and watch, as a stationary onlooker, the action rushing past him like an express train. When he is locked into the spatial framework, he tends to grasp of the performance only as much as he can perceive during the present moment. The action arrives from the future and vanishes into the past after a flash of existence that is poorly connected with what preceded or will follow it. In music, this attitude is found in the kind of concert-goer who is present only in space but hardly in time and who perceives little more than a sound picture undergoing kaleidoscopic transformation.

The dilemma of the unsuccessful concert-goer illustrates a more general problem inherent in the witnessing of events. The performance of a piece of music comes and goes, and at any moment no more than a fraction of it is directly perceivable. Strictly speaking, the present amounts to no more than an infinitely short differential of time. In the mind's practice, however, memory expands the percept, which oozes, as it were, beyond its boundaries. This phenomenon was first discussed by Christian von Ehrenfels in an essay of 1890, which gave gestalt psychology its name (4). He pointed out that when one watches a person walking, the movement of a step is perceived as a whole, but that the mind bestows presence upon a sequence of sounds with even more ease than upon a visual sequence. A melody extending over several bars can be perceived as a unified whole. This perceptual difference between media, according to von Ehrenfels, has an influence on memory. "When a dancer, to the accompaniment of a melody, executes movements which . . . possess an articulation and complexity analogous to that of the melody, it will be possible for many to reproduce the melody even after listening to it only once, whereas hardly anybody can do the same with the movements of the dancer."

This may or may not be so. But in any case the length of the present depends on the structure of the perceived situation. A stroke of lightning makes for a short present, whereas a roll of thunder makes for a longer one. Lightning and thunder together can unify in an expanded present at the next higher level, and thus the experience of what is present can reach out to ever-broader units of a hierarchic structure, depending on the capacity of a person's awareness. A viewer of limited skill will grasp little more than a single movement of a dancer's performance; with better understanding he will survey a complete phrase, and the expert can apprehend the entire composition in simultaneity. Not for nothing were the Muses the daughters of Memory.

The necessary transformation of sequence into simultaneity raises peculiar problems, since only the sense of sight really makes this possible. Strictly speaking, simultaneity in music cannot go beyond the tones of a single chord. The contraction of any sound sequence into one moment would produce a shapeless noise. It follows that in order to survey a work of music as a whole, one has to imagine its structure as a visual image—an image pervaded by a one-way arrow, to be sure. But the thought of this necessary translation is awkward nevertheless.

In literature, which is also a sequential medium, the same requirement leads to the question of how much of an extended verbal description remains active in the reader's or listener's mind. In a novel by Novalis, explorers enter a cave strewn with the bones of prehistoric animals (10). The explorers meet a hermit who has made the cave his dwelling, and his story soon monopolizes the reader's attention. The remnants of a savage past strewn about the cave present a necessary counterpoint to the precious books, graven art work, and song surrounding the hermit in the cave; but they easily slip the reader's mind as he concentrates on the foreground story. If the reader's attention is not very comprehensive, he may need a repeated reference to the skeletons to maintain the complete image in his mind. In a strict sense, no element of a work of art can be understood without the concomitant input of every other element contained in the work as a whole. But since the complexity of many works surpasses the human brain's attention span, they are apprehended only approximately—by the perceivers and also, I suspect, by their own creators.

The processing of information in the organism is essentially sequential. Even the retina of the eye, which faces the world with a two-dimensional dish antenna, develops in the higher animals a fovea, a center of acute vision, which scans the world like a narrow beam. Although a painting is preferably viewed from a distance that lets it appear in its entirety within the visual field of the viewer, articulate perception is limited at any moment to a tiny area, and the painting can be comprehended only by scanning. Sequential perception, therefore, characterizes experience in all aesthetic media, the spatial as well as the temporal ones. What distinguishes the media in this respect is that in music, literature, film, etc., the sequence is inherent in the presentation and is therefore imposed as a constraint upon the consumer. In the timeless arts of painting, sculpture, or architecture, the sequence pertains to the process of apprehension only: it is subjective, arbitrary, and outside the structure and character of the work.

In painting, according to Lessing, action is represented indirectly by the interplay of objects. Therefore, when we turn from the temporal to the timeless media, we are not simply exchanging a world of verbs for a world of nouns, that is, lively action for inert things. The representation of action by painted or sculpted shapes would be totally ineffective if it could rely on nothing better than the viewer's knowledge that in the corresponding physical scene the horseback rider would vigorously gallop or the angels would fly. In that case, abstract painting or sculpture, unable to point to such past experience, could mobilize no action. It is of course the visual dynamics, the directed tension inherent in all shapes, that creates the action in painting, sculpture, or architecture.

This dynamics also sustains the causal relations between the components of a pattern. In a spatial manifold, causal relations are not limited to a linear sequence but occur simultaneously in the many directions offered by a two-dimensional or three-dimensional medium. The attractions and repulsions, for example, that obtain between the components of a painting create an interplay that must be understood synoptically. Only when the scanning eye has collected and related them all does an adequate conception of the total dynamics emerge. This dynamics is inherent in the work and quite independent of subjective exploration. For example, even though someone may scan a picture from right to left, he may discover in doing so that a principal vector of the composition points from left to right. Symmetry, balance, and other spatial characteristics can become apparent upon sequential observation, but they can never be experienced linearly.

The composition of a painting, piece of sculpture, or work of architecture is perceived only when the crisscross of relations between the elements is apprehended synoptically. The same is true, as I mentioned earlier, for the temporal media. Physically, of course, a performance of music dispenses chord after chord and a verbal description word after word, but these materials simply form the channel of communication. The aesthetic structure they transmit—the piece of music, the poetic image—is not limited to a one-way sequence. While listening to music, the hearer weaves relations back and forth and even coordinates phrases as matched pendants, e.g., in the return of the minuet after the trio, although in the performance they are delivered one after the other. The ample use of repetition in the temporal arts serves to create correspondences between parts following one another in time and thereby to compensate for the one-way structure of the performance. To be sure, in a temporal medium such a correspondence can never display the perfect symmetry of a pair of stone lions flanking the steps of a building. The difference in position within the time sequence is acknowledged, for example, when in music a theme is restated at a different pitch level or modified by augmentation, inversion, or similar change. And even the identically repeated refrain of a poem is intended to be affected in its mood and meaning by the differences between the stanzas in which it occurs.

In music, it seems, repetition can have two different effects. It can be experienced either as a repetition of, or as a return to, the phrase that appeared earlier. In the former case the time sequence of the music proceeds undisturbed but offers an analogy to what was heard and remains in the past. In the latter case the listener interrupts the time sequence and returns the phrase to "its proper place" earlier in the composition. I suggest that this happens when the repeated phrase refuses to fit the structure of the music at the new place, as opposed to what it does when it is perceived as a repetition (Figure 7a), and therefore is returned to the only place where it fits (Figure 7b). This alternative amounts to a reshuffling of the musical time sequence (7).

The distinction between the sequential and the synoptic arts loses weight as one realizes that in either case a sequential transmission of information leads to the acquisition of a structure not restricted to linearity. Information theory based on the conception of a one-way channel is incapable of accounting for compositional structure because it deals with the performance of the transmission instead of the multidimensional image produced by that transmission. The relational network of a picture cannot be accounted for by a linear scanning beam, which may indeed produce the picture technically—e.g., on the television screen or the weaver's loom—but can never describe its structure.

The image that emerges in the reader's mind from a literary descrip-

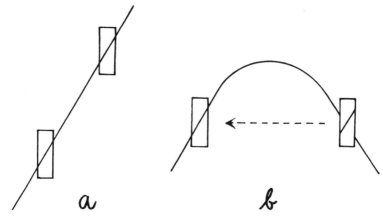

*Figure 7.*

tion vies in its multidimensionality with the spatial complexity of an actual perceptual experience. Even so, the sequence in which a temporal work discloses aspects of the intended structure exerts a decisive influence on the result. When Emily Dickinson describes in a one-sentence poem

> An everywhere of silver,
> With ropes of sand
> To keep it from effacing
> The track called land.

she closes in on the island concentrically, from the outside—a dynamics not prescribed by the image but imposed upon it by the sequence and, to be sure, by the wording (3, p. 88). Inversely, Dickinson has us move from the center outward when she begins another poem (3, p. 108) thus:

> The mountain sat upon the plain
> In his eternal chair,
> His observation omnifold,
> His inquest everywhere.

Or, to use a different example: A linguist who would try to persuade us that the two sentences "The boy chases the cat" and "The cat is chased by the boy" contain the same information would reveal only his illiteracy.

The spatial aspects of the arts may also be examined with regard to distance—a term of several meanings. There is, first, the physical distance between a person and an art object. It concerns us here because it determines whether or not the person can directly handle the object. Also, physical distance influences perceptual distance, i.e., how far away a work of art is experienced to be. There is, however, no simple correspondence between physical and perceptual distance: an object may look closer or farther away than it is. In addition to physical and perceptual distance there is what I will call personal distance, which refers to the degree of interplay or intimacy between person and art object.

The effect of physical distance became evident in recent years when the performing arts tried to undo the separation introduced by the theaters and concert halls of recent centuries between players, actors, and dancers tucked away on the stage and the audience congregated in the house. It is true that even the traditional stage set conformed in some ways to the spatial framework of the hall in which the audience dwelt, just as many paintings implied a viewpoint available somewhere in the viewer's physical space. Even so, the stage presented a remote world, and the dramatic business was an isolated, self-contained event. The frontal exposure of the soloist in an opera or ballet acknowledged the presence of the audience only in the sense of performing for it, but he neither addressed it—for an exception see the prologues and epilogues of Shakespeare—nor called for an active audience response.

The attempt to do away with the distance between stage and audience, however, showed that a mere rearrangement of spatial logistics was insufficient as long as the plays and acting techniques adhered to the old separation. Actors running through the aisles or front-row customers tangling with Chekhov's three sisters in a "theater in the round" accomplished little beyond creating territorial disorder. It became clear that such a reintegration would require nothing less than a return to a different social relation between performers and audience, that is, a return to collective gatherings in which actors and spectators were participants in rituals embracing them both. Such a change could not be persuasively accomplished within the limited confines of mere art events; it would have to be undergone by society as a whole.

On a smaller scale, physical distance makes a major difference between a statue looked at from afar and, for example, *netsukes*, those small figures of wood or ivory worn "for some 300 years by every well-dressed Japanese at the sash of his kimono as an attachment to his purse, pouch, or lacquer box" (2). While the fondling of such miniature sculpture is not only permitted but expected as an essential manner of enjoying it, a similar practice has been frowned upon for larger pieces. Thus Hegel, in his *Aesthetics*, decreed that "the sensuousness of art refers only to the two theoretical senses of sight and hearing, whereas smell, taste, and touch remain excluded from artistic enjoyment"; and he warned that "the pawing of the soft marble portions of the female goddesses recommended by a fellow aesthetician has no place in the comtemplation and enjoyment of art" (5).

Apart from the puritan aspects of this taboo, the demand that the user keep his distance reflected the classicist notion that the aesthetic attitude, for the sake of purity, required detached contemplation, free from the possessive impulses of the "will." Sight, the distance sense *par excellence*, was preferred to the bodily contact of touch.

Here again a recent change of attitude tends to modify the purist demand for detachment—not only by calling for the fullness of perceptual experience as, under the fashionable guidance of phenomenologists like Merleau-Ponty, body meets body, but also by stressing the importance of a natural functional interplay between art work and consumer. What matters aesthetically about the difference between visual and tactile experience is not the psychologically erroneous notion that vision gives us only the image of an object, whereas touch gives us the object "itself." (All percepts are images.) Rather, what matters is the varying degree of perceived interplay between object and person and the corresponding degree of "real presence." To the sculpturally inclined person, only the solid resistance of a physical material conveys the sense that the object and its formal properties of shape and texture are "really there."

By its physical presence, sculpture partakes of the world of furniture and other implements that exist to be handled for practical purposes. These objects, however, are mostly looked at just for the purpose of being handled. Only exceptionally are they thought worthy of contemplation. Perhaps this is why so many museum visitors hardly glance at the sculpture, while they concentrate on the pictures on the walls. One does not contemplate a chair or an umbrella; one uses it or leaves it alone.

At the same time, the physical presence of sculpture as an object of weight and three-dimensional volume contributes to making it perceptually "more real" than pictures. The magical power of a religious statue tends to be greater than that of an altar painting. The faithful respond to statues more readily with worship and sacrificial offerings. Not without reason were the iconoclasts less tolerant of graven images, whose physical presence invited direct idolatry, than of pictures, which were more like illustrations of things to be learned about.

The difference between an art object's presence in physical space and its purely visual appearance is strikingly revealed when one compares a canvas covered with pigment to the visual image it carries. The former is the physical object at which the curator scratches with an authorized finger; the latter can be reached only by pointing at it. The pigmented canvas as a physical object is seen at its physical distance, whereas the depicted view of a remote landscape makes the glance penetrate pictorial space to an indefinite depth. This difference was eliminated only recently, when painters ceased to aim at creating illusionary space and presented instead boards with painted surfaces, which no longer were intended to differ in principle from sculpture.

Even less tangible than distant painted objects are, of course, the mental images produced by literary narration and poetry. The painted vista is connected to the viewer at least by a shared physical space, but no such spatial continuity connects the reader to the images in his mind. They appear in a phenomenal world of their own, detached but not at a defined distance.

The lack of such a perceptual bridge can be offset, however, by the strong resonance that unites the reader to the described scene. In this way "personal distance," as I called it earlier, can be reduced to a minimum. The degree of personal involvement also influences perception proper considerably. Note here, for example, that true aesthetic experience is not limited to the passive reception of the art object arriving from afar, but involves an active interplay between the artist's work and the viewer's, listener's, or reader's response. The exploration of a painted or musical composition is experienced as an active shaping of the perceptual object, and the object, in turn, imposes its shapes as constraints upon the freedom of the explorer: "This I will let you do, but not that!"

Two side observations may be added here. First, the direct handling of art material, such as clay or pigment, encourages the sense of what suits or does not suit a given medium. This objective control is not easily provided by the imagination. Thus the architect, whom one may describe, unkindly and unjustly, as an atrophied builder, may find that his shapes work well on paper but do not go with the materials chosen for the structure. Like a scriptwriter for the cinema, the architect is a Raphael without hands.

Second, the necessary segregation of the maker from his product does not always require a physical distance between the two. Both can be accommodated in the same organism, even when they do not fit as naturally as a dance fits the dancer's body. A startling example is that of the *onna-gata*, or impersonator of women, in the kabuki theater. A mature man interprets the movements and voice of a graceful girl, not by perverting himself into effeminacy or by simply adopting a girl's behavior, but by shaping a stylized image of her external character through the instrument of his own body, which remains recognizable under the disguise of costume and mask. It is an extreme example of the artist's awesome ability to form with his own mind and body creatures profoundly different from himself. Think of an old man—Maillol, Renoir, Matisse— shaping a young woman in clay or paint, imbued with his own character yet true to her nature.

Of course, the dancer's or actor's daily feat differs only in degree from the spectacular performance of the *onna-gata*. Although the figure created by the performer commonly resembles his own body and mind more closely, he, too, produces a human being by transfusing his own nature into a figment, which nevertheless does not absorb his identity but leaves him in remote control.

In the end, however, the power of the imagination is most impressively demonstrated by the narrator or poet, because he creates without the help of any bodily vehicle at all. To quote an observation from Novalis's aforementioned story:

Of the art of the poet nothing can be discovered externally. Nor does it create anything with tools and hands. The eye and the ear perceive nothing of it, for the mere hearing of the words is not the true effect of this secret art. Everything is internal, and as other artists fill the external senses with pleasurable sensations, the poet fills the inner sanctuary of the mind with new, wondrous, and agreeable thoughts.

## References

1. Arnheim, Rudolf. *Rundfunk als Hörkunst*. Munich: Hanser, 1979. Eng.: *Radio, An Art of Sound*. New York: Da Capo, 1972.
2. Bushell, Raymond. *An Introduction to Netsuke*. Rutland, Vt.: Tuttle, 1971.
3. Dickinson, Emily. *Selected Poems*. New York: Modern Library.
4. Ehrenfels, Christian von. "Ueber 'Gestaltqualitäten.'" In Ferdinand Weinhandl, ed., *Gestalthaftes Sehen*. Darmstadt: Wissensch. Buchgesellschaft, 1960.
5. Hegel, Georg Wilhelm Friedrich. *Vorlesungen über die Aesthetik*. Introd. III, 2, and Part III: "Das System der einzelnen Künste, Einteilung."
6. Hornbostel, Erich Maria von. "Die Einheit der Sinne." *Melos, Zeitschrift für Musik*, vol. 4 (1925), pp. 290–97. Eng.: "The Unity of the Senses." In Willis

D. Ellis, ed., *A Source Book of Gestalt Psychology*. New York: Harcourt Brace, 1939.

7. Kramer, Jonathan D. "Multiple and Non-Linear Time in Beethoven's Opus 135." *Perspectives of New Music*, vol. 11, (Spring/Summer 1973), pp. 122–45.
8. Marks, Lawrence E. *The Unity of the Senses*. New York: Academic Press, 1978.
9. Nietzsche, Friedrich. *Der Wille zur Macht*. 1886.
10. Novalis. *Heinrich von Ofterdingen*. Frankfurt: Fischer, 1963.

# A STRICTURE ON SPACE
# AND TIME

THIS INQUIRY was suggested by the observation that in many instances the notion of time is not an element of common experience where generally accepted thinking would hold it should be. Elsewhere I have used the example of a dancer leaping across the stage. I asked: "Is it an aspect of our experience, let alone the most significant aspect, that time passes during the leap? Does she arrive out of the future and jump through the present into the past?" (1, p. 373). Obviously not. And yet the event of the leap, like any other event when it is described by the physicist, takes place in the time dimension. Are we then led to realize that for the description of common perceptual experience the notion of time must be used in a special, more limited sense?

The kind of example I just gave is not confined to events as brief as the dancer's leap. An entire choreographic work, and indeed an entire concert of such works, may be performed without our sensing in it a component that can be described only by reference to time. We simply witness an event unrolling, unfolding in a sensible order. Similarly, an animated debate may go on someplace for two hours without the sense of time entering anybody's consciousness—so much so that when someone observes, "Time is up!" everybody is surprised. When I watch a waterfall, there is no before or after, only an ongoing production of happy abundance; but when I stand at the baggage claim area of an airport waiting for my suitcase, time is distinctly a part of what I feel. Impa-

First published in *Critical Inquiry*, vol. 4, no. 1 (Summer 1978).

tience, boredom, fear are conditions calling up time as a special, fairly exceptional, ingredient of perception.[1] The archetype of the time experience is the waiting room, which has been described by Howard Nemerov as

> A cube sequestered in space and filled with time,
> Pure time, refined, distilled, denatured time
> Without qualities, without even dust ... (7)

Fortunately such experiences are exceptional.

It is tempting to interpret the more typical perception of daily events as "the spontaneous transposition of the temporal into the spatial." This is in fact the hypothesis of Paul Fraisse. He speculates that spatiality corresponds to visual perception, which, as the "most precise" of the sensory modes, takes biological preference over the other modes, among them the mode of temporality (4, p. 277). In what sense is space more precise than time? Perhaps the most convincing reason for the biological priority of space is that normally it takes things to serve as vehicles for action and that therefore in perception things are prior to what they do. Things, however, dwell in space, whereas time applies to action.

Moreover, spatial simultaneity facilitates synopsis and thereby understanding. Therefore the theoretical conception of the world of things is commonly derived from a state of immobility or, more precisely, from a static point in space.[2] This germinal point "grows" the spatial dimensions one after the other until it reaches three-dimensionality. To the full-fledged object mobility is added as the separate, fourth dimension of time. Hence the priority of space.

Transposition of the temporal into the spatial mode can indeed be said to occur, especially when it is interpreted as succession being replaced by simultaneity. This happens not just for convenience' sake, but by necessity when the mind turns from a participatory to a contemplative attitude. In order to comprehend an event as a whole, one must view it in simultaneity, and that means spatially and visually. Succession, by its very nature, limits attention to the momentary, to a differential of time. Synopsis, as the term indicates, is visual. (Touch, the only other sense

---

[1] In Wolfgang Zucker's formulation: "Time is the condition of experience that threatens my existence when that existence of mine is no longer in accord with me." The present paper owes much to an exchange of ideas with the late Dr. Zucker.

[2] Fraisse (4, p. 286) cites Pierre Janet as saying that philosophers have a particular horror of time and have endeavored to suppress it. Bergson (3) says in the first sentence of his essay on consciousness, "et nous pensons le plus souvent dans l'espace."

modality with access to spatial organization, is too limited in its range to contribute much to the spatial aspects of images.) Gaston Bachelard has reminded us that memory is not animated by time. "Memory—a strange thing!—does not register concrete duration, in Bergson's sense of duration. Once durations are brought to a close one cannot revive them. One can only think them, think them along the line of an abstract time that has no thickness. Only through space, only in space, do we find the beautiful fossils of duration concretized by a long stay" (2, p. 28).[3] This transposition of succession into simultaneity leads to the curious paradox that a piece of music, a drama, novel, or dance must be perceived as some kind of visual image if it is to be understood as a structural whole. Painting and sculpture are manifestations of the contemplative attitude. They show the world of action transformed into simultaneity.[4] But this is not the subject of my present concern.

For the purpose of the present study, transposition in the above-mentioned examples changes succession into simultaneity; but the role of time and space in such processes remains to be considered. Furthermore, examples such as that of the dancer's leap, from which I took off, involve no transposition of a primarily temporal experience into a spatial one, but are spatial from the outset. Also, space can be shown to exhibit some of the same problems I pointed to for time. Space, like time, figures in perception only under particular conditions. Therefore, I shall deal first with space and return to time afterward.

The apparent absurdity of my assertions is dispelled as soon as one remembers that categories such as space and time are created by the human mind for the apprehension of facts in the physical and psychological realms, and that therefore they become pertinent only when such categories are needed for the description and interpretation of those facts. For certain practical and scientific purposes, it is necessary to pre-establish a framework of spatial coordinates and chronological sequence to which all facts are automatically fitted. The grid of a geographical map makes it possible to relate the locations of any points on earth, and standardized clock and calendar time lets us establish events in the course of the world's history as preceding or succeeding one another or occurring at the same moment.

---

[3] See also Koffka (5, p. 446) on the similarity of spatial and temporal memory.

[4] See Arnheim (1, p. 374). See also Merleau-Ponty (6, p. 470), who asserts that even in the "objective world" the course of water from mountain glaciers to the river's meeting the sea is not a sequence of events but "one single, indivisible entity that does not change."

Although indispensable for certain purposes of coordination, such pre-established frameworks are what Germans call *strukturfremd*, i.e., alien to the structures they concern. The Cartesian space net tags everything that ventures into its reach, regardless of how the components of things thus measured hang together or are separate from one another. Meridians and parallels cut with ruthless insensitivity across coastlines, mountain ranges, and city limits, and the standards of the clock interfere so patently with local rhythms of day and night that time zones must be used as concessions to local needs.

While for practical and scientific purposes or, for example, in analytic geometry these alien impositions on the live structure of things apply inevitably, they do not necessarily do so in ordinary perception. Things in action are what is primarily given in spontaneous perception. Perception is neither able nor willing to analyze behavior by differentiating the four dimensions. Think of the laborious efforts of dance notation to break down this unity. In actual experience, a dancer's performance admits of no such reduction. Instead, she stands erect or tilts, turns to the left or right, bends or straightens up, moves or stops, in integrated action.

Just as complex behavior resists any perceptual reduction to the three coordinates of space, any distinction between the shape of static bodies and the shape of motion is artificial. As the dancer performs a thrust, there is no sensible way of telling the contribution of the shapes of arms, trunk, and legs from that of the trajectories of the dancer's curved or straight or jagged motions. This is even more obvious in the figurative arts of painting or sculpture, in which the visual dynamics of the bodily shape of, say, a tree or a pyramid is rendered by the same means as the locomotion of a jumping horse or an ocean wave. Visual dynamics is an indivisible unity, not broken down into space and time. We conclude that we shall do justice to perceptual experience only if we abandon the pre-established frameworks of space and time and instead look with unprejudiced eyes for the categories the experience requires.

What matters most for the present purpose is that the various dimensions of appearance and action are perceived as properties of the performing object itself, not as those of some superordinate framework or agency. It is the dancer who moves and turns and stops. The thundercloud grows and advances. The leaning tower deviates from a vertical that is perceived as potentially inherent in the tower's own "true" position or as actually given in the surrounding buildings. By the same token, these dimensions or properties reach only as far as the object. There is something curiously humorous about Aristotle's pointing to the equivalent in empty space of the volume occupied (*Categories* 6.5a10, and *Physics* 4.1.208b). A punning relation is established between the shape of the object and an alien area outside the object to which the object's dimensions do not apply.

The dimensions and categories needed to describe the examples just cited are clearly spatial. Not only size and orientation but also the direction and velocity of movement are experienced as spatial. But the spatial standards to which they refer are not provided by an externally given framework. The object itself provides the framework, which governs what I will call the object's intrinsic or inherent space. In the meantime we have lost time entirely. In our examples it figured neither intrinsically nor extrinsically. I shall undertake to look for time a little later on.

First, however, we must cope with the problem that arises when we assert that the object provides its own spatial framework. How can this be correct, since we know that perceptual features such as size, direction, and speed are relative, i.e., dependent on their context? For the answer we must look at what is meant by the range of the object.

Since we are talking perception, we cannot establish the boundaries of the object simply by physical or pragmatic criteria. What matters is how far the object reaches perceptually. I am looking at a painting by Goya that depicts a bullfight (Figure 8). In the center of the scene a picador on horseback faces a charging bull. The horseman is perceptually defined by a forward-pointing axis provided by the symmetrical shape of man and animal. This symmetry axis pushes beyond the figure into the surroundings, where it meets a similar vector sent out by the equally symmetrical shape of the charging bull. The horseman's spear and the bull's horns reinforce the vectors, which cross at an angle.

Each of the two vectors belongs to its object, but their crossing may be said to belong to neither. It can be perceptually nonexistent, somewhat like a lap dissolve in a film. In that case the two arrows ignore each other. No relation exists between them. Their crossing does not count. They are emissaries from disparate systems, each minding its own business. Or else the crossing does exist as a perceived relation. In that case, where does it belong? There are two solutions.

1. When the contending parties, in our example the horseman and the bull, keep their independence as self-contained and complete systems, the crossing of their axes comes to belong to an additional system, represented by no object of its own but consisting entirely of the relations between other systems. This calls for an additional perceptual compo-

*Figure 8.* Goya y Lucientes, *The Bullfight.* 1822. Metropolitan Museum of Art, New York, Wolfe Fund.

nent, which I will call *extrinsic space*. Extrinsic perceptual space is closest to the objective or absolute space of Newtonian physics. Although not of universal range, it is a comprehensive spatial system in which particular systems are embedded.

Extrinsic space controls the relations between independent object systems and provides them with standards of reference for their perceptual features. The horseman and the bull may be said to meet in extrinsic space. Goya's painting offers many such encounters between systems. There are groups of performers and groups of spectators. There is the square-shaped arena containing the fight, and there are buildings. Each of these units constitutes a system of perceptual forces that reach beyond the object's boundaries into its surroundings. The interplay between the forces of several neighboring systems can create an independent space field, separate from other such fields. This happens often in architectural settings. There may be a small enclosed piazza created perceptually by the size and shape properties of the surrounding buildings. It is held together by an extrinsic space system of its own, which separates it from the adjoining streets.

But this way of seeing particular perceptual objects embedded in an additional system of extrinsic space would seem to violate one of the principal properties of works of art. It patches a work together out of its self-contained components and neglects its unity. To obtain that unity, the overall structure must control the place and function of the parts. If I am to understand Goya's painting, I must see it as such a totality. The way we have talked so far is a useful approximation of what is called pictorial space, but it is an approach "from below," which must be supplemented by an approach "from above."

2. This leads to what I referred to earlier as a second way of looking at the pictorial situation. We begin by asking whether it would not be more natural and appropriate to see the picador and the bull as belonging to one and the same comprehensive system, rather than as two self-contained systems that meet in extrinsic space. This different view, however, involves a profound restructuring of the perceptual situation. Extrinsic space vanishes; it becomes a mere interval between two components of a more comprehensive single "object." It becomes nothing but an internal gap, which no more belongs to an extrinsic space than does the hollow of a pot or, to use another example from the arts, the varying distances between two steel bars moving back and forth in a mobile by George Rickey.

Apply this changed approach to a work as a whole and you arrive at a conception of the work as a single "object," whose *intrinsic space* consists of the relations between its various components, controlled by the total structure. Not that we are dismissing the notion of extrinsic space as incorrect. Instead we are asserting that there are two ways of analyzing pictorial space, both of which are to be considered in all cases. Starting from a composition as a whole, we see a tissue of interwoven units and intervals, all fitting in one unbroken overall system and held together by intrinsic space. When, however, we start from the units, we see subsystems meeting, crossing, repelling, or paralleling one another, all this taking place in the arena of an extrinsic space system. The meaning of the work requires the apprehension of both structural versions: the nature of the whole and the behavior of its parts.

The difference between the two approaches becomes evident when one compares works that emphasize the one or the other. In European painting of the nineteenth century there is an increasing tendency, culminating in Monet's late works, to treat the realm of the picture as an unbroken whole. The interspaces, instead of belonging to a detached background, acquire figure character of their own. Everything is foreground, and only with some perceptual effort, although not without reward, does one succeed in identifying subwholes and setting them against one another. In comparison, if one looks at traditional paintings showing a group of figures or a single portrayed person, there is often a clear distinction between the systems of vectorial forces issuing from the objects and the environment into which these forces flow. The counteraction of the extrinsic space is often so weak that the vectors of the objects appear to have an empty scene all to themselves, a scene that seems to continue as an *apeiron* beyond the frame with no structure-bearing form of its own. This second way of treating pictorial space is the simpler one. It resembles practical perception in daily life, where extrinsic space is reduced to a neutral foil and may therefore be entirely ignored—a mode of vision reflected in amateur snapshots that focus on nothing but the foreground scene.

*     *     *

Does the distinction between extrinsic and intrinsic space hold also for time? It looks as though time figures in a perceptual situation only when it pertains to an extrinsic system, whereas the function of intrinsic time is taken over by intrinsic space.

I stated in the beginning that time is not usually a component of the perception of events, even though in the natural sciences and for certain practical purposes, such as time schedules, all events are automatically assigned a place in an independent temporal framework. The example of the dancer's leap showed that such actions are normally perceived as involving space rather than time. I get up from my chair, walk to the bookshelf, reach for a book, and return to my desk. Such a piece of behavior consists of intention and mobilized muscular action, of changes of place, etc. It is a sequence of events, but by no means all sequences are temporal. The sequence of the letters of the alphabet does not involve time, nor does the sequence of the numbers (Aristotle, *Categories* 6.5a 15ff.). The features of a human face have to come in the right sequence: forehead, eyes, nose, mouth, chin. What counts in experience is the order of things, regardless of whether the sequence dwells in simultaneity or occurs in succession. The difference between simultaneity and succession matters, of course, and is noticed. But it is a difference perceived as one between properties or dimensions within the object itself. To characterize the object perceptually, no reference to time is pertinent. This becomes evident when one looks, in comparison, at situations that do involve time.

Begin with the simple case of a person walking toward a goal. We know by now that the perception of this event involves extrinsic space when the moving person and the goal are perceived as belonging to different systems so that the diminishing distance between them does not belong to either. As the person moves, person and goal approach spatial coincidence in extrinsic space. Our event also consumes clock time, let us say twenty seconds, but perceptually it will involve time only if we ask: "Will he reach his goal in time?" Let us assume a man is running to board a subway train before the doors close. In that case, the visible, spatial goal is invested with a second connotation. Needed for the runner's success is not only coincidence in space but also a particular relation in the time sequence: his arrival must precede the closing of the doors. Under such conditions, time is an active feature of the perceptual situation and is therefore needed to describe it.

Such a time event is not necessarily paralleled by a corresponding action in space. In films, suspense is often obtained by a discrepancy between a visual situation that remains static and the progression of time toward the deadline. This is true for the countdown at the launching of a rocket or for the annoying kettle that will not boil. Time figures conspicuously in the tension between the visually immobile system expected to explode and the mental image of the anticipated explosion as the goal system. Such a tension-loaded discrepancy need not relate to a visual situation. The impassive ticking of a clock, with its static monotony, creates an irritating contrast to time "running out" in a suspenseful situation. Note, however, that whenever the event occurs in a unitary time system rather than as a relation between two independent systems, time drops out of the percept and space takes over. Two men approach each other to shake hands. Usually we see them do so in space, not in time. Intrinsic time is not perceived, probably because the time dimension possesses no sensory medium of its own.

This seems to be true also for music. Extrinsic time may be experienced when components of a piece are perceived as separate systems, for example, in the overlappings of a fugue. But this condition is not easily brought about. Music, as distinguished from painting, where we were able to separate the horseman from the bull without much trouble, acts strongly as a unified flow, one whose components are subdivisions of the whole rather than self-contained subwholes. The voices of a fugue are as tightly integrated in their musical flow as shingles on a roof. They resist emancipation. Music pours forth like a waterfall so that ritardandos and accelerandos are perceived as properties inherent in the music's behavior. The standard speed from which slowing down or speeding up is heard to deviate, like the regular beat that syncopations distort, is commonly perceived not as an external standard, but as a structural norm inherent in the music itself, its heartbeat, as it were—similar to the vertical orientation from which the leaning tower deviates and which can be perceived as a virtual property of the tower itself.

Yet it seems inappropriate to say that these musical events occur in intrinsic time. They are experienced as sequential, of course, but the sequence is no more temporal than the dancer's leap. The music, like the dancer's action, cannot be said to arrive out of the future and move through the present into the past. It occurs in "musical space," a medium whose particular perceptual qualities have been discussed in writings on the psychology of music. Here again, intrinsic time does not seem to exist.

Musical experiences involving extrinsic time are clearly different. The most radical examples are found in some modern music, where the continuity of the melodic flow is deliberately fractured so that even short intervals are strong enough to turn elements into self-contained, often point-sized systems. Time is called upon as the only substratum in which the fragments can organize. Accordingly the listener experiences "waiting for the next tone."

More commonly, extrinsic time can be observed in music when the melodic and harmonic structure of a work announces the approach to a climax, for example, the finale. A goal is established in the awareness of the listener and acts as an independent system toward which the music is striving. Most other examples that come to mind are extramusical, that is, they refer to music in relation to something outside it. A listener who instead of moving with the flow of the musical event remains outside it and watches the arriving and passing of phrase after phrase as though he were watching a parade from a viewing stand places himself in a separate temporal system whose relation to that of the music itself is governed by time. Compare also the radio performance scheduled to finish on the hour, or the state of mind of a concert-goer anxious to make the 11:20 suburban train home.

Like music, a literary narrative tends to be perceived as an ongoing flow. No references to time is appropriate for the description of the sequential action. The work sprouts and grows, and the various actions take place in intrinsic space. But whenever an interruption of continuity makes for a break in coherence, e.g., when the reappearance of a character does not connect back to his or her earlier presence, the two appearances may be experienced as separate systems. The only medium that can bridge the gap may be time, in which both are embedded. This is generally considered a compositional flaw. A skillful narrator avoids such a break by providing a filament that connects past and present appearances "amodally," as psychologists call it, that is, the way a train's progress is seen as remaining uninterrupted even when it is hidden for a moment by a tunnel.

Suspense also makes for extrinsic time. When the reader waits to see whether Stendhal's Fabrice will succeed in escaping from the prison before his enemies poison him, the two strands of action—the preparation for the escape and the fiends' scheming—grow as independent systems whose meeting in time is what matters. And when time is embodied as an authentic literary character, such as the "devouring Time" of Shakespeare's nineteenth sonnet, which blunts the lion's paws and plucks the tiger's teeth, it becomes an active system of its own and thus deserves capitalization.

Our findings help us to characterize complex structures such as the novels or films of the Nouvelle Vague. The shattering of the narrative sequence challenges the reader or viewer to reconstruct the objective order of the events. In trying to do so, he tends to assign the scattered pieces to their place in a structurally separate system offered by time and space. However, if the reader or viewer limited his effort to this reconstruction of objective reality, he would miss the point of the work's structure. Although discontinuous and therefore disorderly with regard to objective reality, the presentation must also be understood and accepted as a valid sequence of its own, a flow of disparate fragments, complexly and absurdly related to one another. When this very "cubist" order is perceived as a unified whole, neither time nor space may enter this aspect of the literary experience.

It remains for me to meet an objection to the thesis of this paper. The strictures I have imposed on space and time seem to place intolerable limits on the language needed to describe works of art. What will critics and historians do when they are prevented from talking about space and time? No such curb is intended. I merely maintained that when space is implicit, it does not figure in the percept as one of its components. When we describe a picture as made up of blues and greens, we can do so without referring to the concept of color. The blues and greens are perceived as properties of the pictorial objects. "Color" is no such property. But we need the concept "color" when we generalize. The collective term required for the purpose of classification hovers at a level of abstraction that can remain above the individual percept. Similarly we speak of forward and backward, straight and curved, fast and slow, without mentioning space as an additional perceptual component. For perceptual description, the term "space" must be reserved to cases of "extrinsic space," in which space operates as the medium for the meeting of separate systems. But a book on "Space in Painting" would correctly use the term to denote both kinds of phenomena. In the same way, time may have been present in only a few of the examples I cited. But if one asks me what I have written about, I will properly reply: "I wrote about time and space."

## References

1. Arnheim, Rudolf. *Art and Visual Perception.* New version. Berkeley and Los Angeles: University of California Press, 1974.
2. Bachelard, Gaston. *La poétique de l'espace.* Paris: Presses Universitaires, 1964. Eng.: *The Poetics of Space.* Boston: Beacon Press, 1964.
3. Bergson, Henri. *Essais sur les données immédiates de la conscience.* Paris: Presses Universitaires, 1948. Eng.: *Time and Free Will: An Essay on the Immediate Data of Consciousness.* London: 1959.
4. Fraisse, Paul. *Psychologie du temps.* Paris: Presses Universitaires, 1957. Eng.: *The Psychology of Time.* New York: Harper, 1966.
5. Koffka, Kurt. *Principles of Gestalt Psychology.* New York: Harcourt Brace, 1935.
6. Merleau-Ponty, Maurice. *Phénoménologie de la perception.* Paris: Gallimard, 1945.
7. Nemerov, Howard. "Waiting Rooms." In *The Western Approaches.* Chicago: University of Chicago Press, 1975.

# LANGUAGE, IMAGE, AND CONCRETE POETRY

OURS IS an age that offers theorists and critics few occasions on which to comment on great masterworks of their own time. Rather, there is much fluctuation in the media—a situation not propitious for peak performances, but attractive to the experimenter and of great interest to the analyst. All media of sensory expression border upon others, and although every one of them tends to do best when it relies on its own most characteristic properties, they all can be rejuvenated at times by cohabitation with their neighbors. Confrontations of immobile with mobile art, three-dimensional with two-dimensional, polychrome with monochrome, audible with visible, alert the observer to qualities taken for granted as long as they rule unchallenged in the precincts of one form of expression. Concrete poetry offers an illuminating encounter of printed language with pictorial image.

Although image making and writing grew indivisibly out of each other and have never been wholly separate, their recent mutual attraction has come like the healing of a wound that had torn them unhealthily apart. The avalanche of writing and printing brought about by the industrial revolution of the eighteenth and nineteenth centuries, the rapid writing skill made available to everyone by the public schools, the devel-

This is a shortened and slightly altered version of "Visual Aspects of Concrete Poetry," published in *Yearbook of Comparative Criticism*, vol. 7 (1976). I am indebted to Mary Ellen Solt and Merald E. Wrolstad, editor of *Visible Language*, for their help in the preparation of this paper, and to Eugen Gomringer, Max Bense, and Ronald Johnson for permission to reproduce their poems.

opment of shorthand and typing, and more recently the introduction of personal computers, together with the corresponding need for rapid reading, skimming, and digesting, have led to an unprecedented cheapening of language as a visual, aural, and syntactic form of expression. The constant gulping down of hastily produced masses of verbal material limits the mind to the absorption of "information," i.e., the raw material of facts. "Never have we possessed so much written material," noted the poet and critic Franz Mon in an introduction to a 1963 exhibition, Art and Writing, at the Stedelijk Museum in Amsterdam, "and never has written language itself given us so little. It covers everything like a scab" (2).

Such diagnoses of what happened to language refer to prevailing cultural trends. If we look from the same bird's-eye perspective at what happened to the pictorial image following the Renaissance, we find that a trend toward increasing lifelikeness in painting made the formal qualities of shape and color less conspicuous. The viewer's attention was monopolized by the subject matter—an attitude strongly enhanced by photography and its use by news services. Along with this depreciation of form went a gradual shift from subject matter embodying ideas to the portrayal of factual and attractive landscapes, still lifes, animals, and human figures. Symbolic depictions of religious, monarchic, or humanistic ideas flattened out into illustrations of history or genre scenes.

In sum, both language and the pictorial image were in need of rejuvenation as media of formal expression. The stylistic developments in modern art and modern poetry can be said to have aimed at just such a rejuvenation. In addition, the visual media needed to be enriched by a return to thought. Perhaps, in a small way, concrete poetry serves these purposes. It refreshes the awareness of language as a vehicle of visual expression, and it injects visual patterns with the thought element of meaningful words.

At the simplest level it is difficult to distinguish sign from image. Georg Christoph Lichtenberg tells of a gatekeeper of Frederick the Great who had to record the comings and goings of the young princes and princesses; he indicated each exit and entrance by an I for a boy, an O for a girl (1). Were these marks signs or iconic pictures? Prehistorically, however, explicit images must have developed soon enough. Such images stand for kinds of things more often than they signify individuals. They portray *the* boar, *the* deer, superhuman powers, man and woman. This generality of meaning makes them useful when they develop into ideographs, markers of concepts.

The history of writing tells us how the need to standardize and abbreviate the images transforms them gradually into patterns that are simple and distinct in visual appearance and easy on the brush or the chisel. Their iconic meaning, however, reverberates even after thousands of years so that a modern Japanese in a thoughtful moment can still see the sun rise behind the tree when he looks at the kanji sign for east in the word Tokyo, which signifies the eastern capital. And even when the visual etymology has vanished, there remains at least the correspondence between a particular concept and a particular sign.

This valuable one-to-one relation between the signifier and the signified seems to be forever destroyed when syllabic or alphabetic writing replaces the ideographs. The direct connection between the object and the visual sign is deflected by the sounds of speech. What is worse, writing is instrumental in dissecting the unique sound pattern of each word into a small number of phonemic components, so that we are left with a set of signs whose units and combinations reflect nothing of the objects for which they stand. It is also true, however, that we profit from the complicated system of similarities and differences thus established among the components of words and therefore of concepts. This creates a world of relations almost totally alien to the world of things—a fabulous dream world in which the punster and the poet roam with delight.

Language describes objects as self-contained things. It grants this same autonomy to parts of objects, so that hand and skin and blood come to look like independent entities, just like the whole body. Language even transforms attributes and actions into things and separates them from their owners and performers. A strawberry is one verbal thing, its redness is another; and when we hear about "the slaying of Abel," the slaying is presented as an object coordinated with, but separate from, the victim. Temporal and spatial connections and logical links are equally reified. This means that to speak is to dismember a unified image for the purpose of communication, the way one dismantles a machine for shipping. To understand speech is to reconstruct the image from the disassembled pieces.

A principal device language relies on to reconstruct the image is the spatial relation between words; and the principal spatial relation for this purpose is linearity. But linearity is not inherent in the nature of language. If it had been necessary to remind us of this, concrete poetry would have done so. Language becomes linear only when it is used to code linear events, whether it is reporting on happenings of the outer world, e.g., by telling a story, or on an occurrence in the world of thought, e.g., by making a logical argument. Visual imagery is less dependent on linearity. It surveys and organizes things perceived in three-dimensional space; it can also synthesize actions gathered from the time dimension, as when a painting depicts the gist of a story. If we wish to understand relations by reasoning, however, we must trace linear connections through the sensory universe of simultaneity. This is what happens when we call one thing larger than, or parallel to, another, or when we observe and say that the moon rose and lit up the sea.

When language serves such narrations or arguments, it must become linear. To the eyes this is expressed most adequately by a line of words, a line as long as the story itself. For convenience we chop up such a line into units of standard length, just as we chop up the scroll into pages. The visual aspects of such packaging are alien to the structure of the discourse; i.e., a break in the line or an end to the page indicates no corresponding break in the story.

Commonly, however, written and printed prose does contain subdivisions reflecting structural properties of the discourse. Words are separated by an empty space, and so are sentences. Paragraphs mark the ends of episodes or thoughts. By carrying such visual depiction of content structure further, poetry is distinguished for the eye from prose. This visual distinction is not a superficial one. The breaking up of the body of discourse into smaller units takes us back to the earliest forms of language, the one-word statement, the short phrase. If we compare the typical piece of prose with the typical poem—thereby neglecting the whole range of literary forms that combine characteristics of prose and poetry—we may venture to say that these two shapes of discourse correspond to two basic components of human cognition, namely, the tracing of causal sequences through the perceived world and the apprehension of unitary experiences, relatively self-contained and outside the course of time. Of these two the second is obviously the psychologically earlier one.

Accessible to the early mind is the relatively limited situation, the episode, the striking appearance, desire or fear, the confined event. These stationary units of experience, which correspond to the limited range of the young mind's organizing power, are reflected in the elementary language of, say, the child. But even at the highest level of human awareness, the grasp of confined, synoptic situations remains one of the basic constituents of mental functioning. It expresses itself visually in the timeless images of painting, sculpture, architecture, and the like, and verbally in the lyrical poem.

The poem, in its prototypic shape, is short because it is synoptic like the picture, and its content is to be apprehended as a single state of affairs. Traditionally this does not deprive the poem's content of change, event, and development, but all this fits into one surveyable situation. A poem is basically timeless, like a picture; and just as a picture must not be broken into two separately framed pieces, we resent it when a poem runs over to a second page.

What is true for the poem as a whole is true for its parts. The visual autonomy of each line detaches it somewhat from the continuity of the total sequence and presents it as a situation within a situation. This can be seen clearly in the radical example of the Japanese *haiku*. The progression in time, which runs from the beginning to the end of the poem like the story in narrative prose, is overlaid by an equally important second structural pattern, a coordination rather than a sequence of elements. The attentive reading of a poem requires much going back and forth, not unlike the scrutinizing of a painting, because the poem reveals itself only in the simultaneous presence of all its parts.

This atemporal coordination of the parts is strengthened by repetition and alternation—two devices favored by concrete poetry, which carries atemporality to an extreme. Repetition violates the Heraclitic criterion of flux. The Same does return; and there is no before and after in the relation between identical things. As in music, poetic repetition in assonance, rhyme, or refrain knits things together outside the succession of time and stresses the simultaneity of the whole work. Alternation, which presupposes repetition, also undercuts the poem's overall sequence by presenting rival sequences of the same passages as equally required. The systematic permutation of lines or words, practiced by some writers of concrete poetry, serves this purpose most radically.

On the threshold between more traditional and concrete poems there is one (3, pp. 90, 253) by Eugen Gomringer:

> avenidas
> avenidas y flores
>
> flores
> flores y mujeres
>
> avenidas
> avenidas y mujeres
>
> avenidas y flores y mujeres y
> un admirador

Simple and pleasant, the poem is traditional in its linear sequence of form and content. The poet uses the time dimension to carry his three basic components onto the stage of the image he is building for the reader. He starts with the setting of streets, decorates them with flowers, populates them with women, and springs an old-fashioned *coup de théâtre* by introducing the admirer as the last touch. Verbally, there is a crescendo of growing sizes, which stops with dramatic abruptness before the punch line.

At the same time, however, the poem as a whole is one image—a Goya painting might come to mind. The four nouns, with nothing but a linguistic plus sign to connect them, are self-sufficient bricks of experience, and the successive presentation of all the possible couplings of three of them counteracts the progression of the poem. Equal weight is given to all relations. We are shown a state of being, while becoming is confined to the poem acting as the presenter.

In its more radical form, the concrete poem abolishes the defined relationship between elements by two principal devices. It reduces or eliminates connectives, leaving the poet with "words as hard and as scintillating as diamonds. The word is an element. The word is a material. The word is an object" (3, p. 32). Second, the poem either excludes an overall sequence entirely or counteracts it so effectively by other sequences that none dominates the other.

Think of a few key words pointing to a landscape—sky, lake, boat, tree—sprinkled over a page. The reader's mind, trying to organize the material, may create a unified picture that possesses the principal property of any visual percept: all elements are fused in one organized whole, and all relations are integrated in a unified pattern. There are concrete poems that aim at such a pictorial response, but they are not many. Most of them produce networks of relations.

Networks of relations are what the mind uses in reasoning. These relations do not fuse as they do in a percept, but in order to be readable they must be organizable hierarchically or sequentially. The diagram of a business organization is such a network; the steps of a mathematical proof are another. To serve the purposes of reasoning, the totality of the relations must add up to an unambiguous statement. If there are contradictions, the thinker is called upon to eliminate them by doing more work.

The concrete poem uses networks but does not adopt the logician's criteria of validity. It thrives on the unresolved multiplicity of relations.

**ich**

**denke**     **ist**

**etwas**

*Figure 9*. Poem by Max Bense.

An illuminating example is given by Max Bense, who derives a concrete poem from a philosophical proposition (Figure 9) (4). Descartes's *Cogito ergo sum* presents an unambiguous logical conclusion. Bense arranges the four words *I, think, is, something* in such a way that none of the possible combinations of two, three, or four words dominates any other. If the reader takes the ungrammatical liberty of not limiting the meaning of the two verbs to the first- and the third-person singular respectively, and if he admits the concept *to be* in its double sense of existence and of belonging in a category, he is presented with a slew of statements: I think; I am; something exists; I think something; something thinks I am; thinking is something; and so on.

Here is a challenge that can be met in two ways. As a reasoner the reader can attempt to sort out all this material and come up with an organized argument that might read like Descartes's *Meditations*. To him, in fact, Bense's display is something like the raw material that must have faced Descartes when he started thinking. But the reader can also take those four words as a poem. Then the statement on the page is final, and the multiplicity of unresolved propositions conveys a sense of the complexity of conscious experience, the wealth of human thought, and perhaps the hopelessness of making sense of it all. What is going on here is not thinking in the intellectual sense of the word, but rather the suspension of reasoning. Reasoning is contemplated perceptually as though it were a play of storm clouds or a roused flock of birds.

If we think of language as raw material of the intellect, we can hazard a guess as to why nowadays the medium of concrete poetry has some attraction. It is not simply a disenchantment with language, a shift from the verbal to the visual. If it were, words could be discarded altogether; the media of the visual arts are available for the asking. A special lure of concrete poetry is the opportunity to disavow sequential reasoning by using and dismembering its verbal devices.

An aversion to sequential reasoning cannot be expressed in a medium like painting and sculpture because the atemporal image makes no statements about such sequences. Pictorial reasoning is concerned with facts and events in simultaneity. In a pictorial image, as I mentioned earlier, all particular relations fuse in a unified pattern. This means that all the influences impinging upon any one element balance out to establish an unambiguous visual definition of that element. If shape A is pushed to the left by factor B and to the right by factor C, it will find its particular dynamic character in the resultant of those vectors. In a completed work of visual art, there is no unresolved ambiguity of compositional vectors; they are absorbed in the interaction of their efforts.

It is a different matter when the image is composed of verbal material. Even though the overall sequence may be weakened or entirely absent, the words come in small sequences or suggest such sequences by their juxtaposition. *Ich etwas* is processed inevitably into I am something, or I have or I want something, or there am I and there is something. As the Bense poem showed, such verbal clusters retain their individual autonomy while entering freely into simultaneously possible, varying combinations.

Is concrete poetry one of the antagonistic reactions of recent generations to the kind of reasoning that operates with linear links, especially causal sequences, between concepts? By its very nature, a causal chain has no beginning and no end. It reaches back before the beginnings of any story, and it searches beyond the end to forecast the future. Calling for anamnesis and prognosis, it asks: How did this come about? What could have happened instead? And: What can be done about the future? It suits an activist's approach, and it implies trust in man's ability to understand and tackle problems. Such an attitude underlies the novel, the drama, the narrative film, but also the clinical case study and scientific descriptions of processes. It is resisted by those who distrust psychoanalysis, which is a linear procedure par excellence, and political doctrines that explain the mechanics of history and advocate change.

Granted that immobile images, too, can represent connections and causal relations, but these images do not suggest links that reach beyond the confines of the situation presented. The artist shows Judith beheading Holofernes, but he does not encourage the viewer to ask what made her do it and what will come of the deed. The linearity of sequence is not in the nature of the pictorial medium. It deals with states of being and turns becoming into being.

By arranging words and phrases in nonsequential patterns, concrete poetry points polemically to the inconclusiveness of reasoning. It suggests that there is no beginning and no end, and that there is no way out of contradictions. In a positive mood, it displays tolerance for a multiplicity of relations and endorses ambiguities and contradictions as reservoirs of experience to be drawn on by the contemplating mind.

At the same time it must be admitted that to resist the challenges of the analytical mind is to limit the validity and also the depth of a work of art. If a work is to be a reflection of man, it must engage all the powers of the human mind. This requirement is fulfilled in any good pictorial image. Perhaps, coming to the visual arts from Shakespeare or Dante, one might be struck momentarily by the muteness of Delacroix's Hamlet or the lack of verbal argument between his Dante and Virgil in Charon's bark. But once the absurd requirement that the picture *should* speak is abandoned, it becomes evident that the image articulates characters and their interrelations with the same kind of acute intelligence that is found in literary speech.

Traditional poetry is distinguished by a total engagement of the mind. Beyond the conveying of moods, there is an impressive trove of thought in a poem by Leopardi or Dickinson or Yeats. By contrast, we may feel tempted to complain about the simplicity of the typical concrete poem. We may liken it to the "minimal art" we saw in recent years in painting and sculpture and assert that while a return to the elements may be therapeutic in certain historical situations, we must guard against granting full status to such diminished products. This objection should not be dismissed too lightly. Yet it may make us blind to certain stylistic trends, barely discernible now but perhaps important for the future. What I have in mind involves the fundamental difference between what I shall call *memento* and what I call *message*.

Nicolas Poussin has given us a picture of shepherds who in the carefree setting of their fields come across a gravestone with the inscription *Et in Arcadia ego*. As a piece of information, the fact that death dwells everywhere is commonplace. As a poem the four words would not amount to much. But the inscription is no news item; it is no message, but rather a memento. Instead of seeking us out for the purpose of delivering a communication, it is discovered by us, tied to a place and inseparable from that setting. If we are thoughtful it will make us meditate, as we may meditate on the intricate body of a fruitfly explored under magnification.

At the early stages of many cultures, works of visual art tend to act as mementos. They are monuments providing for a presence that has meaning for the place where they stand. Statues are an obvious example. Murals, reliefs, or tapestries are integral properties of the caves, the tombs, the castles, and the churches for which they were made. We examine them the way we examine the plants and the rocks of a landscape. As mementos such artifacts have certain characteristic properties. They are limited in range and often quite simple, for several reasons. Being parts of an environment, their function is limited to a partial statement. They merely add an element to whatever else is being conveyed by the setting. Furthermore, since they belong to facilities serving such human activities as work and rest, traveling, visiting, delivering, providing, worshiping, they are geared to man in action. They must be relatively concise, adapted to the coming and going of the consumer.

Between the colossal heads of Easter Island and Bernini's marble figures of Daphne pursued by Apollo, there is a difference not only of historical style but of function. The gigantic stone heads are mementos, presumably objects of worship, goals of pilgrimage, tokens of divinity. Bernini's figures, displayed in a museum, deliver a message. They are tied to no place or civic function, but come to us as a statement on the nature of man. As such, they must do the talking, they must deserve our attention, and being isolated in time and space, they must tell the complete story. They are deliverers of thought, whereas the ceremonial stone heads are occasions for thought.

The same distinction holds for works of language. The inscription on the tomb is a memento. It belongs in the company of signs saying *Exit* or *Silence*. Depending on its particular function, the memento gives directions, prescribes behavior, facilitates orientation. The verbal memento also must be concise, and it may invite thought. Just as the bronze cross on an altar is not required to vie in complexity with a crucifixion by Rubens but rather acts as a focus and stimulus for religious ideas in the churchgoer, so the ornamental quotations from the Koran on the walls of mosques are mementos, different in principle from the disquisitions of a philosophical treatise. In the sanctuary of a Zen temple we may see a scroll displaying a single large ideograph, with perhaps a flower in a vase before it. The word and the flower invite our thought.

Such mementos are clearly different from what I am calling messages. The prototype of a verbal message is the letter in the mail. It arrives and asks for the recipient's attention. It does the talking and can be expected to deserve the time spent reading it. The letter informs and conveys thought. The development of the book, from ancient stone tablet to modern paperback, is one from memento to message. One does not approach the tablets with the request: "Astonish me!" as one legitimately may a best-selling novel.

One of the intentions of concrete poetry is to lead poetry from message to memento by delivering it from the book. A book of poetry acts as a message, like the letter, the novel, or the treatise, although it does so less overtly. It approaches the reader from nowhere, intent on supplying him with thought and feelings at a place of his own choosing. It promises to be worth his while and invites the attitude of the judging consumer, who, if he follows the recommendation of Bert Brecht, leans back and smokes a cigar. Judged by such standards, the typical concrete poem does not qualify as a message. We must realize that it aims at being a memento.

# eyeleveleye

Figure 10. Poem by Ronald Johnson.

As an extreme example, Ronald Johnson's poem (Figure 10) will make the point (3, p. 250). It looks like one word, but when read in the conventional manner it is revealed as three words run together, the first identical with the third. *Eye level* reminds the reader of the way he is facing the row of letters, and *level eye* may set off some vague association. The repetition of *eye* suggests that we give up the left-to-right sequence and perceive the pattern in its symmetry. This restructuring is immediately rewarded by the two eyes now looking at us like those of a face. Once attuned to the visual pattern, we discover the regular weave of six *e*'s, which knit the line together, and the two rooted poles of the *y*'s counterbalancing the two rising poles of the *l*'s. Fenced off by the *l*'s, there appears an *eve* and an *Eve*, whose shapely symmetry is underscored by the total pattern, and we are led to ponder the relations between *eye* and *Eve*. All this works best when the mind is but half awake, willing to admit whatever comes by. Reasoning is caught napping, or at least it is relaxed enough not to spoil the drifting images.

Clearly, the attitude called for by the example is not the heightened alertness that the reading of good poetry traditionally stimulates in us. It is rather as if we were watching the gliding transformations of summer clouds, with our minds on vacation. And in fact, the kind of setting most propitious for the concrete poem is outside the book, somewhere in the practical environment. There it may catch the eye of a partially engaged passerby, who will briefly stop and ponder the curious apparition and then walk away musing, his thoughts slightly or profoundly stirred. Mary Ellen Solt quotes Ferdinand Kriwet as saying of his poems that they have, at least at first glance, "sign character, as have all public texts on notice-boards, house fronts, hoardings, signs, lorries, on roads and runways, etc." (3, p. 20).

The makers of concrete poetry join their fellow artists in their desire to escape from the social isolation that has haunted the arts since they tore loose from their moorings during the Renaissance and became ambulant products, made for no one in particular, belonging nowhere, and willing to bed down with anybody for a price. As the artist shies away from the blank walls of gallery and museum, the poet is disenchanted by the neutrality of the blank paper and dreams of seeing his work as a sign or placard or icon in the daily traffic of market, pilgrimage, and recreation. And just as sculptors plough furrows in a desert or wrap buildings with sheets of plastic that are childish when considered by themselves, the hope of the poets is that in a restored context their verbal images will reveal an eloquence worthy of their purpose.

## References

1. Lichtenberg, Georg Christoph. "Sudelbücher. Section J. 298." In Wolfgang Promies, ed., *Schriften und Briefe*, vol. 1. Munich: Holle, 1968.
2. Mon, Franz. *Schrift und Bild*. Staatliche Kunsthalle, Baden-Baden, 1963.
3. Solt, Mary Ellen. *Concrete Poetry: A World View*. Bloomington: Indiana University Press, 1971.
4. Williams, Emmett, ed. *An Anthology of Concrete Poetry*. New York: Something Else Press, 1967.

# ON THE NATURE OF PHOTOGRAPHY

WHEN A theorist of my persuasion looks at photography, he is more concerned with the character traits of the medium as such than with the particular work of particular artists. He wishes to know what human needs are fulfilled by this kind of imagery, and what properties enable the medium to fulfill them. For his purpose, the theorist takes the medium on its best behavior. The promise of its potentialities captures him more thoroughly than the record of its actual achievements, and this makes him optimistic and tolerant, as one is with children, who have a right to demand credit for their future worth. Analyzing media in this way requires a very different temperament than analyzing the use people make of them. Given the deplorable state of our civilization, studies of the latter kind often make depressing reading.

The social critic, in his resentment and disapproval, is tied to the happenings and productions of the day, whereas the media analyst of my kind can display detachment. He, the media analyst, scrutinizes the passing crowd of daily productions in the hope of an occasional catch, some hint at the true nature of the medium in an otherwise insignificant example, or even one of those rare and glorious fulfillments of the medium's finest capacity. Not being a critic, he views photographs more as specimens than as individual creations, and he may not be up-to-date on the names of the latest promising newcomers. Perhaps the photographer can afford to have some sympathy for this remoteness, since, it seems to

First published in *Critical Inquiry*, vol. 1, no. 1 (September 1974).

me, he too, although in a different sense, must practice his trade with a detached stance.

This may seem a strange thing to say about a medium so inextricably involved in the settings and acts of practical behavior. Epitomized by the news photographer, the men and women of the camera invade the haunts of intimacy and privacy, and even the most visionary of photographers has no substitute for going in person to the place that will give shape to his dream. But precisely this intimate involvement with the subject matter necessitates the detachment of which I am speaking.

In the olden days, when a painter set up his easel at some corner to do a picture of the market square, he was an outsider, looked at with curiosity and awe, perhaps with amusement. It is the prerogative of the stranger to contemplate things instead of dealing with them. Apart from sometimes being bodily in the way, the painter did not interfere with the public private life around him. People did not feel spied upon or even observed, unless perhaps they happened to sit quietly on a bench, for it was evident that the painter was looking at and putting down something other than the facts of the moment. Only the moment is private, and the painter looked right through the coming and going at something that was not there at all because it was always there. The painting denounced nobody in particular.

In the portrait studio, a different social code protected both participants. The sitter, his spontaneity suspended and his best appearance displayed, has invited scrutiny. The amenities of intercourse are abrogated, there is no need for conversation, and the I is fully authorized to stare at the Thou as though it were an It. This was true for the early phase of photography as well. The equipment was too bulky to catch anybody unawares, and the exposure time was long enough to wipe the accidents of the moment from face and gesture. Hence the enviable timelessness of the early photographs. A sort of otherworldly wisdom came symbolically across when all momentary motion vanished from those metallic plates.

Later, when photography drew the stylistic consequences from the technique of instantaneous exposure, it began to define its objective in a way that was totally new in the history of the visual arts. Whatever the style and purpose of art, its goal had always been the representation of the lasting character of things and actions. Even when depicting motion, it was the abiding nature of that motion that the artist portrayed. This remained true also for the paintings of the nineteenth century, although we are accustomed to saying that the Impressionists cultivated the fleeting moment. If one looks carefully one realizes that those contemporaries of the first generations of photographers were not intent primarily on replacing scenes of some permanence with quickly passing ones. They did not try to stop motion. Rather they may be said to have supplemented the fundamental attitudes of the human mind and body, which occupied traditional paintings—the expression of thought and sorrow, of care and love, repose and attack—with the more extrinsic gestures of daily behavior, and to have found a new significance in them. They often replaced the rooted stance of the classical poses with a more casual slouch or stretch or yawn, or the steady illumination of a scene with a twinkling one. But if one compares those washerwomen, *midinettes*, or *boulevardiers*, those smoke-filled railroad yards or milling street crowds, with photographic snapshots, one realizes that, for the most part, even those "momentary" poses (Figure 11) had none of the incompleteness of the fraction of a second lifted from the context of time (Figure 12). In terms of time, a Degas ballerina fastening her shoulder strap is just as

*Figure 11.* Edgar Degas, *Four Dancers.* c. 1899. National Gallery of Art, Washington, D.C., Chester Dale Collection.

collected and reposes as firmly as the winged goddess of victory untying her sandal on a marble relief of ancient Athens.

Profiting from the mobility of the snapshot camera, photography reaches into the world as an intruder and therefore creates a disturbance, just as in the physics of light the single photon at the atomic level upsets the facts on which it reports. The photographer takes a hunter's pride in capturing the spontaneity of life without leaving any trace of his presence. News reporters enjoy recording the undisguised fatigue or embarrassment of a public figure, and the photographic manuals never tire of warning the amateur against the frozen poses of the family lined up for their picture in front of some famous landmark. Animals and infants, the

*Figure 12*. Courtesy Carpenter Center for the Visual Arts, Harvard University.

prototypes of unselfconsciousness, are the darlings of the trade. But the need for precaution and trickery highlights the congenital problem of photography: inevitably the photographer is a part of the situation he depicts. A court order may be necessary to keep him away, and the more skillfully he hides and surprises, the more acute is the social problem he creates. It is in this connection that we should think of the irresistible fascination that photography, film, and video have for young people today.

I shall not try to account here for all aspects of that fascination. It would be malicious to emphasize the tempting opportunity offered by photography to produce acceptable pictures without much training, toil, or talent. It may be more relevant to note that by opting for the camera, some young people may be demonstrating against form. Pronounced form is the characteristic distinction of traditional art. Form is suspected of serving the establishment, of detracting from the raw impact of passions and dreams psychologically, and that of injustice, brutality, and deprivation politically and socially.

But of course, such a denunciation of form would be misguided. Far from emasculating visual messages, form is the only way of making them accessible to the mind. We need only glance at the work of a great social photographer such as Dorothea Lange to realize the forceful eloquence of form. And conversely, the current video work that records interviews, debates, and other events without sufficient control of perspective, light, and camera movement proves by default that the gray evasiveness of the noncommittal image sabotages communication.

Form is indispensable. But there is still another source of fascination, one that derives from the photographer's ambiguous relation to the scenes he records. In the other arts, the problem arises only indirectly. Should the poet write revolutionary hymns at home or mount the barricade in person? In photography, there is no geographic escape from the conflict. The photographer must be where the action is. It is true that limiting oneself to observing and recording in the midst of battle, destruction, and tragedy may require as much courage as participating; however, when one takes pictures, one transforms life and death into a spectacle to be viewed with detachment. This is what I meant to suggest earlier: the detachment of the artist becomes more of a problem in the photographic media precisely because they immerse him bodily in situations that call for human solidarity. It is true that photographs, once they are produced, can serve as an effective instrument of activism, but at the same time photography as an occupation enables a person in the midst of things to go about his own business without taking part. The photographer overcomes alienation bodily without having to give up mental detachment. Self-deception comes easy in the twilight of such ambiguous conditions (6).

So far I have mentioned two phases in the development of photography: the early period, during which the image, as it were, transcended the momentary presence of the portrayed objects because of the length of exposure and the bulkiness of the equipment; and the second phase, which exploited the technical possibility of capturing motion in a fraction of time. The ambition of instantaneous photography, I noted, was that of preserving the spontaneity of action and avoiding all indications that the presence of the picture-taker had any influence on what was depicted. Characteristically enough, however, our own century has discovered a new attraction in the very artificiality of picture-taking and has endeavored to use it deliberately for the symbolic representation of an age that has fallen from innocence. This stylistic trend has two main aspects: the introduction of surrealist apparitions, and the frank acknowledgment of photography as an exposure.

Surrealist painting depended by its very nature upon the *trompe l'oeil* illusion of the settings it presented. In this the painter now has a powerful competitor in the photographer, for, although the incisive presence of realistically painted images is not easily matched by the camera, a photograph has an authenticity from which painting is barred by birth. Fashion photography may have started the trend by showing in the midst of an authentic setting—a hotel terrace on the Riviera, or the Spanish Steps in Rome—a grotesquely stylized model, the body reduced to a scaffold and the face to a mask, in a deliberately angular pose. Startling though such apparitions in the public domain were for a while, they looked too obviously like artifacts truly to stir the sense of the superreal. They were more like pranks than creations of the bona fide world; and only as an outgrowth of reality can apparitions work their spell. A surrealist shiver was more effectively produced by the more recent practice of photographing nude figures in a forest or living room or abandoned cottage. Here was indubitably real human flesh, but since such appearances of nude figures were known only from the visions of painters, the reality of the scene was transfigured into a dream—pleasant perhaps, but also frightening because it invaded the mind as a hallucination.

Another recently explored way of using the artificiality of the photographic medium can be found in reportage, most impressively in the weird documentations of Diane Arbus. Instead of being caught in the act unconsciously, persons are seen acknowledging the presence of the photographer, either by displaying themselves for her cheerfully or ceremoniously, or by watching her with suspicious attention. What we seem to be shown here is man and woman after they have eaten from the tree of knowledge. "And the eyes of them both were opened," says the Book of Genesis, "and they knew that they were naked." This is man under observation, in need of a *persona*, concerned with his image, exposed to danger or to the prospect of great fortune by simply being looked at.

All these applications derive ultimately from the fundamental trait of the photographic medium: the physical objects themselves imprint their image by means of the optical and chemical action of light. This fact has always been recognized but treated in a variety of ways by the writers on the subject. I am thinking back to my own way of dealing with the psychology and aesthetics of film in a book originally published in 1932 (1). In that early book I attempted to refute the accusation that photography was nothing but a mechanical copy of nature. My approach was a reaction to the narrow notion that had prevailed ever since Baudelaire, in his famous statement of 1859, predicted the value of photography for the faithful documentation of sights and scientific facts, but also denounced it as an act of a revengeful god who, by sending Daguerre as his messiah, granted the prayer of a vulgar multitude that wanted art to be an exact imitation of nature (3). In Baudelaire's day, the mechanical procedure of photography was doubly suspect as an attempt by industry to replace the manual work of the artist with the mass production of cheap pictures. Such critical voices, although less eloquent, were still influential when I decided upon my own apologia for the cinema. My strategy was therefore to describe the differences between the images we obtain when we look at the physical world and the images perceived on the motion picture screen. These differences could then be shown to be a source of artistic expression.

In a sense it was a negative approach because it defended the new medium by measuring it with the standards of the traditional ones—that is, by pointing to the range of interpretation it offered the artist, very much like painting and sculpture, in spite of its mechanical nature. Only secondarily was I concerned with the positive virtues that photography derives precisely from the mechanical quality of its images. Even so, the demonstration was necessary then, and perhaps it is worth recalling now; it seems so, at least, to judge from one of the best-known and also one of the more confusing statements of recent years, Roland Barthes's paper on *Le message photographique* (2). Barthes calls the photograph a

perfect and absolute analogue, derived from the physical object by reduction but not by transformation. If this statement means anything, the
meaning must be that the primary photographic image is nothing but a
faithful copy of the object and that any elaboration or interpretation is
secondary. To me, it seems necessary to keep insisting that an image cannot transmit its message unless it acquires form at its primary level.

It is true that we look at photographic scenes not as invented by man
but as replicas of things and actions that existed and took place somewhere in time and space. The conviction that pictures are generated by a
camera and not made by hand profoundly influences our way of viewing
and using them. This point has been stressed by the film critic André
Bazin (4).

Photography, observed Bazin in 1945, derives an advantage from the
fact that "for the first time, between the originating object and its reproduction there intervenes only the instrumentality of a nonliving agent.
. . . Photography affects us like a phenomenon in nature, like a flower or
a snowflake whose vegetable or earthly origins are an inseparable part
of their beauty" (4, p. 13). Looking in a museum at a painting of a
Flemish tavern scene, we notice which objects the painter introduced and
which occupations he gave his characters. Only indirectly do we use his
picture as documentary testimony to what life was like in the seventeenth
century. How different is the attitude with which we approach a photograph showing, say, a lunch counter! "Where was this taken?" we want
to know. The word "caliente" that we discover on the list of foods in the
background points to a Spanish element, but the paunchy policeman at
the door, the hot dogs, and the orange drink assure us that we are in the
United States. With the delighted curiosity of the tourist, we explore the
scene. The glove near the wastepaper basket must have been dropped by
a customer; it was not placed there by the artist as a compositional
touch. We are on vacation from artifice. The different attitude toward
time is also characteristic. "When was this painted?" means mostly that
we want to know to which stage of the artist's life a work belongs.
"When was this taken?" means typically that we are concerned with the
historical locus of the subject. Does a particular photograph offer a view
of Chicago before the great fire, or did Chicago look that way after
1871?

In evaluating the documentary qualities of a photograph we ask three
questions: Is it authentic? Is it accurate? Is it true? Authenticity, vouched
for by certain features and uses of the picture, requires that the scene has
not been tampered with. The masked burglar leaving the bank is not an

actor, the clouds are not printed from another negative, the lion is not posed in front of a painted oasis. Accuracy is another matter; it calls for the assurance that the picture corresponds to the scene the camera took: the colors are not off, the lens does not distort the proportions. Truth, finally, does not deal with the picture as a statement about what was present in front of the camera, but refers to the depicted scene as a statement about facts the picture is supposed to convey. We ask whether the picture is characteristic of what it purports to show. A photograph may be authentic but untrue, or true though inauthentic. When in Jean Genet's play *The Balcony* the queen's photographer sends an arrested revolutionary to get him a pack of cigarettes and pays a police officer to shoot the man, the picture of the rebel killed while trying to escape is inauthentic but probably accurate in what it shows and not necessarily untrue. "Monstreux!" says the queen. "C'est dans les habitudes, Majesté," says the photographer. To be sure, when it comes to truth the problem is no longer specifically photographic.

One can understand why Bazin suggested that the essence of photography "is not to be found in the result achieved but in the way of achieving it" (4, p. 12). It is equally important, however, to consider what the mechanical recording process does to the visual qualities of the photographic image. Here we are helped by Siegfried Kracauer, who based his book *Theory of Film* on the observation that the photographic image is a product of cooperation between physical reality as it impresses its own optical image on the film and the picture-maker's ability to select, shape, and organize the raw material (5). The optically projected image, Kracauer suggested, is characterized by the visual accidents of a world that has not been created for the convenience of the photographer, and it would be a mistake to force these unwieldy data of reality into the straitjacket of pictorial composition. Indefiniteness, endlessness, random arrangement should be considered legitimate and indeed necessary qualities of film as a photographic product—necessary because they alone derive logically from the unique conditions of the medium and thereby create a view of reality not offered by any other medium. If with Kracauer's observation in mind we look attentively at the texture of a typical photographic image, we find, perhaps to our surprise, that the subject matter is represented mostly by visual hints and approximations. In a successful painting or drawing every stroke of the pen, every touch of color, is an intentional statement of the artist about shape, space, volume, unity, separation, lighting, etc., and it should be read as such. The texture of the pictorial image amounts to a pattern of explicit information. If we approach photographs with the expectations instilled in us by the perusal of hand-made images, we find that the work of the camera lets us down. Shapes peter out in muddy darkness, volumes are elusive, streaks of light arrive from nowhere, juxtaposed items are not clearly connected or separate, details do not add up. The fault is ours, of course, because we are looking at the photograph as though it were made and controlled by man and not as a mechanical deposit of light. As soon as we take the picture for what it is, it hangs together and may even be beautiful.

But surely there is a problem here. If what I affirmed earlier is true, it takes definite form to make a picture readable. How, then, can an agglomerate of vague approximations deliver its message? To speak of "reading" a picture is appropriate but at the same time dangerous because it suggests a comparison with verbal language; and linguistic analogies, although fashionable, have greatly complicated our understanding of perceptual experience everywhere. I will refer here once more to the article of Roland Barthes, in which the photographic image is described as coded and uncoded at the same time. The underlying assumption is that a message can be understood only when its content has been processed into the discontinuous, standardized units of a language, of which verbal writing, signal codes, and musical notation are examples. Pictorial surfaces, being continuous and unstandardized in their elements, are therefore uncoded, and this is said to mean unreadable. (This observation, of course, would hold for paintings as well as for photographs.) How, then, do we gain access to pictures? By making the subject matter conform, says Barthes, to another kind of code, not inherent in the picture itself but imposed by society as a set of standardized meanings upon certain objects and actions. Barthes gives the example of a photograph depicting a writer's study: an open window with a view of tiled roofs, a landscape of vineyards; in front of the window a table with an album of photographs, a magnifying lens, a vase of flowers. Such an arrangement of objects, asserts Barthes, is nothing more or less than a lexicon of concepts whose standardized meanings can be read off like a description in words.

It will be evident that such an interpretation denies the very substance of visual imagery, namely, its capacity to convey meaning by full perceptual experience. The standardized designations of things are nothing but husks of information. By reducing the message to meager conceptual fare, one accepts the impoverished practical responses of the modern man in the street as the prototype of human vision. In opposition to this approach we must maintain that imagery can fulfill its unique function—whether photographic or pictorial, artistic or informational—only if it goes beyond a set of standardized symbols and exerts the full and ultimately inexhaustible individuality of its appearance.[1]

If, however, we are correct in asserting that the messages conveyed by pictures cannot be reduced to a sign language, then our problem of how to read them is still with us. Here we need to realize, first of all, that a picture is "continuous" only when we scan it mechanically with a photometer. Human perception is not such an instrument. Visual perception is pattern perception; it organizes and structures the shapes offered by the optical projections in the eye. These organized shapes, not sets of conventional ideographs, yield the visual concepts that make pictures readable. They are the keys that give us access to the rich complexity of the image.

When the viewer looks at the world around him, these shapes are delivered to him entirely by the physical objects out there. In a photograph, the shapes are selected, partially transformed, and treated by the picture-taker and his optical and chemical equipment. Thus, in order to make sense of photographs, one must look at them as encounters between physical reality and the creative mind of man—not simply as a reflection of that reality in the mind, but as a middle ground on which the two formative powers, man and world, meet as equal antagonists and partners, each contributing its particular resources. What I described earlier in negative terms as a lack of formal precision must be valued positively from the point of view of the photographic medium as the manifest presence of authentic physical reality, whose irrational, incompletely defined aspects challenge the image-maker's desire for visually articulate form. This quality of the optical raw material exerts its influence not only when the viewer recognizes in a picture the objects that had been projected on the sensitive coating of the film, but is actually more manifest in highly abstract photographs in which objects have been reduced to pure shapes.

Even so, a medium that limits the creations of the mind by powerful material constraints must have corresponding limitations. In fact, when

---

[1] Ironically, not even a verbal message is coded, only the means of conveying it. Words are discontinuous signs, reasonably well standardized, but the message they transmit consists in the image that induced the sender to verbalize and is resurrected by the words in the mind of the recipient. This image, whatever its precise nature, is as "continuous" as any photograph or painting. What comes across when a person hears "Fire! Fire!" neither consists of two verbal units nor conveys a standardized image.

one compares the artistic development of photography from the days of David Octavius Hill to the great photographers of our own time with the range of painting from Manet to, say, Jackson Pollock, or of music from Mendelssohn to Bartók or Berg, one may conclude that there has been photographic work of high quality, but that it has been consistently limited in its range of expression as well as in the depth of its insights. To be sure, new worlds of subject matter have been opened by the microscope, the telescope, and the airplane, but the manner of looking at them is hardly different from that of the early pioneers. Technical tricks by which to change the appearance of the image as well as the montage of positives or the assembly of negatives certainly make pictures look quite different; but to the extent they abandon the basic realism from which photography derives its unique effect, they tend quickly to look like yesterday's fashion. And as to their depth of meaning, photographs look significant, striking, revealing, but rarely profound.

The photographic medium seems to operate under a definite ceiling. To be sure, every artistic medium limits the range of successful expression and needs to do so. But there is a difference between the productive limitations that intensify a statement by confining it to a few formal dimensions and a narrowing of expressive freedom within the range of a particular medium.

If this diagnosis is correct, I think the difference is due not to the relative youth of the photographic art but to its intimate physical connection with the activities of human life. I would also suggest that this is a liability when looked at from the point of view of the painter, the composer, or the poet, but it is an enviable privilege when we consider its function in human society. Let us consult another medium of artistic expression, one that is much more ancient but is equally bound to physical conditions, namely, dance. Just as photography is dependent on the optical projection of the material objects it portrays, dance is controlled by the structure and motor capacities of the human body. As we look at the historical record of dance, there, too, we seem to find that the resemblance between the dances of remote times and places and those of our own outweighs the difference, and that the visions conveyed, though beautiful and impressive, remain at a relatively simple level. This is so, I believe, because dance is essentially a ritualized extension of the expressive and rhythmical movement of the human body in its daily activities, its mental manifestations and communications. As such it lacks the almost unconditional freedom of imagination accorded the other media, but it is also spared the remoteness that separates the great private visions of the poets, composers, or painters from the commerce of social existence.

Perhaps the same is true for photography. Wedded to the physical nature of landscape and human settlement, animal and man, to our exploits, sufferings, and joys, photography is privileged to help man view himself, expand and preserve his experiences, and exchange vital communications—a faithful instrument whose reach need extend no further than the way of life it reflects.

## References

1. Arnheim, Rudolf. *Film as Art.* Berkeley and Los Angeles: University of California Press, 1957.
2. Barthes, Roland. "Le message photographique." *Communications,* no. 1 (1961).
3. Baudelaire, Charles. "Salon de 1859, II: Le Public moderne et la photographie." In *Oeuvres complètes.* Paris: Gallimard, 1968.
4. Bazin, André. "The Ontology of the Photographic Image." In *What Is Cinema?* Berkeley and Los Angeles: University of California Press, 1967.
5. Kracauer, Siegfried. *Theory of Film.* New York: Oxford University Press, 1960.
6. Sontag, Susan. *On Photography.* New York: Farrar, Straus, 1977.

# SPLENDOR AND MISERY OF
# THE PHOTOGRAPHER

FROM THE very outset there is a difference between singling out the traditional visual arts of painting and sculpture for an undistracted look at their nature and doing the same for photography. It would not be too difficult to remove the visual arts from their environment. One would have to take the pictures from the walls, close the museums and galleries, pull the public statues from their pedestals, and the job would be nearly done. The world would not look noticeably different afterward, and many people would indeed notice nothing amiss. But try to extricate photography from the world it serves today. What would happen to newspapers and magazines without their pictures? To posters and the packaging of merchandise, to passports, family albums, dictionaries, catalogues? It would be vandalism of the first order, a thorough despoliation.

We look further and find that just as the traditional arts are easily detachable from their everyday environment, they do not originate in the visual world they depict. Although painting and sculpture as we know them might not have come about at all without the challenge of that visual world, their nature does not derive primarily from their subject matter, but from the media in which they are created: the sheet of paper, the canvas, the block of stone, and the tools and materials. The perceptual conditions deriving from the chosen medium stimulate and deter-

First published in the *Bennington Review* (September 1979).

mine the conceptions of the artist. This is also true, but to a much lesser extent, for photography. It springs primarily from the environment in which it is so inextricably enmeshed. One understands photography by considering what happens when the skin of physical things is optically projected on film, chemically transformed and fixed, printed, and manipulated. Painting and sculpture come from the inside out; photography comes from the outside in.

Therefore I shall consider photography first in three respects: the way it makes itself practically useful; the relevance of the moment in time; and the relevance of the visible surface.

The usefulness of photography for recording and preserving visible things has been recognized from its infancy; there is no need to belabor the point. Instead it may be instructive to characterize the utility of photography indirectly, by referring to a few instances in which it does less well than hand-made imagery. Take the sketch of a suspect drawn by a police artist. Only general impressions are available to describe the suspect, so the picture must stick to generalities: the overall shape of the face and the hair, the approximate coloring. This sort of generality comes easy to the draftsman. His strokes and shadings are naturally inclined to start from a highly abstract level and would reach individuality only by special elaboration. Photography, on the other hand, would have a hard time presenting a generalized face. It cannot but start from an individual instance. In order to arrive at generality, it would have to blur or otherwise partly conceal the distinguishing details of the individual. Instead of stating abstractness positively, it can only arrive at it negatively, by eliminating some of the primary data.

For a related reason photography lends itself only reluctantly to the production of official portraits, intended to convey a person's exalted position. In the great dynastic or religious hierarchies, such as that of ancient Egypt, the statue of the ruler was expected to characterize the power and superhuman perfection of his office at the expense of his individuality; and even in our time, photographers specializing in the portraits of presidents or business leaders are called upon to tamper with nature in ways that do not enhance the artistic quality of their work. By balking at any sublimation that violates the given truth, photography reveals its allegiance to the reality from which it springs.

But even the rendering of reality in the strictest rigor of the term calls for capacities not easily provided by photography. Consider its use for scientific purposes. The photographic medium is immensely valuable for documentation; it is reliable, fast, faithful, and complete. But it is less well suited to interpret or explain relevant aspects of what is being shown. This is a serious drawback. For the most part, illustrations are intended to clarify spatial relations, to tell what belongs together or apart, and to sharpen the distinctive characteristics of particular shapes and colors. This is often achieved more effectively by the trained draftsman because his drawings can translate into visual patterns what he has understood about the subject. The photographic camera cannot understand, it can only record; and the photographer has a hard time introducing scientifically or technologically relevant perceptual features by the mere control of lighting, retouching, airbrushing, or other manipulation of negatives and prints. The reproductive medium is not geared to formal precision because much of the world at large did not come about for the purpose of offering instructive visual images to the eyes.

The reality of a physical subject comprises, in the strictest sense, the total course of its existence in time. To render it in the timeless medium of painting, the artist has to invent an equivalent that translates a synthesis of the time sequence into an appropriate immobile image. For that same purpose, the photographer is limited to selecting a momentary phase of the sequence. It is true that in special instances photography can go beyond the single moment. When the shutter remains open for an extended period of time, it produces an overlay of moments, adding up to a larger whole—e.g., when the apparent rotation of the stars reveals a beautiful pattern of concentric curves. Prolonged exposure also compensates for the passing twists and tensions in a portrait sitter and thus obtains a kind of timeless monumentality, as in the portraits of David Octavius Hill. But such intensification by summation does not suit many subjects. The photographer has the choice between stopping the natural traffic of life—a procedure symbolized by the metal clamp that kept the heads of early photographic subjects immobile—and putting his trust in the significance of a fraction of time. But such significant moments are not easily come by. Works of art such as dances or theatrical performances often compose their action to culminate in high points that synthesize external events and can be photographed. In the traditional kabuki theater of Japan, for example, the leading actor's play peaks in the *mi-e*, literally "picture viewing," as he freezes in a stylized pose, accompanied by the roll of wooden clappers, and is wildly cheered by the audience. The reality of the photographer's world, however, is under no obligation to stop for "picture viewing." Even so, and quite remarkably, photography has taught us that the unposed happenings of daily life yield significant fragments of time much more often than one might expect.

What is more, the rapid course of events is found to contain hidden moments which, when isolated and fixed, reveal new, and different, meanings.

These uniquely photographic discoveries owe their existence to two psychological principles: first, the mind is geared to the apprehension of totalities and needs time to grasp details; and second, an element extracted from its context changes character and reveals new properties. Offhand it would seem most improbable that a single phase of an ongoing process would meet a good photograph's requirements of composition and symbolic meaning. But like a fisherman or hunter, the photographer bets on improbable accident and wins more often than seems reasonable.

Another limitation, this one shared with the other visual arts, restricts the photographer's imagery to what shows on the outside of the objects he portrays. Under special conditions, painters or sculptors not committed to the rules of a realistic style are free to present the inside with the outside—the Australian bushman showing the innards of a kangaroo, or Picasso constructing a guitar that is closed and open at the same time. A photographer would have to resort to risky tricks to acquire a similar freedom. Thus he has to worry about the extent to which the outside represents the inside. Of primary assistance is what the Renaissance mystic Jakob Böhme called the *signatura rerum*, the signature of things, by which outer appearance reveals inner nature. How would photography manage to portray humans, animals, and plants if their visible shapes had no structural correspondence to forces governing their insides? What would remain of the pictures of people if their states of mind were not directly reflected in the muscular behavior of their faces and limbs?

Fortunately, the visual world conveys the nature of many events through the immediacy of their appearance. It shows pleasure and pain expressed in external response. It also preserves the scars left by traumas of the past. At the same time, however, pictures neither explain what they show nor do they tell us how to judge it. In our century, the total coverage of the news by photography, film, and television has provided us with significant insights. The technical perfection of instantaneous photography has been accompanied in our Western civilization by the increasing freedom to show in public things that in the past remained hidden for reasons of morality, modesty, or what used to be called "good taste." Photographs of violence, torture, destruction, and sexual license have provided the shocking impact of confrontation. The citizen is exposed to the visible presence of events that verbal descriptions could conjure up only indirectly through the reader's imagination. But these recent practices have also taught us that the shock effect of such sights wears off quickly and that, in any case, it does not necessarily carry a message, certainly not a controllable one. Nowadays children are routinely exposed to horror scenes of crime, war, and accident, apparently without suffering the catastrophic afflictions one would fear. This is so partly because children are first exposed to such sights at an age at which they cannot tell the difference between a real act of violence and the similar-looking smashes, explosions, and demolitions in animated cartoons or similar slapstick.

To be touched by the impact of pictures takes more than eyesight. In more ways than one, pictures are not self-explanatory. Their meaning depends on the total context of which they are a part. It depends on motives and attitudes of the persons depicted that may not be apparent from the pictures, and it also depends on the value attributed by the viewer to life and death, to human well-being, to justice, freedom, private profit, and so forth. In this respect, the traditional visual arts are at an advantage because everything in a painting or drawing is understood to have been put there by intention. Thus when the graphic "activist" George Grosz depicted a well-to-do gentleman with a bulging paunch, we know that he introduced the anatomical deformation to characterize the social deformities of capitalism. But when a press photographer shows some similarly heavy men at a convention, their obesity may pass as an accidental feature, not necessarily symbolic of attitude or social role. In that sense, the photograph is beyond good and evil.

It is true that photography puts the viewer in the direct presence of relevant facts. It thereby exposes him to what may be called the raw effect of matter, the impact created by the immediately given. If the viewer is at all sensitive to what he is being shown, this impact may set him to thinking. But what his thoughts will be when he looks at a good shot of a political demonstration, a sports event, or a coal mine will depend on his own intellectual orientation, to which the picture will accommodate. A picture may be glamorous but be seen by someone as a repulsive symptom of decadence; it may be as heartbreaking as a scene of starving children and yet be dismissed as nothing but the consequence of governmental inefficiency or as the deserved punishment for refusal to practice the correct religion. Consequently when photography wishes to convey a message, it must try to place the symptoms it exposes into the proper context of cause and effect. More often than not, this will require the help of the written or spoken word.

The photographer may be willing to acknowledge this dependence. But as an artist he cannot be blamed for being particularly concerned with photographs that stand on their own, the way many paintings or sculptures make their statement without much outside help, appearing as they do in the empty space of an exhibition wall and in something of a social vacuum. I will therefore attempt now to explore some of the specific properties of photography as a visual medium by referring to two characteristic subjects, the nude and the still life.

In the classical tradition of Greece and Rome the nude figure emerges as a principal subject of art. During the Middle Ages, nudity is limited mostly to depicting the deplorable condition of those who have fallen from grace. It makes its reentry in the secularized art of the Renaissance and its descendants in recent centuries. Apart from its erotic appeal, the nude body depicted by the Renaissance artist in the Greek tradition shows beauty and virtue in a state of purity and generality that does not tolerate the limiting features of clothing.

In keeping with this symbolic function, the artist presents the human body cleansed of the accidents of imperfection and individuality. Sometimes the shape of the body is determined by standardized numerical proportions, and curves are smoothed to an all but geometrical simplicity. I observed earlier that such generality of form comes easy to the "manual" arts because by their very nature they take off from an inventory of elementary shapes and colors. They approach the particulars of physical objects only gradually and to the extent that this is warranted by the needs of culture and style. In periods in which the sense of form and the notion of art as an embodiment of ideas gives way to realistic copying for its own sake, we are presented with products in which the discrepancy between form and intended meaning creates an offensive and ludicrous effect. Adolf Hitler's favorite painter, a Professor Ziegler, was called in subversive circles the Master of the Pubic Hair because of the silly meticulousness with which he depicted, for example, a female model as the life-size symbolic figure of the "Goddess of Art." His case has become less spectacular since in recent years a number of our own painters and sculptors have betrayed a similar mindlessness and have been praised for it by critics.

In photography, the detailed rendering of an individual human body is not the rarely approached extreme of a particular stylistic development. On the contrary, it is the base from which the medium commonly starts. A normally focused shot of a human body displays all the imperfections of the particular specimen. Hence, for example, the depressing effect of pictures taken in nudist camps. This idiosyncrasy of the medium leaves the photographer as an artist with several choices. He can emphasize the given shape and texture and interpret it as the result of the interaction between the biologically "intended" type and externally induced wear and tear. The skin of an old farmer or the crusty bark of a tree are prototypes of this approach, which can produce very moving symbols of the natural condition.

Or the photographer can search for the rare specimens of perfection that show the human body in the healthy exuberance of a young woman, the disciplined strength of the athlete, or the almost dematerialized spirituality of an aged thinker. Such images are ideals, like their counterparts in painting and sculpture; but given the differences in medium, their connotation is not the same. The photographic documents are not the creations of an idealizing imagination that responds to the imperfections of reality with a dream of beauty. Instead, they are the trophies of a hunter who looks for the unusual in the world of what actually exists and discovers something exceptionally good. It is like coming across a particularly regular and large diamond. In such a picture, the photographer offers the sensational news that something superhumanly good can be found in our own midst, embodied in a fellow creature, not in a Platonic *eidos*. Therefore his picture is remarkable in a special way. Rather than make us humble, it can make us proud.

But the photographer may also choose to transfigure the ordinary into the exalted by the magic of light and thereby wipe out textures or conceal them in darkness. He can use the tricks of optics and chemistry to transpose his image to the realm of graphics. But here again the conception stirred in the viewer should differ in principle from that suggested by a lithograph or etching. If it is to remain a photograph, the picture should be seen as an artful disguise of the real body of the model, which continues to lurk in whole and worldly actuality behind the transformation. Although the photographer needs true imagination to make such a transformation successful, the result may be said to resemble that of Japanese bonsai—artistic creations whose main point would be missed if they were not understood as a spell cast upon actual creatures of nature.

Let me conclude with a few observations on another subject matter, the still life. In painting, the still life may be said to be the most artificial of subjects, in the sense that in all other types of pictorial representation the "story" of the picture accounts for what it contains. This is true for portraits, landscapes, genre scenes, and even for allegories. Still lifes, however, more often than not are arrangements determined by nothing but the demands of the composition and its symbolic meaning. For the most part, nothing resembling those arrangements of fruit, bottles, dead fowl, and drapery can be found anywhere in the world. But there is nothing wrong with this artificiality, since painting as a medium has no commitment to faithful documentation.

In photography, examples of the same type can be found occasionally, under the influence of traditional painting. But wherever the photographic medium imposes its own character, still lifes look like the objective record of some corner of the environment, furnished by the inhabitants for their practical needs and imprinted with the effects of human presence. Or we see a sample of nature, shaped by plant and animal and perhaps by the intrusion of man. Whereas the pictorial composition, arranged by the artist, shows a self-contained world enclosed in its frame, the authentically photographic still life is an open segment of a world that continues in all directions beyond the limits of the picture. And the viewer, instead of merely admiring the artist's invention, also acts as an explorer, an indiscreet intruder into the privacy of nature and human activity, curious about the kind of life that has left its traces and searching for telltale clues.

Through a prodigious combination of the opportunities offered by untampered reality and the shrewdness of the photographer's sense of form, a successful photograph is derived from the active cooperation of model and artist, the signified and the signifier. The stubbornness of the photographer's subject matter, which will give up its life rather than let him clumsily coerce it, makes for much misery. But the successful union of the character and needs of both contributors yields a very special splendor.

# THE TOOLS OF ART—
# OLD AND NEW

IT IS sensible and practically useful to call the most recent centuries of our history the age of technology. We assign the beginning of this age to the period in which tools, in the older meaning of the term, were being supplemented by machines. Machines are tools that no longer rely on a human operator for the power of action and the steering of the production process, but themselves supply all of the power and much of the control. There can be no doubt that the psychological, economical, and political changes brought about by industrialization are fundamental. The age of technology has given us mass production, rapid transportation, and the electrical generation of light, heat, and cold. It has replaced large amounts of human labor with faster and more accurate factory work, and it has severed man's intimate ties to the work of his hands and to the elementary resources of nature. For all these reasons the age of technology certainly is distinguishable in principle from earlier periods. For these reasons, too, one is fully justified in looking for the particular cultural traits that characterize life with modern technology and for the specific benefits and threats it has in store for cherished human values.

But no novelty can be entirely new. Made *by* man and *for* man, the new must rely on the same basic principles, resources, and needs as the old. We are bound to misinterpret the nature of a novelty if we give it exclusive credit for qualities it shares with much more general condi-

First published in *Technicum* (School of Engineering, University of Michigan, Summer 1979).

tions. Take, for example, the once fashionable assertion that the invention of the printing press converted our culture to linear thinking. As it happens, linearity of thought did not have to wait for Gutenberg. Written speech was linear from the beginning. But even this extension of our view does not suffice; we must realize that sequential speaking and writing are not the cause but only a manifestation of sequential thinking. The ability to think in sequences must have emerged at a primordial stage of human development, and only when we consider this ancient acquisition of the mind can we hope to approach the root of a psychological phenomenon that may have been bolstered since the Renaissance by the mass production of printed language but certainly did not originate as a specific symptom of so recent a cultural period.

Once we see technology in the more general context of man's relation to his tools, we also react less one-sidedly to the suspicions that have been voiced against the machine—a fear expressed most movingly in one of Rainer Maria Rilke's *Sonnets to Orpheus*, which begins with the assertion: "Alles Erworbene bedroht die Maschine." The machine, says Rilke, threatens everything man has acquired, as it insolently claims to be "the inspiring lead" rather than limit itself to obedience. Unhesitatingly it "orders, creates, and destroys." We acknowledge the complaint, but we also realize that in Western history the onset of modern technology coincided with the age of Romanticism, and that the one-sidedness of Romantic thought is no less to blame for the conflict than the one-sided character of the machine.

The problem has become particularly poignant in the arts. Here again it is not sufficient to point out the ways in which the new instruments created by technology—say, photography or computer graphics—differ from the manual arts. It is equally necessary to know how these new devices handle the timeless invariants of artistic creation. There exist certain indispensable conditions without which art is not art, and we must find out what becomes of them when new techniques tackle the old job.

Looking back to the origin of man's relation to his tools, we are reminded that all willful human activity is generated by the mind for the mind, and that the first instrument to serve all that activity is the human body. No mental conception can generate material action or shape directly. The task must be entrusted to the body, which is not necessarily a very satisfactory piece of technology. For example, even if one excludes the hand and creates a drawing of an object by recording the draftsman's eye movements with the help of electro-oculography (1), one is far from producing a faithfully direct materialization of a mental image. In a sense, the whole problem is already there. The physical instrument, the human body, offers the means of giving tangible presence to the images conceived by the mind, but like every other tool, acting as an intermediary and translator, it has its own idiosyncrasies. Inevitably the special traits of the tool influence the product.

Certain formal qualities suit the instrument so well that they flow from it almost spontaneously. Others require special efforts, lead to painfully artificial results, or are not obtainable at all. For example, since the human arm is a pivoted instrument, it takes naturally to curved movements and curved shapes. A straight line movement requires special control, not only in drawing but also in the handling of a violin bow or in a dance gesture. The opposite bias distinguishes, for example, the loom. The weaver has no trouble with straight shapes when they run parallel to the woof, but the loom has its own rules: to produce a diagonal or a curve, it is necessary to coerce the weave's structure. A good craftsman knows how to reconcile the freedom of his conceptions with the character traits of his tools.

Most tools have an affinity to geometrically definable shapes, especially to straightness and rectangularity. Organic shapes, however, tend to be biomorphic. They eschew the straight line and the right angle and defy mathematical formulae. Human life in what is sometimes called a "carpentered" environment is largely an interplay between the flexibility of the organism and the configurations of cubic shapes, which facilitate work and orientation but may frighten us by their stern impersonality. The city dweller's escape to the inexhaustible multiformity of nature is a response to this contrast, and the recent rebellion of architects against the neatly regular skyscrapers of the so-called international style is equally symptomatic of the unsteady relationship between man and his technological products.

These same examples, however, warn us not to view the situation too simply. After all, it is man himself who opted for all those cubic shapes and made machines to help him build them. In architecture, the international style came about in response to a desire for clarity, simplicity, and efficiency. Mathematically precise slabs, cubes, cylinders, and pyramids are the embodiment of one of the extremes on the scale on which every organic and inorganic thing finds its particular kind of shape. The five regular stereometric bodies described by Plato in his *Timaeus* (4, sec. 55, 56) as the elementary building blocks of all existing things are a pleasant reminder of our willingness to accept geometrical shapes as the manifestation of the fundamentally simple laws of nature, to which all complexity can be reduced.

In the history of art we note a give and take between simple shapes simply combined and complexities that tax the most refined organizational powers of the human nervous system. It looks as though the mind, in the course of its history, feels impelled to explore the many positions on the scale that leads from elementary constituents to their richest combinations. Thus, when in the arts of recent generations we observe a tendency toward mathematically definable shapes, it is not sufficient to explain such works as responses to, or products of, all the technology we happen to have around. Technology itself must be understood as a swing of the human mind toward a way of life that happens to be congenial to some of our present attitudes.

Note here also that not all technical devices affect the style of their products in the same direction. For example, photography, the first technological artform in the more specific sense of the term, does more nearly the opposite. It keeps picture-making away from the simple elements of shape and leads it toward the other extreme, the full complexity of the world in its actual appearance. The idiosyncrasy of the camera did not find the Western mind unprepared. By no means can one assert that photography came about in the nineteenth century simply because at that time the optics of the camera obscura happened to be joined by the discovery of photosensitive substances. Rather, it took a civilization inclined toward mechanically faithful recording to give the new invention its opening. Photography was a welcome ally in the quest for a realistic style of picture-making, which Western art had been seeking for centuries (2).

The example of photography can also help us to refine our notion of the role played by technological hardware in the artist's dealings with his environment. What is decisive for the character of the photographic product is not the technical equipment as such, but what it brings about—namely, the mechanical imposition of the physical world's projective image. This imposition, however, is only the most radical step in a long evolution that started when organisms developed eyes to obtain information about the environment beyond the reach of their bodies. In vision, the optical information is the raw material shaped by the nervous system. The eyes receive retinal images, and the brain processes them. Even more indirect is the relation of the painter to the visual images offered him by his nervous system. He responds to them by inventing images of his own. But in the photographic camera, the visual world itself may be said to impose its projection directly upon the pictorial surface. The environment itself becomes a decisive component of the picture, and this is like saying that the tool, halfway between the world and the human being, is a part of the environment as much as it is an extension of the person.

I am influenced here by a striking remark I found in an article by a California computer artist, Christopher William Tyler (5, p. 88). He observes that "one of the trends of recent art has been the tendency to operate by selecting from an environment entities that have significance to the artist rather than creating from scratch on a tabula rasa." And he continues: "The instruments which are thought of as tools at the disposal of the artist become part of the environment in which the art is produced." In a more general sense we arrive at the insight that our problem is not so much the relation of the artist to his tools as the relation of the mind's conceptions to the opportunities and constraints presented by the environment. To invent a new tool is to change that environment. If we identify the human being with the mind, the body is not only the primary tool of man, but also his closest neighbor in the world that surrounds him. The boundary line can be traced either way.

In the arts the question arises to what extent the direct contribution of environmental factors must be acknowledged by the viewer if he is to perceive certain types of art appropriately. This is certainly relevant in photography. A photograph can be understood and appreciated only when the viewer acknowledges the contribution of the optical projection (see "On the Nature of Photography," above). Photography displays its particular value only when it is understood as a collaboration between the projected optical environment and the shaping mind of the artist. The artistic value of a photograph depends on the success of this collaboration. The same is true for other recording techniques, such as photocopying or the casting of molds in plaster or plastic. While we respect the documentary value of a mechanical reproduction, say, the imprint of a person's face preserved in a mask that was made after death, we have reason to object to the casting of a body when it is presented as sculpture.

To a lesser extent this is true for the geometric fundamentals to which I referred earlier. Although they can be conveniently supplied by tools, they are also essential creations of the mind itself and as such can, but need not, rely upon the help of tools. The potter's wheel or the lathe, for example, imposes upon the object a mathematically strict circularity in the rotational plane, while along the axis the craftsman creates "free" forms that need not obey any geometrical formula. For the appreciation of a typical ceramic vase it is necessary to realize, at least intuitively, the interplay between rigid circularity in the horizontal dimension and freedom of shape in the vertical. But it is not necessary, although perhaps helpful, to attribute the former to the technological tool, the latter to the free judgment of eye and hand. In principle, the same ceramic pot could be made without the wheel, although the skill would really be wasted and the result would hardly match the perfection of the "thrown" product.

Moreover, the use of the mechanical tool and the realization on the part of the viewer that the tool has been used sharpen the distinction between mathematical regularity and free invention. The mathematical condition of circularity is a constraint imposed by the artist upon his visual imagination, and the potter's wheel is the technological device that introduces the constraint with the utmost precision.

It is useful to realize that the imposition of rational, i.e., intellectually definable, shapes by the lathe, the wheel, the plane, the saw, the straightedge, or the draftsman's compass, is similar in principle to the intellectual constraints adopted without the aid of such tools by painters or architects when they rely on modular proportions, the golden section, or other ratios. In literature one can refer to the rules for the form of sonnets or haiku or to Dante's use of the number three in the composition of the *Divine Comedy*. The same poet's funnel-shaped hole of the Inferno and the conic mountain of Purgatory as well as his concentric galleries of sins and virtues were built without the help of engineers. The case of music is too obvious to mention. Everywhere the mind craves the rationalization of shapes and, if necessary, produces tools to achieve it.

In this connection it is instructive to look at computer graphics. A computer is a steering device and as such has been compared, misleadingly, to the human brain. It differs from the brain in at least two fundamental aspects. A computer cannot invent but only execute instructions. To be sure, it can deliver combinations that no brain ever conceived of, and it can produce random patterns that might enchant and aid artists. But neither combinations nor random behavior amounts to invention, or even thinking.

Computers differ from brains also by being incapable of organizing data in field or gestalt processes, which are the privilege of perception and as such a decisive resource of the artist. Computers, as we know them today, produce only combinations of fixed elements. They receive information in the form of bits, and they dictate only patterns whose shapes and spatial relations are reducible to the formulae by which they were constructed. Therefore the technique of computer graphics is particularly suited to geometrical ornament. It is a godsend for weavers and for the designers of fabrics and wallpapers because not only does it execute tediously repetitive work with supreme accuracy and speed, it also can deliver all possible variations of a given set of elements and thereby supply the designer with an inexhaustible choice of themes. By the same token, however, certain types of computer graphics presented as works of art remind us all too often painfully of Christmas tree decorations or grandma's cross-stitch embroideries. In such works there is frequently a pathetic discrepancy between the sophistication of the program fed into the computer and the simplism of the visual results.

Such disappointment is to be expected when the work is entirely determined by a computer program. Elsewhere in the arts the same aridity distinguishes certain works of so-called minimal or conceptual art that are derived entirely from intellectual measurements. In the search for proportions that would reveal the secret of beauty, there has been a similar belief that once the happy formula was found, it would deliver the perfect composition. This, however, is an illusion. Wherever such measurements are used, they serve only to give simple accuracy to relations prescribed by intuition. This is true, for example, of symmetry. And it took Le Corbusier's ingenious sense of design to make the *modulor* a useful aid.

The good sense of a good artist makes him realize that the unchallenged dominance of particular mental powers leads to poverty and boredom. In successful products of computer graphics all elements, whatever their origin, fit a visual pattern whose compositional order and originality reveal themselves to the eye but are not reducible to the sum of the elements that may have given rise to them.

When intuition controls the design, technologically created shapes can exercise a particular charm and enrich the artistic statement. This effect is evident elsewhere in the arts when geometrically simple shapes such as squares, circles, or even simple straight lines appear in pictorial compositions. Modern nonfigurative painting offers examples; so do sculpture and, of course, furniture design and architecture. The antagonistic interplay of rationally defined elements and the elusive freedom of intuitive conception reflects symbolically the dual character of the mind. It also symbolizes man's productive dealings with nature and with his own rationalized environment.

A good example is the use of typographic elements in so-called concrete poetry (see "Language, Image, and Concrete Poetry," above). In this recent branch of graphic art, letters and numbers are combined to form visually meaningful compositions. Here again the results are most successful when the printed shapes are arranged with intuitive imagination. The patterns often lack interest when they are confined to the standard horizontal and vertical rows and columns or to a few regular distances. The technique also fails, however, when the letters or numbers look hand-drawn. It takes the crisp precision and perfection of printed type to make the contrast compelling. In this connection it may also be mentioned that the reflections of the technological age in modern painting and sculpture are most convincing when actual samples of machine production are used in collages, assemblages, or constructions of *objets trouvés*, whereas the pictorial imitation of technological shapes, for example, in the stovepipe figures of Fernand Léger's paintings, rarely go beyond ingenuous make-believe.

As long as we are dealing with art, perceptual experience remains the final objective and the final judge. A sobering admonition to this effect came half a century ago from one of the most influential pioneers of technological art, László Moholy-Nagy. In his book *From Material to Architecture* he wrote:

Since ancient times people have labored to discover formulae for laws that would decompose the intuitive quality of human expression into scientifically manipulable elements. One tried repeatedly to establish canons that would guarantee harmonious results in some particular medium. We have become skeptical about this sort of doctrine of harmony. We do not believe that works of art can be produced mechanically. We know by now that harmony does not reside in an aesthetic formula, but in the organic, unhampered functioning of any one being. Therefore the knowledge of some kind of canon is much less important than the existence of a true human equilibrium. To approach a piece of work in this way is almost tantamount to giving it balanced, harmonious shape and true meaning. When this is done, the work attains its lawfulness by itself, organically. (3, p. 188)

I will conclude with one more reference to the so-called applied arts, for which technological means of production are most frequently and most happily employed. The applied arts make constant use of geometrically simple, intellectually definable shapes, which appear in the fine arts only exceptionally. Of course, this is so for practical reasons. A building reposes most safely on right-angled relations. A table, a chair, or a vase uses symmetry to stand up. The cylinder and its piston will not fit each other unless they are perfectly smooth and regular. Easy cleaning, measuring, stacking call for simple shapes. And precisely those simple shapes are most readily produced by tools and machines, because tools and machines themselves function best when they are designed of simple shapes. Tools and machines make objects of their own kind, and what suits the functioning and efficiency of the producing mechanism suits the functioning of the product.

Not only do all organic or man-made things fulfill certain functions, they all participate in artistic expression. It has often been observed that well-designed machines are beautiful. Why do we welcome geometrically simple, intellectually definable shapes in the applied arts, whereas we reject such a preponderance in the fine arts? The reason seems to be that a painting or a piece of sculpture—and the same is true for musical compositions—is expected to represent and interpret the various aspects of human experience in all their fullness. If the image they offer is one-sided, they fall short of their task. Each of the works of painting or sculpture we see in our museums and each musical composition we hear at a concert is, one might say, a complete and closed world of its own. These works are either detached from the broader context of the environment they represent, in which they and we dwell, or they occupy within that environment a central place that calls for such completeness of representation.

Most objects, however, serve a more limited function. A wine glass, for instance, is shaped to facilitate drinking. Therefore artistically also it should express the limited functions of containing and dispensing and should do so in a manner that befits a festive occasion. If such an implement goes beyond its limited program, if it pretends to be painting or sculpture, we are puzzled and suspect bad taste. Benvenuto Cellini's exuberant saltcellar can embarrass. There is, then, a meaningful correspondence between the range of an object's function and the range of its expression. Modesty of expression suits a pocketknife or a pair of scissors. When a hunting gun or a telephone is enriched beyond practical necessity, we diagnose a tendency to glorify its function.

Although the so-called applied arts rely so rightly on simple, rational shapes, even they are seldom reducible to such elementary geometry. Even a beer bottle supplements its straight cylinders with curved transitions and endings that may follow no simple formula. An elementary tool like a hammer or pair of pliers has angles, proportions, and curves whose aesthetic rightness in relation to their function can be judged only intuitively. But the machines and tools that fabricate these objects cannot make free forms. They can only cast or stamp them out from models created by designers.

The conclusion seems to be that the outcome of the encounter between man and the machine will be determined more by the former than the latter. It is true that in many ways an airplane is more coercive than a buggy, and an electronic word processor more than pen and paper. But whether or not we get carried off by the waters that swept away the sorcerer's apprentice will depend more on the swimmers than on the flood.

## References

1. Cross, Richard G. "Electro-oculography: Drawing with the Eye." *Leonardo* (1969), pp. 399–401.
2. Galassi, Peter. *Before Photography*. New York: Museum of Modern Art, 1981.
3. Moholy-Nagy, László. *Von Material zu Architektur*. Mainz and Berlin: Kupferberg, 1968.
4. Plato. *Timaeus*.
5. Tyler, Christopher William. In Ruth Levitt, ed., *Artist and Computer*. New York: Harmony Books, 1976.

# Part IV

# A PLEA FOR VISUAL
# THINKING

IN RECENT years the notion of visual thinking has made its appearance everywhere. This cannot but give me some personal satisfaction (1). But it also astonishes me, because in the long tradition of Western philosophy and psychology the concepts *perception* and *reasoning* have not belonged under the same blanket. One can characterize the traditional view by saying that the two concepts are believed to require each other, but also to exclude each other.

Perceiving and thinking require each other. They complement each other's functions. The task of perception is supposed to be limited to collecting the raw materials for cognition. Once the material has been gathered, thinking enters the scene, at a supposedly higher cognitive level, and does the processing. Perception would be useless without thinking; thinking without perception would have nothing to think about.

But by the traditional view, the two mental functions also exclude each other. It was assumed that perception can deal only with individual instances, that it cannot generalize; but generalization is precisely what is needed for thinking. For the purpose of concept formation, one must go beyond the particulars. Hence the belief that perception ends where thinking takes over.

Derived from two papers, "Visual Thinking in Education," in *The Potential of Fantasy and Imagination*, ed. Anees A. Sheikh and John T. Shaffer (New York: Brandon House, 1979), and "A Plea for Visual Thinking", in *Critical Inquiry*, vol. 6 (Spring 1980).

The habit of separating the *intuitive* from the *abstractive* functions, as they were called in the Middle Ages, goes far back in our history. Descartes, in the sixth *Meditation*, defined man as "a thing that thinks," to which reasoning came naturally; whereas imagining, the activity of the senses, required a special effort and was in no way necessary to the human nature or essence. The passive ability to receive images of sensory things, said Descartes, would be useless if there did not exist in the mind a further and higher active faculty, capable of shaping these images and correcting the errors that derive from sensory experience. A century later Leibniz spoke of two levels of clear cognition (10). Reasoning was cognition of the higher degree: it was *distinct*; that is, it could analyze things into their components. Sensory experience, on the other hand, was cognition of the lower order: it also could be clear, but it was *confused* in the original Latin sense of the term; that is, all elements fused and mingled together in an indivisible whole. Thus artists, who rely on this inferior faculty, are good judges of works of art but when asked what is wrong with a particular piece that displeases them can only reply that it lacks *nescio quid*, a certain "I don't know what."

George Berkeley, in his *Treatise Concerning the Principles of Human Knowledge* (3), applied the dichotomy to mental images and insisted that nobody can picture in his mind an idea, such as "man," as a generality: one can visualize only a tall or a short man, a white or a black one, but not man as such. Thinking, on the other hand, is said to handle only generalities. It cannot tolerate the presence of particular things. If, for example, I try to reason about the nature of "man," any image of a particular man would lead me astray.

In our own time, the old prejudice has survived with particular clarity in developmental psychology. Thus Jerome S. Bruner, following the lead of Jean Piaget, has asserted that the cognitive development of a child passes through three stages (5). The child explores the world first through action, then through imagery, and finally through language. The implication is that each of these cognitive modes is confined to a specific range of operation, so that, for example, the "symbolic" mode of language is capable of tackling problems at a level not accessible to the perceptual mode. Thus Bruner notes that when "perceptual-iconic representation" becomes dominant, it inhibits the operation of symbolic processes. The very title of a recent collection of Bruner's articles suggests that to arrive at knowledge, the human mind must go "beyond the information given" by direct sensory experience. Thus when the child learns to go beyond a particular constellation that he sees directly in front of him, the ability to restructure the situation in a more appropriate way Bruner attributes not to the maturing of perceptual capacity, but to a switch to a new processing medium, namely, language.

Let me illustrate the crucial theoretical point by reference to the best-known demonstrations in the field, namely the conservation experiments (11). A child is shown two identical beakers, each filled with the same amount of liquid. The content of one of them is poured into a third container, which is taller and thinner. A young child will assert that the taller beaker contains more water even though he has watched the pouring. A somewhat older child will realize that the quantity has remained the same. How is one to describe the change that has occurred during this development of the child's mind?

There are two basic approaches. One has it that when the child is no longer fooled by the different shapes of the two containers into believing that they hold different amounts of liquid, he is escaping from the appearance of things to the realm of pure reason, where he is no longer misled by perception. Thus Bruner: "It is plain that if a child is to succeed in the conservation task, he must have some internalized verbal formula that shields him from the overpowering appearance of the visual displays" (5).[1] The other approach maintains that to judge the two columns of liquid by, say, their height is a legitimate first step toward solving the problem. To go beyond it, the child does not leave the domain of visual imagery—there is in fact nowhere else to go—but proceeds to view the given situation in a more sophisticated fashion. Instead of considering just one spatial dimension, he looks at the interplay between two, namely height and breadth. This is true progress on the scale of mental development, achieved not by going "beyond the information given" in perception but, on the contrary, by going more deeply into it.

The fact that thinking of this kind must take place in the perceptual realm because there is no place else to go is obscured by the belief that reasoning can only be done through language. I can refer here only briefly to what I have tried to show more explicitly elsewhere, namely, that although language is a valuable aid to much human thinking, it is neither indispensable nor the medium in which thinking takes place (1).

---

[1] In a personal communication, Professor Bruner has assured me that he agrees with my approach and that he sees the source of cognitive growth "in the *interaction* of the three modes of processing knowledge." It makes a decisive difference, however, whether one believes that perceptual imagery at its own inferior (because "stimulus-bound") level can supplement the workings of nonperceptual reasoning or that the restructuring of a given problem-situation typically occurs within the perceptual realm itself.

It should be obvious that language consists of sounds or visual signs that possess none of the properties that have to be manipulated in a problem situation. In order to think productively about the nature of a fact or problem, whether in the realm of physical objects or in that of abstract theory, one needs a medium of thought in which the properties of the situation to be explored can be represented. Productive thinking operates by means of the things to which language refers—referents that in themselves are not verbal, but perceptual.

As an example let me use a puzzle cited in an article by Lewis E. Walkup (13). The solution should be attempted without the help of an illustration. Imagine a large cube made up of twenty-seven smaller cubes, that is, three layers of nine cubes each. Imagine further that the entire outer surface of the large cube is painted red and ask yourself how many of the smaller cubes will be red on three sides, two sides, one side, or no side at all. As long as you stare at the imagined cube as though it were nothing but a pile of inert building blocks, and as long as you take only a diffident, haphazard nibble at this or that small cube, you will feel uncomfortably uncertain. But now change your visual conception of the cube into that of a centrically symmetrical structure, and in a flash the whole situation looks different! What happens first is that suddenly the imagined object looks "beautiful"—an expression mathematicians and physicists like to use when they have attained a view that offers a surveyable, well-ordered image of a problem's solution.

Our new view shows one of the twenty-seven cubes surrounded by all the others, which cover it like a shell. Shielded from the outside, the one central cube obviously remains unpainted. All the others touch the outside. We now look at one of the six outer surfaces of the large cube and notice that it presents a two-dimensional version of the three-dimensional image from which we started: we see, on each of the six surfaces, one central square surrounded by eight others. That central square is obviously the one painted surface of a cube—which gives us six cubes with one surface painted. We now look at the twelve edges of the large cube and find that each edge belongs to three cubes and that the cube in the center rides on two surfaces, like a gable. The two surfaces it exposes to the outside make for a cube painted on two sides, and there are twelve of those cubes. We are left with the eight corners, which cover three surfaces each—eight cubes with three of their sides painted red. The task is done. We hardly need add one + six + twelve + eight to make certain that we have accounted for all twenty-seven cubes, so sure are we of the completeness of our solution.

Did we go beyond the information given? In no way. We only went beyond the poorly structured pile of blocks a young child would be able to perceive. Far from abandoning our image, we discovered it to be a beautiful composition, in which each element was defined by its place in the whole. Did we need language to perform this operation? Not at all; although language can help us codify our results. Did we need intelligence, inventiveness, creative discovery? Yes, some. In a modest way, the operation we performed is the stuff both good science and good art are made of.

Was it seeing or was it thinking that solved the problem? Obviously, the distinction is absurd. In order to see we had to think; and we would have had nothing to think about if we were not looking. But the claim of the present discussion goes further: I assert not only that perceptual problems can be solved by perceptual operations, but that productive thinking must solve any kind of problem perceptually because there exists no other arena in which true thinking can take place. Therefore it is now necessary to show, at least sketchily, how the human mind goes about solving a highly "abstract" problem.

Let us ask the old question whether free will is compatible with determinism. Instead of looking up the answer in Saint Augustine or Spinoza, I watch what happens when I begin to think. In what medium does the thinking take place? Images start to form. The motivational forces of the "Will," in order to become manipulable, take the shape of arrows. These arrows line up in a sequence, each pushing the next—a deterministic chain that does not seem to leave room for any freedom (Figure 13a). Next I ask What is freedom? and I see a sheaf of vectors issuing from a base (Figure 13b). Each arrow is free, within the limits of the constellation, to move in any direction it pleases and to reach as far as it can and will. But there is something incomplete about this image of freedom. It operates in empty space, and there is no sense to freedom without the context of the world to which it applies. My next image adds an external system of a world minding its own business and thereby frustrating the arrows that issue from my freedom-seeking creature (Figure 13c). I must ask: Are the two systems incompatible in principle? In my imagination I start restructuring the problem constellation by moving the two systems in relation to each other. I come across one pattern in which the arrows of my creature remain intact by being fitted to those of the environmental system (Figure 13d). The creature is no longer the prime mover of its motivational forces, each of which is fitted now into a sequence of determining factors of the type shown in Figure 13a. But in no

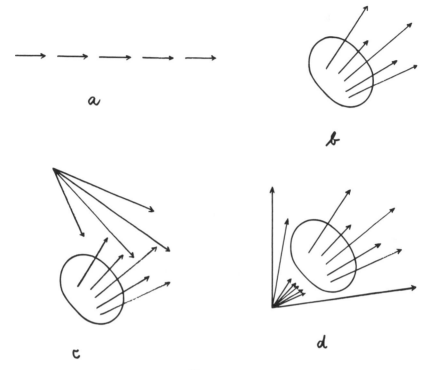

*Figure 13.*

way does this determinism impair the freedom of the creature's vectors.

The thinking has barely started, but the description of these first steps will suffice to illustrate some remarkable properties of this thought model. It is a wholly concrete percept, although it does not spell out the images of particular life situations in which freedom arises as a problem. While concrete, the model is entirely abstract. It draws from the phenomena under investigation only those structural features to which the problem refers, namely, certain dynamic aspects of motivational forces.

The example offers an answer to a question that is of particular interest to psychologists: In what medium does one think about mental processes? The example shows that one embodies motivational forces in perceptual vectors—visual ones, perhaps supplemented by kinesthetic sensations. An illustration from the history of psychology may help to make the point. Sigmund Freud, in one of the few diagrams that accompany his theories, illustrated the relation between two triads of concepts: id, ego, and superego, and unconscious, preconscious, and conscious (Figure 14) (7). His drawing presents these terms in a vertical section

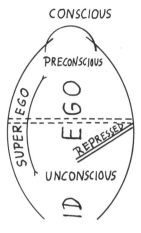

*Figure 14.*

through a bulgy container, a kind of abstract architecture. The psychological relations are shown as spatial relations, from which we are asked to infer the places and directions of the mental forces that the model is intended to illustrate. These forces, although not represented in the picture, are as perceptual as the space in which they are shown to act. It is well known that Freud made them behave like hydraulic forces—an image that imposed certain constraints on his thinking.

Note here that Freud's drawing was not a mere teaching device used in his lectures to facilitate the understanding of processes about which he himself thought in a different medium. No, he portrayed them precisely in the medium in which he himself was thinking, well aware, undoubtedly, that he was thinking in analogies. Whoever hesitates to believe this is invited to ask himself in what other medium Freud—or for that matter any other psychologist—could have done his reasoning. If the hydraulic model was imperfect, it needed replacement by a more suitable image. But perceptual it had to be, unless Freud, instead of engaging in productive thinking, had limited himself to trying out new combinations of properties his concepts already possessed, in which case a simple computer would have done equally well.

Earlier I mentioned a basic objection that seemed to indicate that visual images could not serve as the medium of reasoning. Berkeley had pointed out that perception, and therefore mental images, could refer only to individual instances, not to general concepts, and was therefore unsuitable for abstract thinking. But if this were so, how could diagrams be used everywhere as vehicles for thinking at a highly abstract level?

Take as an example the syllogism, that triumph of inferential logic. The device has been famous since antiquity because it permits the thinker to draw a valid conclusion from two valid premises. One obtains a new piece of reliable knowledge without any need to consult the facts of reality for confirmation. Now, when the syllogism formula is recited in words, the listener experiences a fine case of scampering in search of a thought model. He hears: "If all A are contained in B, and if C is contained in A, then C must also be contained in B." Is this proposition right or wrong? There is no way of finding out without recourse to the kind of image that turns up in Janellen Huttenlocher's splendid experiments on strategy in reasoning (8). I want to refer here to the oldest syllogistic diagrams, introduced around 1770 by the mathematician Leonhard Euler in his book *Letters to a German Princess* (6). One glance at Figure 15 proves that the syllogistic proposition of the *modus barbara* is correct, and must be correct not only in the present example but in all possible cases. In the drawing, the factual relations are shown as spatial relations, just as in Freud's diagram.

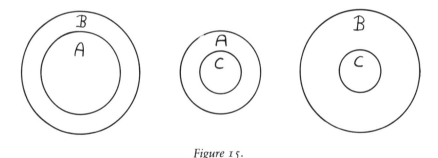

*Figure 15.*

Evidently the syllogism uses concepts at a very high level of abstraction. They are despoiled of all particular characteristics except that of spatial inclusion. The syllogism can serve to prove that Socrates is mortal or that cherry trees have roots, but neither Socrates nor cherry trees figure in the proposition. Visually, the circle is the most denuded shape we possess. But when we look at the drawing, we seem to find Berkeley's assertion confirmed: we see a particular instance of entangled circles and nothing else. How, then, do we reason so abstractly with particulars?

The answer comes from the psychological principle for which philosophers are searching when they discuss the problem of "seeing as" (14). I would formulate this principle by saying that all perception is the perceiving of qualities, and since all qualities are generic, perception always refers to generic properties. Seeing a fire is always seeing fieriness, and seeing a circle is seeing roundness. Seeing the spatial relations between Euler's circles lends itself quite directly to seeing the range of enclosure; and the topological aspects of enclosure are presented by Euler's images with the disciplined economy required by all good thinking.

I would like to return to a problem to which I referred briefly when I asserted that all truly productive thinking has to occur in the perceptual realm. I implied that perceptual thinking tends to be visual, and in fact, vision is the only sense modality in which spatial relations can be represented with sufficient precision and complexity. Spatial relations offer the analogies by which one visualizes such theoretical relations as the logical ones presented by Euler or the psychological ones investigated by Freud. Touch and kinesthesis are the only other sensory medium that conveys such spatial properties as inclusion, overlap, parallelism, size, etc., with some precision. But in comparison with vision, the spatial universe presented by tactile and muscular sensations is limited in range and simultaneity. (This should have consequences for the range of theoretical thinking in the blind, which would be worth investigating.)

Thinking, then, is mostly visual thinking. But, someone might ask, could one not solve theoretical problems in an entirely nonvisual way, namely, by means of purely conceptual propositions? Could one? We have already excluded language as an arena of thought since words and sentences are only a set of references to facts that must be given and handled in some other medium. But yes, there is a nonvisual medium capable of solving a problem in an entirely automatic fashion as soon as all pertinent data are supplied. Computers function in this way, without any need to consult perceptual images. Human brains can produce approximations of such automatic processing if they are subjected to sufficient deprivation or educational pressure, even though a brain is not easily prevented from exercising its natural inclination and ability to approach a problem by structural organization.

But it can be done. The other day, my wife bought twenty envelopes at seven cents each at the local university store. The student at the cash register punched the seven key twenty times and then, to make sure she had done it often enough, proceeded to count the seven on the sales slip. When my wife assured her that the sum of $1.40 was correct, she looked at her as though she were privy to superhuman enlightenment. We supply children with pocket calculators; but we must consider that the saving in time and effort is made at the expense of precious elementary training of the brain. Genuine productive thinking starts at the simplest level, and the basic operations of arithmetic offer fine opportunities.

To repeat, when I assert that thinking is impossible without recourse to perceptual images, I am referring only to the kind of process for which terms like "thinking" or "intelligence" ought to be reserved. A careless use of these terms will lead us to confuse purely mechanical, though immensely useful, machine operations with the human ability to structure and restructure situations. Our analysis of the cube was an example of a solution that a machine could arrive at only mechanically. Another example comes from the performances of chess players (4). It is well known that the ability of chess players to retain whole games in their memories does not rely on a mechanical copy of the arrangements of pieces on the board, preserved in eidetic memory. Rather, a game presents itself as a highly dynamic network of relations in which each piece comes with its potential moves—the queen with her long, straight outreach, the knight with his crooked hop—and with the risks and defenses of its particular position. Each piece is meaningfully held in its place by its function in the overall strategy. Therefore, any particular series of moves does not have to be remembered piecemeal, which would be much more cumbersome.

Or think of the difference between a machine reading letters or digits—a purely mechanical procedure—and a young child figuring out how to draw a picture of a tree (Figure 16). Trees as seen in nature are intricate entanglements of branches and foliage. It takes truly creative structuring to discover in such a jumble the simple order of a vertical trunk from which the branches issue, one by one, at clear angles and serve in turn as bases for the leaves. Intelligent perceiving is the child's principal way of finding order in a bewildering world.

One more testimonial to visual thinking deserves to be cited, this one from an unexpected source, a presidential address by the psychologist B. F. Skinner, to which, it seems to me, not enough attention has been paid (12). In opposition to the usual statistical treatment of experiments based on a large number of subjects, Skinner recommended the careful scrutiny of individual cases. Mass experiments are based on the rationale that by aggregating the behavior of many subjects, one causes accidental factors to cancel one another out, which lets the underlying lawful principle emerge in uncontaminated purity. "It is the function of learning theory," said Skinner, "to create an imaginary world of law and order and thus to console us for the disorder we observe in behavior itself." He became disenchanted with this procedure through his interest in the

*Figure 16.*

training of individual animals. For that purpose the lawfulness of average behavior offered little consolation. The performance of the particular dog or pigeon had to be flawless to be usable.

This led to attempts to rid the individual case of whatever was not pertinent to it. In addition to perfecting the practical performance of the animal, this method had two advantages. It induced a positive scrutiny of the modifying factors, which in the statistical procedure simply dropped out as so much "noise." In addition, however, the method reduced the scientific practice to "simple looking." Whereas the statistics divert the psychologist's attention from the actually observed cases to the manipulation of purely numerical data, that is, to the refuge "beyond the information given," the cleaned-up individual case makes a type of behavior directly perceivable. It displays before the observant eye the interaction of the relevant factors.

With this enjoyable spectacle of the behaviorist all but holding hands with the phenomenologist who endeavors to see the essential truth through the unhampered inspection of the perceptually given experience, I rest my case. Perhaps we are witnessing the beginning of the convergence of approaches that, under the impact of the evidence, will restore the intelligence of the senses to its rightful place.

*     *     *

The foregoing demonstrations were intended to show that all productive thinking is based by necessity on perceptual imagery, and that, conversely, all active perception involves aspects of thought. These claims cannot but be profoundly relevant to education, and therefore I will devote the remainder of this paper to a few more specific remarks on this subject. If all good thinking involves perception, it follows that the perceptual base of the student's and the teacher's reasoning must be explicitly cultivated in all areas of learning. But it is equally true that all training of perceptual skills must explicitly cultivate the thinking on which they rely and which they serve.

This means that art education is destined to play a central role in the curriculum of a good school or university, but that it can do so only if studio work and training in art history are understood as means of coping with the environment and the self. This responsibility is not always clearly faced. The way art educators describe their function often falls short of making the main point. We are told that the arts are needed to create a well-rounded person, although it is not obvious that being well-rounded is better than being slim. We hear that the arts give pleasure but are not told why and to what useful end. We hear of self-expression and emotional outlets and the liberation of individuality. But rarely is it made evident that drawing, painting, and sculpture, properly conceived, pose cognitive problems worthy of a good brain and every bit as exacting as a mathematical or scientific puzzle. Nor can it be said that the study of the arts makes true sense unless we are led to understand that the efforts of the great artist, the lowly art student, or the client of the art therapist are means to the end of facing the problems of life.

How does one render in a picture the characteristic aspects of an object or event? How does one create space, depth, movement, balance, and unity? How do the arts help the young mind comprehend the confusing complexity of the world it is facing? These problems will be productively approached by students only if the teacher encourages them to rely on their own intelligence and imagination rather than on mechanical tricks. One of the great educational advantages of artwork is that a minimum of technical instruction suffices to provide students with the instruments needed for the independent development of their own mental resources.

Artwork, intelligently pursued, lets the student take conscious possession of the various aspects of perceptual experience. For example, the three dimensions of space, which are available for practical use in daily life from infancy on, must be conquered step by step in sculpture. Such competent handling of spatial relations, acquired in the art room, is of direct professional benefit for activities such as surgery or engineering. The ability to visualize the complex properties of three-dimensional objects in space is necessary for artistic, scientific, or technological tasks. In a less technical sense, it is of general educational value to study in concrete detail how Michelangelo visualized problems of morals and religion in his *Last Judgment*, or how Picasso symbolized the resistance to fascist crimes during the Spanish Civil War in the figures and animals of his *Guernica*.

In terms of visual thinking there is no break between the arts and the sciences; nor is there a break between the uses of pictures and the uses of words. The affinity between language and images is demonstrated first of all by the fact that many so-called abstract terms still contain the perceivable practical qualities and activities from which they were originally derived. Such words are mementos of the close kinship between perceptual experience and theoretical reasoning. Beyond the purely etymological virtues of words, however, good writing, in literature as well as in the sciences, is distinguished by the constant evocation of the live images to which the words refer. When we remark regretfully that nowadays scientists no longer write like Albert Einstein or Sigmund Freud or William James, we are not voicing a merely "aesthetic" complaint. We sense that the desiccation of our language is symptomatic of the pernicious split between the manipulation of intellectual schemata and the handling of live subject matter.

The study of language as a means of effective communication is the business of poets and other writers, just as the skillful use of visual imagery is the task of artists. Therefore academic courses in writing fail to serve their purpose when they graduate students who have enjoyed the easy pleasures of "creative" writing but would not know how to describe a spoon or to formulate a regulation. Similarly, studio courses must do better than assuage the emotions or play games with shapes. Beyond their own specialty, they must face the responsibility of preparing the perceptual abilities of the mind for their indispensable work in all the disciplines of learning.

If I were asked to describe my dream university, I would have it organized around a central trunk composed of three disciplines: philosophy, studio art, and poetry. Philosophy would be asked to return to the teaching of ontology, epistemology, ethics, and logic, to remedy the shameful deficiencies in reasoning now common among academic specialists. Art education would refine the instruments by which to carry out such thinking. And poetry would make language, our principal medium for communicating thought, fit for thinking in images.

A glance at the practice of secondary and higher education today indicates that imagery has its representatives in the classroom. The blackboard is the venerable vehicle of visual education, and the diagrams drawn in chalk by teachers of social science, grammar, geometry, or chemistry indicate that theory must rely on vision. But a look at these diagrams also reveals that most of them are the products of unskilled labor. They fail to transmit their meaning as well as they should because they are badly drawn. In order to deliver their message safely, diagrams must rely on the rules of pictorial composition and visual order that have been perfected in the arts for some 20,000 years. Art teachers should be prepared to apply these skills not only to the exalted visions of painters whose work is fit for museums, but to all those practical applications the arts have served, to their own benefit, in all functioning cultures.

The same consideration holds for the more elaborate visual aids, the illustrations and maps, the slides and films, the video and television shows. Neither the technical skill of picture-making alone nor the faithful realism of the images guarantees that the material explains what it is intended to explain. It seems to me essential to go beyond the traditional notion that pictures provide the mere raw material and that thinking begins only after the information has been received—just as digestion must wait until one has eaten. Instead, the thinking is done by means of structural properties inherent in the image, and therefore the image must be shaped and organized intelligently in such a way as to make the salient properties visible. Decisive relations between components must show up; cause must be seen to lead to effect; correspondences, symmetries, hierarchies must be clearly presented—an eminently artistic task, even when

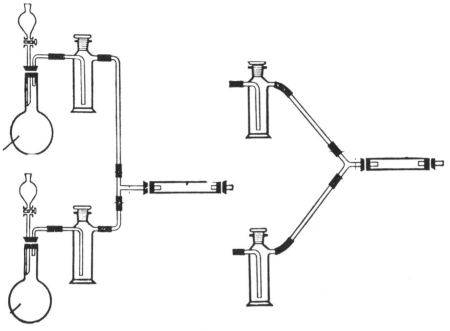

*Figure 17.*

it is used simply to explain the working of a piston engine or a shoulder joint (2).

I would like to conclude with a practical example. Some time ago I was asked for advice by a German graduate student at the Pedagogical Academy in Dortmund. Werner Korb was working on the visual aspects of classroom demonstrations in the high-school teaching of chemistry, and having discovered that gestalt psychology has worked out principles of visual organization, he asked for my permission to send me his material. From what I saw I gained the impression that in general school practice a classroom demonstration is considered to be doing its duty when the chemical process to be understood by the students is made physically present. The shape and arrangement of the various bottles, burners, tubes, and their contents are determined by what is technically required and what is cheapest and most convenient for the manufacturer and the teacher. Little thought is given to the manner in which the visual shapes and arrangements reach the eyes of the students, or to the relations between what is seen and what is understood (9).

Here is a small example. Figure 17 shows the arrangement suggested

*Figure 18.*

for demonstrating the synthesis of ammonia. The two component gases, nitrogen and hydrogen, each in its bottle, combine in a single straight tube, from which a short connection takes off with a sharp, right-angled break and leads the two gases to the container in which they form the ammonia. The single straight vertical tube is the simplest and cheapest way of making the connection, but it misleads the visual thinking of the students. It suggests a direct connection between the two components and bypasses their merging for the synthesis. A Y-shaped combination of two tubes, perhaps a trifle more troublesome for the teacher, leads the eye correctly.

My next example, also taken from Mr. Korb's material, shows a typical classroom demonstration of the production of hydrochloride (Figure 18). The array of bottles on the shelf in the background has nothing to do with the experiment. It is the teacher's storage space, meant to be ignored by the students. But the visual discrimination of figure and ground does not obey nonperceptual prohibitions. In a perceptual statement, whatever is seen is supposed to belong; and since the crowded shelf is part of the sight but not of the experiment, the contradiction threatens to sabotage the demonstration.

There is no need to comment on the virtues of the counterproposal illustrated in Figure 19. A sense of well-being and order distinguishes the

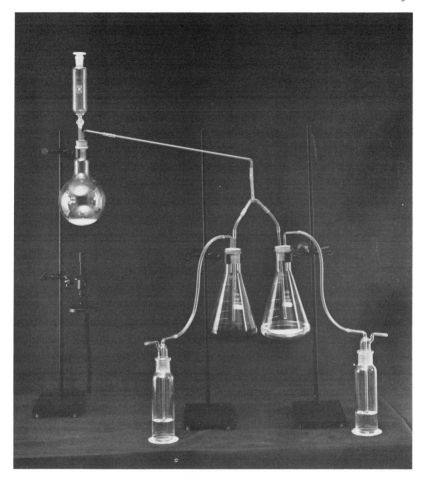

*Figure 19.*

image. The eye is securely led, even before one has any conception of the particular nature of the chemical process.

As my modest examples will have indicated, visual thinking is unavoidable. Even so, it will take time before it truly assumes its rightful place in our education. Visual thinking is indivisible: unless it is given its due in every field of teaching and learning, it cannot work well in any field. The best intentions of the biology teacher will be hampered by half-ready student minds if the mathematics teacher is not applying the same principles. We need nothing less than a change of basic attitude in all teaching. Until then, those who happen to see the light will do their best to get the ball rolling. Seeing the light and rolling the ball are good visual images.

# References

1. Arnheim, Rudolf. *Visual Thinking*. Berkeley and Los Angeles: University of California Press, 1969.

2. ———. *Art and Visual Perception*. New version. Berkeley and Los Angeles: University of California Press, 1974.

3. Berkeley, George. *A Treatise Concerning the Principles of Human Knowledge*. London: Dent, 1910.

4. Binet, Alfred. "Mnemonic Virtuosity: A Study of Chess Players." *Genetic Psychology Monographs*, vol. 74 (1966), pp. 127–62.

5. Bruner, Jerome S. "The Course of Cognitive Growth." In Jeremy S. Anglin, ed., *Beyond the Information Given*. New York, 1973. See also, "The Course of Cognitive Growth." *American Psychologist*, vol. 19 (Jan. 1964), pp. 1–15.

6. Euler, Leonhard. *Lettres à une princesse d'Allemagne sur quelques sujets de physique et philosophie*. Leipzig: Steidel, 1770.

7. Freud, Sigmund. *New Introductory Lectures on Psychoanalysis*. New York: Norton, 1933.

8. Huttenlocher, Janellen. "Constructing Spatial Images: A Strategy in Reasoning." *Psychological Review*, vol. 75 (1968), pp. 550–60.

9. Korb, Werner, and Rudolf Arnheim. "Visuelle Wahrnehmungsprobleme beim Aufbau chemischer Demonstrationsexperimente." *Neue Unterrichtspraxis*, vol. 12 (March 1979), pp. 117–23.

10. Leibniz, Gottfried Wilhelm von. Nouveaux essais sur l'entendement humain. Paris, 1966. Book 2, chap. 29.

11. Piaget, Jean, and Bärbel Inhelder. *Le développement des quantités physiques chez l'enfant*. Neuchâtel: Delachaux et Niestlé, 1962.

12. Skinner, B. F. "A Case History in Scientific Method." *American Psychologist*, vol. 11 (May 1956), pp. 221–33.

13. Walkup, Lewis E. "Creativity in Science through Visualization." *Perceptual and Motor Skills*, vol. 21 (1965), pp. 35–41.

14. Wittgenstein, Ludwig. *Philosophical Investigations*. New York: Macmillan, 1953.

# NOTES ON THE IMAGERY OF DANTE'S *PURGATORIO*

NOT A systematic study but a few chance observations made during a
rereading of some cantos of the *Purgatorio* will be presented here. Since
I wanted to be brief I intended to limit myself to those explicit similes
that Dante uses to illustrate some item of his narrative by citing an analogous scene from daily experience—for instance, when we are told in
the *Inferno* that the dead souls strained their eyes to see the two strange
wanderers "*come vecchio sartor fa nella cruna,*" that is, like an old tailor
puckering his brow on the eye of his needle (Inf. XV 21). But my reading
of the cantos soon reminded me that the particular nature of the metaphorical comparison was strongly influenced by the fact that the entire
*Commedia* is metaphorical, from the Inferno at the bottom to the Paradiso at the top, in its subject matter as well as in the detail of the descriptive language. In a setting in which each action and each sight were
the transparent carriers of ulterior meaning, the simile ceased to be a
mere analogy. It had to meet the demand that it contribute to the foreground story, just as the rest of the metaphorical subject matter was
doing. Confronted with a figurative reality, the figure had to be more
real. This meant to me that I had to look at the simile in context. The
investigation had to concern itself with the imagery as a whole.

Metaphor derives from the desire for sensory concreteness. Such concreteness is essential to poetical language in general and distinguishes it

First published in *Argo: Festschrift für Kurt Badt* (Cologne: Dumont, 1970).

most particularly when the poet profits from the sharp-sightedness of a culture still close to the soil. In the seventh canto of the *Purgatorio*, the poet Sordello, wishing to explain to Virgil and Dante that after sunset they cannot hope to continue their journey another inch, bends down and furrows the ground with his fingers: "Not even this line could you cross" (VII 52). From such concreteness of reasoning derives the verbal concreteness of the poet. It is most radical when it reduces an object to its mere shape or color, as when the serpent of temptation, approaching from a distance, is described as *la mala striscia*, the evil stripe (VIII 100).

More often Dante captures a gesture or stance with the immediacy that reminds us so inevitably of his contemporary, Giotto. The lazy Belacqua sits and embraces his knees, holding his face low down between them (IV 107). Often again, the enlivening concreteness is in the very texture of Dante's language, most liable to be bulldozed into flatness by translation. Thus, the optics of light and shadow acquire the masculine strength of fighting and chopping when the light is said to be broken or split in front of the observer's body and the sun wounds him from the left (*che da sinistra n'eravam feriti*) (III 17, III 96, IV 57, V 5). The imagery is drawn from the entire inventory of the perceivable world, and nature is humanized by psychological references. Dawn defeats the morning breeze, which flees before it, and the evening bells weep for the dying day (I 115, VIII 6).

This sort of thing is, of course, customary poetical practice. What is unique is that the cross-references between the terrestrial and the cosmic, the physical and the mental, operate in an explicitly conceived and systematically organized universe of sensory experience, in which the metaphor serves to define each element by its references to the others. Man appears in the center between the earthly realm and the divine, and is freshly seen as a product of animalism and spirit. When he is at his most common behavior he is characterized by images taken from the barnyard. The shadows of the dead, meeting the living stranger, act like sheep, which come forward from the fold by one, by two, by three, and the others stand timid, lowering eyes and muzzle to the ground; what the first does the others do, piling on it if it stops, simple and quiet, and not knowing the why (*semplici e quete, e lo perchè non sanno*) (III 79). And when they are frightened away they disperse like pigeons. Yet, even at this lower end of the human scale, there are faint overtones of the higher range, since the very choice of sheep and pigeons could not but remind the faithful of the noble appearance of these same animals in the symbolic mosaics of the Byzantine churches. At his best, man unites in himself his disparate heritages. Thus, much more than the usual perceptual enhancement is achieved when the bearded Cato "moves those honest plumes" (*movendo quell'oneste piume*) while his face shines as though the sun were in front of it (I 42). The vestiges of animal hair go with the splendor of the heavens—a balance not often achieved by mortal man. Man tries, uneasy, to maintain himself at the hub of the great panorama, whose sweeping boundary is drawn by a stroke of the poet's pen when he says of the setting sun that it retires to its nest, or when he describes an angel as "the divine bird," *l'uccel divino* (VII 85, II 38).

The *Commedia* may be the only literary narrative whose geographical setting conforms entirely to its symbolic purpose. The hollow crater of the Inferno furnishes the idea of sinfulness with the pervasive theme of descent, and this descent is coupled with an increasingly stifling convergence of space, until the icy paralysis of complete evil is reached at the bottom of the funnel. And inversely, the mountain of Purgatory and the spheres of Paradise beyond it make for continuous rising. As the mountain narrows toward the peak, body and mind move more and more freely. Thus the topology of the landscape not only supplies a static hierarchy of shelves for the display of the sins and virtues, it also produces the wealth of symbolic motion that goes with falling and climbing, with the Fall and the Ascension—all the nuances of eager speed and retardation, of steepness and gentle slope, of stumbling and surefootedness, fatigue and effort, yielding and overcoming.

We are told that this symbolic setting came about by an event that has all the hearty concreteness of good folk art: Lucifer, thrown out of heaven, drops to the ground, digs a crater like a meteor, and gets stuck in the center; and the dirt displaced by the thrust is pushed out as a mountain on the opposite side of the earth. The result of this fantastic piece of geology, however, may seem distressingly arid. The geometric simplicity of the spherical globe, modified by the two complementary cones, the hollow and the solid, with the concentric shells of the heavens surrounding the whole, may seem quite suitable as a visual aid for a systematic presentation of sin, penitence, and grace, but as artistic invention it may remind us of the naked poverty of "minimal art." Are these shapes not too directly derived from the intellectual skeleton of the theme, a textbook diagram rather than a living image?

In fact, Francesco de Sanctis, in the brilliant chapters devoted to the *Commedia* in his history of Italian literature (1), maintains that the didactic tradition of the literature of his time trapped Dante in the pitfall of allegory.

The allegory has made available to Dante an unlimited freedom of shapes, but it has also made him incapable of shaping them artistically. Since the figure has to represent its referent it cannot be free and independent, as required by art, but is merely a personification or sign of an idea. The only traits it is permitted to contain are those relating to the idea, the way a true comparison expresses by itself only what serves to depict the thing compared. Therefore, the allegory broadens Dante's world and slays it at the same time; it deprives it of a personal life of its own and makes it the sign or cipher of a concept foreign to it. (vol. 1, p. 123)

And de Sanctis points to the many conventional figments and allusions that are indeed as dead as the costumes and props of a forgotten play.

The danger is real. Our sense of what an early morning feels like is not refreshed when we read that "the concubine of ancient Tithonus was turning pale in the distant East" (IX 1), nor is the mythological reference likely to have done this service for Dante's contemporaries—although the image of the eternal youth of the morning arising from the bed of old age is by no means arbitrary. De Sanctis maintains that the poem was saved only because the poet was unwittingly overcome by his poetical instinct and talent; but the great critic would seem to have overstated his case because he was subject to the nineteenth-century dichotomy of art versus reason. To be sure, didactic illustrations of concepts tend not to have a life of their own. Any attempt today, for example, to parallel the behavior of atoms or electrons in a specific chemical process by a parable in which the roles of the particles were acted out by the members of a human family would probably be sterile and even ridiculous. Yet the elective affinities of the chemist became the guiding metaphor of one of the great novels of our age, Goethe's *Wahlverwandtschaften*, and many other concepts of natural science have been successfully reflected in poetry. I cannot here speculate on the underlying reasons for what, at first glance, looks like a lucky coincidence, by which the events of nature seem to parallel the strivings of the human mind and therefore lend themselves to reflecting them poetically. I will merely suggest that the logical development of a concept is not alien to the natural manifestations of the phenomenon for which the concept stands. The concept was drawn from these manifestations in the first place, and in using them to symbolize the concept the poet merely reverses the process by which the thinker obtained it originally. This holds particularly for those psychological categories that describe the inmates of the various circles in Hell and Purgatory. The poetic truth of Francesca da Rimini's story reflects the inner logic of her particular "case," as psychologists would call it, and this case study in turn fits the concept to be illustrated—the incontinence of erotic passion—so naturally that by its own economy the narrative contains nothing but what is needed to unfold the concept.

It would be quite unfair to accuse the poet, as I almost did a moment ago, of locating his story in a textbook diagram; for the geometrical diagram I described does not actually appear in the *Commedia* itself but is used by commentators to explain it. It is like the compositional lines drawn across paintings by teachers of art appreciation. It is there and it is not there. In the *Commedia*, the spheres and cones are nothing but an armature, overgrown almost everywhere with living matter.

If nevertheless we notice the didactic skeleton more readily in this work of art than we do in others, it is not because the poet failed to be a poet but because his works stands, in the history of literature, at the equinoctial turning point between medieval rationalism and modern worldliness. The exact ratio of percept and concept in a work of art is, of course, a matter of style. In the morality plays of the Middle Ages a simple label explicitly dominates each personification, whereas in the individualized figures and plots of modern novels the concept reverberates only vaguely. Dante, standing as he does between his two great compatriots, Thomas Aquinas, the man of thought, and Giotto, the man of images, holds the exact balance between thought and image, and within his work the *Purgatorio* is in a similar central position between the robust corporality of the *Inferno* and the disembodied ideas of the *Paradiso*.

The resulting balance is precarious, but it is also the key to the unique greatness of the *Commedia*. Here I can refer back to what I said in the beginning about the peculiar obligation facing the explicit metaphor in a story whose subject matter itself is so thoroughly metaphoric. The spirituality of man, who leaves his body behind like a garment, is symbolized in the *Commedia* by the incorporeal shadows of the dead; but this lack of physical substance is also quite real: it is the natural consequence of death. Since the usual gap between the literal and the figurative is all but closed, many of Dante's metaphors fit the foreground story rather directly. In the opening lines of the *Purgatorio,* the poet lets the little boat of his wit hoist its sails to travel on better waters (I 1)—a figure of speech not remote from the actual situation of the man who is in fact traveling on symbolic ground and who will, in a moment, meet an angel in charge of aquatic transportation. Similarly, the dew that serves to wash the dirt of the Inferno from Dante's face serves at the same time to unfog his mind's eyes and mingles with the tears of repentance. The sustained intelligence of a presentation for which there is no seeing without thinking and nothing material without reason shows even in the details of the language, for instance, when the equipment of the boat—its oars and sails—is called "the human arguments" (*gli argomenti umani*), which the angelic boatsman can do without (II 31). In such examples one experiences the dizzying symmetry between the figure and the things signified. It leads at times to a reversal of the usual practice of symbolizing the more abstract by the more concrete, as when we are told that at a certain place in Toscana the river Archiano's name comes to nothing, and are expected to understand by this reference to a linguistic change that the river flows into the Arno (V 97), or when the slope of a mountain is said to be steeper than the line that halves the quadrant of a circle (IV 42). No wonder that in such a climate even the allegorical beasts come to life and behave unselfconsciously like any other animal. A heraldic viper steps out of the coat of arms of the Viscontis to prepare the funeral of an unfaithful woman—a less good funeral than she would have received from the cock painted on the arms of another branch of the family (VIII 79). And in the same canto the constellation of the Ram bestrides the bed of the sun with all four feet (VIII 134).

Perhaps my rapid sketch of a particular aspect of the *Commedia* has turned out to be a tribute to the greatness of "padre Dante," as Benedetto Croce calls him with a suitable blend of veneration and affection. Perhaps this study of imagery has suggested why the *Commedia* may have to be called the greatest piece of writing ever done by a human being. Born at the moment of our Western history when reason became as visible as the view of nature became thoughtful, Dante Alighieri was able to present the highest synthesis of human experience.

## Reference

1. De Sanctis, Francesco. *Storia della letteratura italiana*. Milan: Treves, 1925.

# INVERTED PERSPECTIVE AND THE AXIOM OF REALISM

INVERTED perspective is a small matter. It occurs now and then in periods of art history that are not constrained by the stranglehold of central perspective; it is a pictorial device used by artists who are unaware of the geometry of perspective imposed on Western painting in the fifteenth century or who no longer feel bound to obey it, such as Picasso and some other painters of our century.

At the same time, inverted perspective can serve as a particularly helpful example to illustrate two different ways of accounting theoretically for deviations from projective realism, by which I mean the kind of image produced by lenses through optical projection. One of these interpretations relies on a prejudice generated by the particular conventions of Western art since the Renaissance; the other, proposed here, is intended to provide a more appropriate psychological base for the explanation of pictorial phenomena such as "inverted perspective."

## Taking Off From Realism

By definition, representational art derives its subject matter from nature. This implies that at least to some extent the shapes used for such representation must also be taken from the observation of nature since otherwise the depicted subjects would remain unrecognizable. The prejudice

Developed from "Inverted Perspective in Art: Display and Expression," *Leonardo*, vol. 5 (1972).

I am diagnosing here holds that painters of any provenance, young or old, modern or ancient, primitive or sophisticated, would produce likenesses of optical projection if they were not kept from doing so by constraints of one kind or other. If the term "naive realism" were not preempted by epistemologists, it would serve perfectly to label the theoretical approach under indictment here. I will call it "the axiom of realism."

Actually, of course, very few periods or places have ever produced paintings that even approach the standard of optical projection. But as long as the deviations are considered compatible with the intention of meeting the standard, theorists have been willing to explain them as the effects of stylistic convention. The idealizations of a Classicist style are within this range of tolerance. But the Mannerist elongations of an El Greco were sufficiently shocking to plant and keep alive the ludicrous suggestion that the painter must have suffered from astigmatism. This even though as early as 1914 the psychologist David Katz pointed out that astigmatism would apply to the picture as well as to the model depicted and that therefore no deformation on the canvas would result (8).

Pathologists, either professional or amateur, have been busy trying to save the axiom of realism by accusing Van Gogh's eyes of glaucoma or cataract and his mind of schizophrenia. Max Nordau in his book *Degeneration* accounted in 1893 for the technique of the Impressionists by referring to Charcot's findings on nystagmus in the eyes of "degenerates" and partial anesthesia of the retinae in hysterics (12, p. 51). The predominance of golden browns in the late Rembrandts and the unorthodox perspective of Cézanne have similarly been laid to ophthalmic flaws. According to Trevor-Roper, the loss of detail in the late style of painters such as Titian is "perhaps" due to presbyopia of the crystalline lens (17). Of course, pathological effects on a painter's style of representation cannot be ruled out in principle. What is of interest here is that such explanations are so often sought to support the conviction that if those artists had not been physically or mentally impaired, they would have produced realistic pictures.

The same tendency shows up in the assumption that the work of normally endowed artists derives all its motifs and formal devices from observations of nature. This theory ran into difficulty when it had to account for simple geometrical shapes as they occur in ornament and also in representational art, because such shapes are rarely found in nature. If one keeps searching, however, one can come up with likely models. Circular shapes were said to have been suggested by the sun and the full moon. According to Worringer (19, p. 68), the anthropologist Karl von den Steinen asserted that the Brazilian natives favored triangular shapes in their ornaments because their women used triangular loincloths, and that cross shapes were derived from the visual pattern of flying storks. More recently, speculations have become more sophisticated, but the underlying prejudice remains the same. Gerald Oster, for example, has asserted that the elementary symmetrical patterns in the drawings of young children "may be derived in part" from phosphenes, subjective images generated by the eyes in darkness (13).

Alois Riegl's statements on the origins of ornaments are somewhat ambiguous. He seems to share the traditional belief that geometrical shapes are obtained by copying from nature, specifically from the inorganic structure of crystals (15). But some of his formulations remind one of the medieval view that, in the words of Thomas Aquinas, "art is the imitation of nature in her manner of operation" (4, p. 52). Riegl writes:

Since the motifs of the figurative arts are created in competition with nature, they cannot be taken from anywhere but nature. . . . As soon as man feels the urge to fashion from dead matter a work for the purpose of decoration or utility, it is natural for him to employ the same laws as nature does when it wants to give shape to dead matter, namely the laws of crystallization. . . . Symmetry of fundamental form, bounding by plane surfaces meeting at angles, and finally immobility, existence at rest, are the natural conditions given from the outset for any work made of inorganic matter. . . . Only in inorganic creation does man appear as nature's full equal, by creating purely from an inner urge without any external models. (15, pp. 75–76)

## The Demands of the Medium

This inner urge to create simple basic shapes can be described with some psychological concreteness when we state that perception consists in the search for elementary forms in the stimulus material and the imposition of such "sensory categories" upon the raw data (1). It is entirely possible that the formation of these perceptual elements is stimulated and reinforced by the occasional observation of simple geometrical shapes in nature. The basic impulse, however, cannot be explained as an urge to copy nature; it can be understood only when one realizes that perceiving is not passive recording but understanding, and that understanding can take place only through the conception of definable shapes. For this reason art, like science, begins not with attempts to duplicate nature, but with highly abstract general principles. In the arts, these principles take the form of elementary shapes.

Symmetry is one of the features of art to which theorists have given some attention. They commonly attribute its frequent use to the symmetry of the human body. Once again such an influence of experiences in the environment upon what is invented in art is not unlikely; in fact, the kinesthetic striving for balance in the upright body might well carry over to an analogous striving in visual composition. Of much more basic influence, however, are the perceptual impulses evoked within the artist's medium itself. The medium demands equilibrium for its own independent sake and spontaneously obeys the law of parsimony: any statement, artistic or otherwise, must remain as simple as the purpose and the circumstances permit. Thus Pascal acknowledges that symmetry "is founded on the figure of man, whence symmetry is sought only laterally, not in height or depth"; but he cites as its primary rationale that symmetry occurs in "what has no reason to be shaped differently" (14, part I, sec. 29). Applied to the artistic statement, this interpretation shifts the emphasis from the demands of the natural model to the demands of representation.

For the sake of a tidy analysis it pays to distinguish between factors deriving from the nature of visual perception and others deriving from the medium of representation, even though in practice the two are not clearly separable. Both are modifying factors that are not limited to particular cultural conventions, as are the styles of art history, but apply across the board wherever human beings create artifacts. In the following I turn more specifically to the demands of the medium.

In drawing and painting, images are not taken simply from what is observed in nature but originate on the flat surface of paper, canvas, or walls. The surface imposes constraints that derive from its own perceptual properties: it favors certain procedures and discourages others. When these idiosyncrasies of the medium are ignored and their effect is attributed to what can be observed in nature, misinterpretations result. A few examples, selected at random, will lead to the principal exhibit of the present paper.

Cubist painters such as Picasso have sometimes combined several aspects of the same object in a single image. In principle, this device is used almost universally wherever pictorial representation does not adhere to the rule that all elements shown in a picture must have been viewed by the painter from the same point of observation. Of the Cubist paintings it has been said that to perceive them requires the beholder to move in his mind to the spatial positions he would have to assume if he were to see the model object the way it is represented in the picture. The experience of time and motion would thereby be added to the perception of the immobile image (9). This erroneous interpretation is derived from the axiom of realism, i.e., from the assumption that the work of art duplicates visual situations occurring in physical space. The space in which a picture comes about, however, is the two-dimensional surface of an immobile medium, not the physical arena in which we move around. The pictorial surface and what is on it can be perceived from a single vantage point, and the images it carries are conceived accordingly. The observer need not imagine moving through space in order to properly distinguish the side view of a painted pitcher from the top view; and the object represented is no monstrous distortion, just as the profile figures of ancient Egyptian art are not seen as walking around with twisted shoulders.

Rather, experiences gathered in physical space over time are translated into their two-dimensional equivalent outside time. The various aspects of the model are rendered and combined in the manner most appropriate to the artist's purpose. This procedure is not adopted because of lack of skill or by accidentally acquired convention. It is derived logically, from the perceptual nature of the artist's medium (2, p. 132).

In an illustration of the Manesse Codex (Figure 20) we see Count Otto von Brandenburg being checkmated by his lady. By the standards of "naive realism" the chessboard is wrongly placed upright rather than horizontal, probably because the medieval painter did not know how to draw a foreshortened board. But the board would stand upright only if the scene were taking place in the living room of the Count. Instead, it is being produced on the artist's flat drawing surface. By the rules of that medium, all objects remain in the plane of origin unless there is reason to remove them from it. At the given level of representation, there is no reason for such a differentiation of spatial dimensions. On the contrary, the less distorted the board, the more clearly the constellation of chessmen will show up. Far from making a mistake, the artist has made his subject most visible by conforming to a principal property of his medium; and this solution has been selected by him to make the viewers of his picture see what they are meant to see.

A further example comes from a commonly used interpretation of isometric perspective. In this type of perspective the sheaves of parallel lines or edges are shown not as converging toward vanishing points on the horizon, as they are in central perspective, but as retaining their par-

*Figure 20.* Manesse Codex. Early 14th century. Universitätsbibliothek Heidelberg.

allelism. How is this deviation from optical projection to be explained? Our interpreter, rummaging through the stores of everyday perception, finds that parallels remain parallel when they are looked at from sufficiently far away. Hence the assertion that isometric perspective depicts the world as it looks from an infinite distance. Here the error is compounded by the false assumption that the normal perception of space is identical with the optical image projected upon the retina. Actually, projective distortions are observed only by the select few who have been trained to watch out for them. Ignoring this fundamental fact, our interpreter assumes that normally people see parallels as converging but that under special circumstances, namely when they happen to look from far away, they discover that parallels can remain parallel. This theoretical approach offers no discernible reason why whole civilizations use this special case as the norm for their pictorial representation of nearby space.

Where does one find a better explanation? Commonly, people perceive parallels as parallels wherever they occur around them. But this fact alone does not suffice to account for the ubiquitousness of isometric perspective, which serves to depict architecture and other man-made objects in Far Eastern art and at early stages of representation in folk art and children's art, as well as in the technical drawings of designers, engineers, and mathematicians. Isometric perspective solves a problem that does not arise in the world at large, but only on the artist's and engineer's drawing board: how to recede from the frontal plane into depth with a minimum of shape distortion. Inverted perspective is a solution to a related problem.

## Scale of Size

The term "inverted perspective" refers essentially to two pictorial features: the rendering of relative size and that of geometrically shaped planes, hollow enclosures, and solids. In the art historical literature, the discussion began with an attempt to interpret the alleged inversion of size relations.

Byzantine and medieval painting had insisted on a puzzling, seemingly paradoxical way of scaling the size of human figures and other objects. Late traces of this tradition were still observed in the high Renaissance. Moreover, the same perverse procedure was met in Oriental art, quite independent of European practice. It seemed to reverse one of the basic principles of visual experience or at least of optical projection, namely, the larger things look, the closer they are to the observer and, therefore, the lower down they are in the visual field. This principle is respected in Renaissance perspective, but violated with ease in long and important periods of Western and Eastern art. A simple example is offered by a Japanese mandala of about A.D. 1000, showing Vairocana seated in the center and surrounded symmetrically by eight smaller figures belonging to lower religious echelons (Figure 21). If we force ourselves to see the picture as an attempt at perspective representation—and nothing but brute force can make us do it in this case—we notice the absence of the prescribed gradient, which would mean the upper figures would be the smallest, the lower ones the largest. In fact, nothing points to the representation of a horizontal floor.

An interpreter committed to the axiom that all pictorial representation derives from the optical projections produced in the eyes by three-

*Figure 21.*

dimensional visual space will be perplexed. What models for such perverse aberrations from the norm can we find in nature? The notion of "inverted perspective" was introduced in 1907 in a paper by Oskar Wulff (20). Significantly, Wulff does not base his argument on such clear-cut examples as the Japanese mandala, but rather on paintings of the high Renaissance in which puzzling deviations from the size gradient occur in compositions that otherwise obey the rules of realistic perspective. In Dürer's altar painting *Adoration of the Trinity by All the Saints* (Figure 22), the representation of the heavenly assembly respects realistic perspective to the extent that the figures of the crowd of saints in the lower

*Figure 22.* Albrecht Dürer, *Adoration of the Trinity by All the Saints.* 1511. Kunsthistorisches Museum, Vienna.

half of the picture are presented as closer to the observer and therefore larger than the figures in the upper half, including the relatively small central Christ on the cross. However, at the bottom of the painting there appears in sudden smallness a terrestrial landscape with one standing figure, a tiny self-portrait of the artist. As a second example, painted during the same period, Wulff cites Raphael's *The Vision of Ezekiel*, in which again a large heavenly scene borders on a small landscape at the bottom, a landscape containing the minute figure of the prophet who receives the vision. Such an interference with the size gradient is not compatible with the view an external observer of the scene would receive. But instead of diagnosing a clash between two different principles of representation, Wulff is bound by the axiom of realism to search in the world at large for a situation that would fit the scale of sizes adopted by the painters tolerably well. He concludes that we are dealing with examples of *Niedersicht*, i.e., a view from above, a bird's-eye perspective, which scales the diminishing sizes from the point of view of the most important person in the picture. In Dürer's painting, therefore, the figure of the painter is small because it looks that way to the heavenly personages above the clouds. "The artist raises us to the aerial realm by exercising his sovereign right to let us see the picture from a point of view completely independent of any possible standpoint of the observer outside." Wulff contends that only by psychological analysis can we hope to understand this subjectivistic treatment of space, and he refers to Theodor Lipps, whose theory of empathy had been made public a few years earlier.

Lipps theorized that observers give life to inanimate objects by projecting their own experience of physical activity upon the shapes they perceive, e.g., the columns of a temple (11). In no way can this theory be held accountable for the psychologically unacceptable use Wulff made of it. Lipps limited empathy to instances in which the observer's subjective projection supplements but does not contradict what he sees; whereas the perspective size scale attributed by Wulff to the perceptual experience of a person within the picture space would directly oppose the size scale the external observer could find in the picture. The observer looking at the picture is expected, by empathy, to see objects as farther away that to him look closer.

Wulff's thesis was rejected by other art historians from the beginning, mostly with the argument that it attributed subjective size perspective to cultures whose art did not possess it and were therefore even less likely to practice the inversion of that principle.[1] Positively it was pointed out, first in a brief critical note published in 1910 by Doehlemann (5), that the treatment of sizes in the works under discussion could be interpreted more convincingly as a hierarchic scaling, with the more important figures given larger size. More recently, John White in his book on perspective in European painting dismissed inverted perspective as a "mythical monster" (18, p. 103). He explains: "The difficulty is that the variations in figure scale are neither dependent on any spatial relationships within the composition nor upon the relationship of the scene as a whole to the observer. The deciding factor is invariably the importance which, for one reason or another, is attached to each particular figure."

In the course of the Renaissance, hierarchic scaling made its peace with the demands of realistic size perspective. At a time when small donor figures praying in a corner of the picture became unacceptable, Dürer, in the altarpiece misinterpreted by Wulff, justified the smallness of his self-portrait by placing the figure in a distant landscape. Painters like Tintoretto or El Greco endowed hierarchically prominent figures with the appropriate large size by locating them in the foreground. More generally any intelligent painter took advantage of the prescribed size scale not only to balance the visual weights of the figures and other pictorial objects in his composition, but also to create the hierarchy that he wanted to convey. The spontaneously evident expression of bigness and smallness, closeness and distance, serves to reflect the intended symbolic meaning. This was and is true also for photography and film.

It is worth mentioning in passing that projective space representation created an important visual paradox. The topography of the framed picture plane suggests that the dominant motifs should be located in the center or the upper portion of the composition and only exceptionally in the border area at the bottom. Placed at the bottom, the distinguished figures or objects would appear close and large. A central location on the canvas, however, assigns to the principal theme a relatively distant place on the depth scale. In consequence, that theme is given small size (e.g., the small and distant crucifix in Dürer's painting). The resulting contradiction between visual appearance and thematic importance creates a

---

[1] Curt Glaser accepted Wulff's interpretation in 1908 and applied it to Oriental art: "Die Raumdarstellung in der japanischen Malerei." *Monatshefte für Kunstwiss.* vol. 1 (1908), pp. 402ff. Later he rejected much of it in his *Die Kunst Ostasiens* (Leipzig: Insel, 1920). Erwin Panofsky criticized Wulff in "Die Perspektive als symbolische Form," *Vorträge d. Bibl. Warburg,* 1924/25, p. 310.

tension that begins to be utilized artistically during the Renaissance, for example, in Raphael's *Fire in the Borgo*, where the dominant figure, the miracle-working Pope Leo, appears in the center of the picture but tiny and at a large distance. The paradox is most deliberately exploited in the Mannerist style of a Tintoretto or Bruegel. The principal theme is often all but removed from sight.

In our own century, artists became free to abandon the continuous depth scale of traditional painting. The simplest example of this innovation is the photomontage, which juxtaposes fragments of totally different spatial systems. The sizes of various pictorial objects can no longer be compared within the represented space. A large human figure clipped from one photograph and a small tree clipped from another are not relatable except in the pictorial space of the composition, which must remain unified in order to be readable. Similarly, a painter like Chagall combines scenes of different size scale without any pretense of a continuous natural space. The perceptual and artistic effect of this new freedom deserves systematic investigation.

## *What Makes Shapes Diverge*

As long as the symbolic hierarchy of largeness and smallness is obtained without violating the rules of Renaissance perspective, it creates no problem for the kind of interpretation I am trying to discredit here. When the conflict does exist, however, it is psychologically inappropriate to ask: Why did the artist deviate from the realistic projection of physical space? Realistic styles of art require justification as much as nonrealistic ones; they are fairly rare and late and have no priority. The question to be asked is: For what visual purpose did the artist present his subject in this particular manner? This brings me to the second and perhaps more interesting aspect of "inverted perspective," namely, the representation of geometrically shaped solids in a manner contradictory to optical projection and the rules of central perspective.

Wulff refers to linear perspective only in an extensive footnote. He mentions as a specific example the Justinian mosaic of San Vitale in Ravenna, in which the ceiling beams above the heads of the emperor and the archbishop converge toward the observer. Here again he contends that in the pertinent art styles, the ceilings, table tops, stools, beds, and steps are mistakenly rendered the way the most significant person in the picture would see them. Other authors have made misleading references to the perspective treatment of buildings and other geometric shapes in

Japanese paintings. The contention that rectangular surfaces are often rendered as diverging toward the back derives from a well-known optical illusion: edges drawn as parallels in isometric perspective appear to diverge toward distance. If one measures Japanese examples, one finds that, on the whole, the edges are strictly parallel, with occasional deviations either way, as will happen when parallels are drawn by the judgment of the eye rather than with mechanical aids (Figure 23). One might surmise that Western viewers, accustomed to strong depth effects in pictures, see more depth in these scenes than Japanese do, and therefore perceive divergence where Easterners probably intend and see parallels.

Returning to our base of departure, the two-dimensional pictorial surface, we note as a fundamental condition that no more than one opaque thing can ever be visible at any one place on the surface. Now, when physical space is projected upon a surface, locations in the projective plane correspond inevitably to more than one object or portion of object. Foreground hides background, frontal plane hides backplane. Furthermore, when one faces a cube head on, only its frontal face will be seen (Figure 24a). In a photograph, such an object will look like an upright square, not like a cube, because the sidefaces converge behind the front. Central perspective, which has adopted convergence from optical

*Figure 23.*

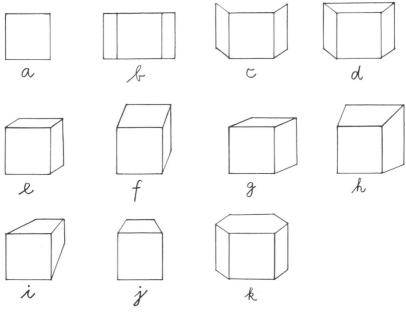

Figure 24.

projection, has little trouble as long as hollow spaces are represented. For example, when one looks into an interior, one sees the room depicted as a truncated pyramid (Figure 25). The floor, the bottom, and the three sidefaces, although distorted, are sufficiently visible. The back wall is seen head on, and the other four surfaces, which extend in depth, are conveniently opened toward the observer.

Seen from the outside, however, the cube looks three-dimensional only when it is shown obliquely and thereby reveals some of its sidefaces (Figure 24i). But this solution should not be acceptable to those who advocate optical projections. If the frontal face remains frontal and un-distorted, the cube cannot be shown obliquely at the same time. Figure 24i is a compromise, recommended by the rules of central perspective, but in violation of optical projection. Moreover, the sidefaces are badly shortened and distorted by perspective convergence. If they are to be displayed clearly, the procedure is unsatisfactory. This is the sort of prob-lem all draftsmen have to struggle with whenever they attempt to depict the third spatial dimension by means of the second.

The quest for a good solution does not start from optical projection, but from the surface of the drawing board. In children's drawings and at

*Figure 25.* (after Dieric Bouts).

and at other early stages of art, a cube is represented by a square (Figure 24a). The square is the appropriate two-dimensional equivalent of the cube, but it does not reveal the difference between a square and a cube and offers no information on the sidefaces. To remedy this limitation, e.g., in drawings of houses, children at a somewhat advanced stage of development add two lateral sidefaces (Figure 24b). This in turn becomes inadequate when the draftsman wishes to show the different spatial orientation of front and sides. He obtains what he wants by slanting the sidefaces upward (Figure 24c); and finally, the solid is completed by a top (Figure 24d).[2]

It will be seen that when this representation of cubic shape is correctly explained as the solution to a problem arising on the pictorial surface, it becomes a perfectly logical and valid equivalent of the three-dimensional object on the two-dimensional surface. Looked at inappropriately as an optical projection, however, it presents the opposite of the truth—"inverted perspective." Perhaps by now it is evident that this label is misleading. Nothing has been inverted. The solution of Figure 24d is arrived at before anybody ever conceives of convergent pictorial projections.[3]

Figure 24d employs parallel edges and is, in this sense, a variation of isometric perspective. Compared with the orthodox version of that principle (Figure 24e), it has for certain purposes a distinct advantage. Orthodox isometric perspective can show the object only from the side, and therefore it cannot display the left and right sidefaces at the same time. It sacrifices the completeness and symmetry of the solid. The wish to combine frontality with a display of the sides favors the use of divergent, symmetrically attached sidefaces. For this reason, examples of this device can be found in a variety of different cultures, where it is discovered and developed from the perceptual requirements of the pictorial medium. Its visual virtues can also be observed in architecture. Bay windows with slanted sidefaces, for example, display the three-dimensionality of the protrusion to the eye.

The diverging top surface has the additional advantage of offering a more generous base to objects resting upon it. The converging edges of central perspective cut visually into the Christ child in Figure 26b, whereas in Figure 26a it is comfortably embraced by the diverging borders of the cubic crib. In the larger context of the painting from which the example is taken (Figure 27), the divergent top of the crib gives access

---

[2] Observe here that the sidefaces in Figure 24b and 24c are not "folded over" or "bent down," as we are still told in explanations of children's art and other early stages of pictorial representation. This misinterpretation is based on the axiom of realism. The sidefaces of the cube were never in the position prescribed by optical projection. Hence, there is nothing to bend.

[3] Derivation from the properties of the drawing surface also explains why isometric as well as central perspective tolerates the undeformed frontal square in cubes shown obliquely (Figure 24e, 24i). The square is what remains of the original conception, from which the sidefaces deviate at a later stage of development. Perspective, far from being simply obedient to projection, limits deformation to the minimum required for the depth effect. Therefore the projectively monstrous cube looks unobjectionable. See Arnheim (2, p. 267).

also to the figures of Mary and Joseph and receives them in partial enclosure. Convergent perspective would produce the opposite effect.

Granted these desirable properties, the top surface of the divergent cube (Figure 24d) has the disadvantage of being an asymmetrical trapezium. I am convinced that the hexahedrons and octahedrons frequently found in art styles that use forms of early space representation (Figure 24k) are popular because they add more complete symmetry to divergent perspective; sometimes they may even have to be interpreted as representations of cubes. Similarly, polyhedral buildings such as baptistries and certain product containers profit from the same visual advantage. In the last analysis, of course, divergent sidefaces can be related to roundness, which in columns, towers, and spheres displays the three-dimensionality of solids so convincingly.

Isometric perspective, as I mentioned earlier, cannot represent an object frontally. This creates a problem when the symmetry of head-on presentation is essential to conveying solemn repose. If the steps of the throne on which the Madonna or other exalted figure sits in state are shown isometrically, they create discord with the symmetry of the rest. This is acceptable as long as the enthroned figure takes part in the lateral action, as, for example, in the *Adoration of the Magi* at Santa Maria Maggiore in Rome (Figure 28), but it would disturb the overall symmetry of an altar painting such as Giotto's *Madonna Enthroned* in the Uffizi. Undoubtedly it is for this reason that Giotto represents the step with divergent sidefaces (Figure 29).

*Figure 26.*

One more predicament that can be remedied by divergent perspective should be mentioned here. Whenever it is desirable to show the top and side of a cubic solid rather extensively, the orthodox isometric procedure hampers a successful presentation because an enlargement of the topface narrows the sideface and vice versa (Figure 24f, 24g). If both surfaces are given their due simultaneously, the result is divergent perspective (Figure 24h). The altar on which Abel and King Melchizedek are making their

*Figure 27.* Spanish School, *Nativity, Ayala Altarpiece.* 1396.
Art Institute of Chicago.

offerings in the lunette mosaic at San Vitale is a good example (Figure 30). The divergent edges enable the artist to show the sacrificial objects on the altar without raising the sideface from the ground at an unduly steep angle.

It is worth citing the interpretation of this mosaic by the art historian Decio Gioseffi, who in obedience to the axiom of naive realism asserts that there can be no other perspective but that of optical projection, and

*Figure 28.*

*Figure 29.* (after Giotto).

that the examples of "inverted" perspective are nothing but the in-between spaces that come about when two systems of central perspective are used next to each other: "When in one and the same painting two or more centers of vision are introduced, there exists between two adjacent centers a zone of reconciliation (*una zona di raccordo*): all objects that happen to be located in that sector should grow rather than taper with

*Figure 30.*

increasing distance" (6). He contends that if the whole scene of the Ravenna mosaic were constructed with one common vanishing point, the altar would hide parts of the two figures and this would also create too much depth. Therefore, each figure is given its own perspectively convergent "niche," which makes the altar, between them, divergent. The interpretation is puzzling because the drawing Gioseffi uses to illustrate his theory (Figure 31) deviates from the original in at least two crucial aspects: it depicts the altar as symmetrical, with both sidefaces showing, and it gives the right sideface as converging, whereas in fact it diverges in the original. The drawing also omits the buildings, which in no way conform to central perspective. Abel's hut on the left is in frontal position, and the king's palace on the right diverges like the altar. The example shows to what lengths the vision of even a trained observer can be misled by the axiom of realism.

## Some Modern Examples

During the centuries following the introduction of central perspective into the pictorial practice of the West, the rules were not applied literally. Artists modified them to suit their own visual judgment, but these deviations did not conspicuously violate the underlying principle; they rather supported it, by helping the geometrical construction look more convincing. Only in our own time have the arts returned to the freedom of spatial representation they enjoyed outside the dominion of Renaissance perspective. The unorthodox handling of perspective, however, cannot be dismissed as arbitrary neglect. In artists like Picasso, it can be shown to serve essential pictorial effects.

*Figure 31. (after Gioseffi).*

In some instances, as in the historical examples discussed earlier, the inversion of perspective is used mainly to display relevant aspects of three-dimensional objects in the picture plane. Picasso paints a birdcage and playing cards on a table (Figure 32). The cards, being flat objects, are rendered without distortion as the tabletop is made to run parallel to the picture plane, like the chessboard of the medieval nobleman. The birdcage poses more complex spatial problems. The painter wishes to show the captive birds pushing their heads, wings, and tails through the wire screens of the cage on all sides. Convergent perspective would hide the side views; divergence provides the beholder with a dramatic spectacle.

Picasso's *Three Musicians* (Figure 33) brings to mind what was observed in the Spanish altarpiece (Figure 27). In the divergence of its sides and top, the table offers an ample expanse, an area of tranquillity, on which various objects are readily displayed. It also opens out toward the musicians, with whom it forms a visual unity. In addition, the convergence of the tabletop toward the front serves a compositional function. It produces a wedge or arrow shape, somewhat like the hood of an automobile, pointing at the viewer. The viewer is approached aggressively.

*Figure 32.* (after Picasso).

Historically, this indicates a fundamental change in the relation between the picture and its beholder. To be sure, advancing elements have
never been absent from painting, but when one looks back at examples
like Bouts's *Last Supper* (Figure 25), one realizes that the dominant direction of central perspective is one leading the viewer into pictorial

*Figure 33.* (after Picasso).

space toward the apex of the visual pyramid, the vanishing point. In the Bouts painting, the beams of the ceiling, the mosaic pattern of the floor, and the shape of the table receive the viewer with open arms, as it were, and draw him into their embrace. This visual invasion of the picture space makes the encounter with the forward-directed figure of Christ and the fireplace backing him all the more powerful.

The reversal of the dominant direction observed in the Picasso examples is related to a more general trend in the art of our century, which has reduced or even eliminated the hollow space behind the window of the frame. It frequently builds the composition as a central mass protruding from a plane base that lies parallel to the surface of the canvas. This tendency is evident in many cubist paintings and, more recently, for example, in Vasarely.

When Picasso depicts the opening of a fireplace (Figure 34), he uses a carefree variety of traditional convergence, which is passively receptive

*Figure 34.* (after Picasso).

and has feminine connotations. As a visual counterpoint, the mantle narrows toward the viewer and thereby reverses the pictorial vector. Van Gogh also was consciously aware of such motion effects. Meyer Schapiro quotes him as saying about one of his drawings: "The lines of the roofs and gutters shoot away in the distance like arrows from a bow; they are drawn without hesitation" (16). On the contrary, in Van Gogh's late landscape *Crows in the Wheatfield*, the three roads are, according to Schapiro, presented in inverted perspective: "The perspective network of the open field, which he had painted many times before, is now inverted; the lines, like rushing streams, converge towards the foreground from the horizon, as if space had suddenly lost its focus and all things turned aggressively upon the beholder."

## To Distinguish from Relativism

I have tried to show that the formula of central perspective, which was worked out only once in the entire history of art,[4] is but one method among several to render the experience of three-dimensional depth on a flat surface. Looked at from outside the Renaissance tradition, it is neither better nor worse than the others. It remains for me to make sure that this demonstration of mine is not misunderstood to coincide with the relativistic contention that the choice of methods of representation is due entirely to the accidents of tradition. In the most extreme version of the relativistic approach, pictorial representation is said to have nothing intrinsically in common with the subjects it represents and therefore to rely on nothing better than an arbitrary agreement of the parties concerned (7, p. 15). This trivially shocking challenge to beliefs taken as givens by the rest of the population is the direct opposite of what I meant to demonstrate.

Central perspective resembles optical projection more closely than other methods of depth representation, but it cannot be said to offer the closest equivalent, in the two-dimensional medium, of the way space is experienced in the visual environment. On the contrary, it involves more severe distortions of shape and size, as they are commonly perceived, than any other procedure. It is for this reason that it developed so rarely and so late. Very special cultural conditions must override the constraints it imposes on the painter's natural perception of space. Once the technique has been mastered by realistic painting or photography, observers can be induced, sometimes not without initial trouble, to treat its products as duplicates of the world at large.

Other, more common procedures of representing objects in space, which developed independently all over the world and throughout history and are spontaneously used and understood, differ radically from

---

[4] When isometric perspective is applied to symmetrical and frontal architecture, it looks at first glance like central perspective. Isometric perspective prevails in Pompeian wall painting, on which White (18) bases his claim that central perspective was practiced in antiquity. Beyen (3), White's source, shares this claim, but emphasizes more explicitly how rare, partial, and inexact are the examples of perspective convergence. Besides, Beyen presents his examples in drawings, not photographs of the paintings. In his Figure 23, convergent lines are shown in the diagram where in his own drawing of the painting the vanishing lines in front diverge from those in back. Lehmann (10, p. 149) acknowledges that no example of consistent application is known, but prefers to interpret the inconsistencies of Pompeian perspective as stylistically deliberate variations of spatial representation.

optical projection. What I have tried to show by the example of "inverted perspective" is that these procedures derive no less lawfully than central perspective from the conditions of human perception and the two-dimensional medium. Similar demonstrations can be given for other features of nonrealistic representation and for other media, such as sculpture (2, p. 208). So although we must realize that our continued commitment to a particular tradition of realistic picture-making has induced us to misinterpret other ways of portraying space, we are not left with the nihilistic conclusion that nothing but subjective preference ties representation to its models in nature. On the contrary, we have shown that the observation of nature is only one of the universal determinants that control representations of space and account for their variety.

## References

1. Arnheim, Rudolf. "Perceptual Abstraction and Art." In *Toward a Psychology of Art*. Berkeley and Los Angeles: University of California Press, 1966.
2. ———. *Art and Visual Perception*. New version. Berkeley and Los Angeles: University of California Press, 1974.
3. Beyen, Hendrick Gerard. *Die pompejanische Wanddekoration vom zweiten bis zum vierten Stil*. The Hague: Nijhoff, 1938.
4. Coomaraswamy, Ananda K. *Selected Papers: Traditional Art and Symbolism*. Princeton, N.J.: Princeton University Press, 1977.
5. Doehlemann, K. "Zur Frage der sogenannten umgekehrten Perspektive." *Repert. f. Kunstwiss.* vol. 33 (1910), pp. 85ff.
6. Gioseffi, Decio. *Perspectiva Artificialis*. Trieste: Università degli Studi, 1957, no. 7.
7. Goodman, Nelson. *The Language of Art*. Indianapolis: Bobbs-Merrill, 1968.
8. Katz, David. *War Greco astigmatisch?* Leipzig: Veit, 1914.
9. Laporte, Paul M. "Cubism and Science." *Journal of Aesthetics and Art Criticism*, vol. 7, no. 3 (March 1949), pp. 243–56.
10. Lehmann, Phyllis Williams. *Roman Wall Paintings from Boscoreale in the Metropolitan Museum of Art*. Cambridge, Mass.: Archaeological Institute of America, 1953.
11. Lipps, Theodor. *Grundlegung der Aesthetik*. Hamburg and Leipzig: Voss, 1903.
12. Nordau, Max. *Entartung*. Berlin: Duncker, 1893. Eng.: *Degeneration*. New York: Appleton, 1895.
13. Oster, Gerald. "Phosphenes." *Scientific American*, vol. 222 (Feb. 1970), pp. 83–87.
14. Pascal, Blaise. *Pensées*. Montreal: Variétés, 1944.
15. Riegl, Alois. *Historische Grammatik der bildenden Künste*. Graz-Cologne: Böhlau, 1966.
16. Schapiro, Meyer. "On a Painting of Van Gogh." In *Modern Art—19th and 20th Centuries*. New York: Braziller, 1978.

17. Trevor-Roper, Patrick. *The World Through Blunted Sight*. London: Thames & Hudson, 1970.
18. White, John. *The Birth and Rebirth of Pictorial Space*. London: Faber, 1957.
19. Worringer, Wilhelm. *Abstraktion und Einfühlung*. Munich: Piper, 1911. Eng.: *Abstraction and Empathy*. New York: International Universities Press, 1953.
20. Wulff, Oskar. "Die umgekehrte Perspektive und die Niedersicht." *Kunstwissensch. Beiträge August Schmarsow gewidmet*. Leipzig: 1907.

# BRUNELLESCHI'S PEEPSHOW

WE HAVE been taught that it was Filippo Brunelleschi who first demonstrated the principles of central perspective, and that he did so by means of two paintings. From him Leone Battista Alberti is supposed to have learned the geometrical procedure that he codified in the first book of his *Treatise on Painting*. According to John White, the importance of the two panels on which Brunelleschi portrayed the Piazza del Duomo and the Piazza della Signoria in Florence "can hardly be overestimated" (10, p. 113). He asserts that through these two pictures, rather than by the publication of a treatise, the mathematically based perspective system was heralded during the early years of the fifteenth century. White echoes a conviction prevailing in the professional literature today. But how compelling is the evidence on which these assertions are based?

If someone had found the geometrical principles of central perspective and "chose to publicize his new discovery" (White) by painting pictures, what kind of subject would he be likely to select? First of all, he would want his subject to contain a set of clearly relatable parallel lines or walls, belonging to more than one architectural unit, in order to show their convergence toward a vanishing point. To keep his demonstration simple, he would probably limit himself to one set of parallels, that is, to one-point perspective. For the same reason he would prefer to use as his parallels a set of orthogonals, for which the vanishing point would lie in the viewer's line of sight. The walls of a street vista or the nave of a church would serve this purpose well. A typical example of such a didac-

First published in *Zeitschrift für Kunstgeschichte*, vol. 41 (1978).

tic demonstration is the woodcut of a living room in Viator's *De artifi-ciali perspectiva* (Figure 35).

Instead, for the paintings about which we are informed in the biography attributed to Antonio Manetti, Brunelleschi chose two subjects that meet those conditions quite poorly. A glance at the plan given by

*Figure 35.* Jean Pèlerin Viator, *De artificiali perspectiva.* 1505.

Sgrilli (Figure 36) shows that the view from inside the door of the Florence cathedral does indeed offer sections of two orthogonal street fronts; however, although White sets the visual angle of the picture at a generous 90°, these sections are limited to a narrow range of about 10–15° of that angle and are located at such great distance from each other that they would not show the convergence effect convincingly even if they had the picture space to themselves. But any such effort is defeated by the large mass of the Baptistery (Figure 37), which holds the center of the scene. This octagonal body is hardly suited to illustrate central perspective. The frontal wall, being parallel to the picture plane, is entirely exempt from perspective. Each of the two visible sidefaces can be made to converge, but both are foreshortened to a narrow projective angle and if drawn in perspective would require a two-point perspective, with vanishing points lying outside the limits of the picture.

Such an octagon, however, would be a logical choice for a painter who, using traditional means, wanted to demonstrate his ability to represent architectural space convincingly. Octagonal or hexagonal shapes are used by preference to represent three-dimensionality, e.g., in the Gothic building of Duccio's *Christ's Temptation on the Temple*, for the well in Van Eyck's *Adoration of the Lamb*, in Persian miniatures, and in many instances of the misnamed inverted perspective (see preceding essay). Such structures can be convincingly depicted in the pictorial tradition by means of mere isometric perspective or simple convergence. They

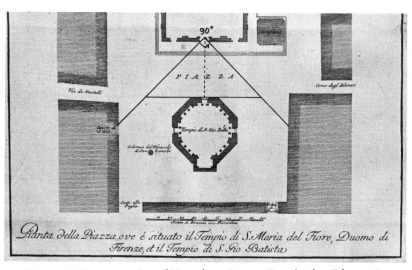

*Figure 36.* Reconstruction of View from Duomo Portal (after Edgerton).

show depth and volume well, without any necessary use of central perspective.

An even less plausible choice for the demonstration of central perspective is Brunelleschi's second subject, a diagonal view of the Palazzo della Signoria. Here no two architectural units run parallel (cf. White's plan, 10, p. 118); and, like the view of the Piazza del Duomo, this one fails to offer the kind of open stage on which convergence toward a vanishing point could be demonstrated. Instead, this sight, too, is monopolized by a powerful central mass, the Palazzo della Signoria, seen

*Figure 37.* Baptistery of San Giovanni, Florence (D. Anderson photo).

obliquely as a strongly receding wedge shape. Here again the painter used the kind of view that would have been selected traditionally to obtain a compelling depth effect without the benefit of central perspective. Panofsky, referring in another context to the practice of placing the architectural elements of a picture at an oblique angle, called it "an archaic audacity." He comments further: "It was an attempt to take space by storm, and frequent though it had been in fourteenth and fifteenth century art, it became correspondingly rare, both in Italy and in the Northern countries, when the representation of space had come to be based on a comprehensive and consistent principle" (6, p. 421). White takes note of these archaic features, but suggests that "in the very compositions with which Brunelleschi chose to demonstrate the new invention, he is careful to respect as far as possible the particular, simple, visual truths which underlie the achievement of Giottesque art" (10, p. 120). Would it not be more economical to assume that, as a painter, the architect Brunelleschi had not gone beyond the preperspective tradition?

Manetti claims for Brunelleschi that he "put forward and into practice (*misse innanzi ed in atto*) what painters today call perspective" (5, p. 9). The term *perspective*, of course, was neither coined for, nor limited to, the geometrical procedure here under discussion. Brunelleschi's accomplishment consisted in his putting down "well and with reason the diminutions and enlargements that appear to the eyes of men from things far away or close at hand." He showed buildings, plains and mountains, figures, etc., in the size appropriate to their distance (*di quella misura che s'appartiene a quella distanza*). It is true, Manetti also insisted that perspective was part of a science, and that from Brunelleschi "is born the rule which is the gist (*importanza*) of all that has been done of that kind from that time on"; but we should bear in mind that Manetti's biography was written after Brunelleschi's death, and this means after the publication of Alberti's treatise.

Let us now look, once again, at Manetti's description of what Brunelleschi did when he painted the picture of the Baptistery: "It seems that in order to portray it he was inside the middle door of Santa Maria del Fiore." From that vantage point he portrayed with the care and delicacy of a miniaturist as much as can be seen at a glance from outside that temple. For the sky he used burnished silver, "so that the air and the natural skies might be mirrored in it; and thus also the clouds, which are seen in that silver, are driven by the wind, when it blows" (5, pp. 10, 11). Since a picture can be seen correctly only from one point of sight if errors in the "apparitions of the eye" are to be avoided, Brunelleschi drilled a hole into his panel, at a point directly opposite the point of sight of a spectator looking at the scene from the church door. In order to view the painting, the beholder was to look through this hole from the back of the panel while holding in his other hand a mirror, in which he saw the image reflected. Viewed that way, the picture looked like "the real thing."

What was the purpose and effect of this tricky procedure? It served, first of all, to make the viewer see the projection at the angle at which it had been traced and thereby to avoid distortions. Although the hole in the picture must have been at the point where the vanishing point would lie for the orthogonal parallels and could be seen at that point in the reflection, there is, as Krautheimer points out, no compelling reason to assume that Brunelleschi was aware of this coincidence of the two points (4, p. 239). To him, the hole in the panel, in addition to preventing optical distortions, served greatly to enhance the picture's depth effect. When a painting is viewed directly, the surface texture of the pigment tends to be visible and to reveal the picture's physical character as a flat plane. Stereoscopic vision, too, brought about by binocular inspection, helps reveal the flatness of the picture. The peephole makes vision monocular and thereby increases perceptual depth. The mirror image diminishes the surface texture of objects reflected in it and thus counteracts flatness, especially when the contours of the mirror are hidden by the peephole.

Krautheimer refers in this connection to the opposite phenomenon, namely, a mirror's ability to reduce perspective convergence to a compelling two-dimensional projection. "The use of the mirror in verifying the phenomenon of linear perspective," writes Krautheimer, "was common Quattrocento practice. Indeed, three-dimensional relationships in a mirror are automatically transferred onto a two-dimensional surface as they would be in a drawing by means of a perspective construction. Filarete probably codified an old tradition when stating that the mirror revealed perspective elements which could not be seen with the naked eye" (4, p. 236). Filarete adds that in his opinion Brunelleschi found his procedure for achieving perspective through the use of the mirror (2, pp. 607, 618). Now a mirror will indeed make projective deformations somewhat more evident if the mirror is relatively small and clearly framed. To the extent the spatial image is visually reduced toward the flatness of the mirror plane, the depth of the mirrored space will look reduced toward a flat projection. A mirror will also permit a painter to trace the outlines of the projected shapes on the reflecting surface. But for Brunelleschi's viewer this condition was explicitly avoided through the peephole setup, which was designed to obtain the contrary, namely to increase the depth effect.

The peephole was not intended to help painters draw foreshortenings correctly.

It has been surmised, however, that in addition to having his picture reflected in a mirror, Brunelleschi painted the picture itself on a mirror surface (3, p. 77). This in fact must have been almost unavoidable because unless the picture was a mirror image of the real scene, the viewer, peering through the hole, would have seen the reflection of the scene laterally inverted. Left and right of the Piazza del Duomo would have been interchanged. A second mirror used as the picture surface would have compensated for this disturbing inversion in the viewing mirror. It also would have allowed the artist to simply trace the outlines of his scene on the reflecting surface. This procedure would indeed go a long way in letting him obtain a projectively correct drawing. But it would have nothing whatever to do with the geometrical construction of central perspective.

Nothing in Manetti's description of Brunelleschi's procedure suggests that it involved any geometrical construction or indeed required it. The attribution of the diagrams worked out by Panofsky or Krautheimer is, of course, conjectural. Vasari, writing around 1550, does assert that Brunelleschi found on his own a way of rendering perspective correctly, establishing it by "plan and profile" and by means of intersection. Strictly speaking even Vasari, whose testimony is often cited, does not say that Brunelleschi applied this procedure to the two panels. He says of the discovery that it was "cosa veramente ingegnosissima ed utile all'arte del disegno. Di questa prese tanta vaghezza, che di sua mano ritrasse la piazza di San Giovanni" (9, p. 142). It was his fondness for drawing, says the text, that made him portray those architectural vistas.

According to Prager and Scaglia, it does not appear "that Filippo himself ever undertook a mathematical or analytic investigation" (8). The theory accepted in the literature, however, has it that Brunelleschi produced his two pictures by using the geometrical constructions known to us from Alberti's treatise. According to Panofsky, he began with two preparatory drawings, the ground plan and an elevation; that is, he surveyed the Piazza del Duomo to obtain the basic objective measurements of the buildings, in both the horizontal and the vertical dimensions. Then, after adding to his drawings the point corresponding to the location of a viewer in the door of the Cathedral, he worked out the geometrical projection following the procedure known as the *costruzione legittima* (7, p. 123). This work would have had to be done on a drafting table. What then was Brunelleschi doing in the doorway of Santa Maria del Fiore, where, according to Manetti, he was when he portrayed the scene? All he needed for the geometrical construction was the location of the point of sight on his ground plan and elevation. Instead, he obviously drew or traced the sight on his panel. If, in addition, he constructed the sight by geometrical projection, he must have done so separately, in order to check on the perspective in his tracing or freehand drawing; unless, conversely, he made the drawing from the real scene to help him flesh out his homemade construction.

In either case it is difficult to be persuaded that the panels could have provided an impressive demonstration of the virtues of the *costruzione legittima*. Regardless of whether or not Brunelleschi knew the geometrical rules of perspective, their value could hardly be illustrated by pictures that did not require them and probably were done without them. He is more likely to have roused the admiration of his fellow citizens by producing unprecedentedly faithful likenesses. This he probably did by tracing his subject on a mirror, and he thereby implicitly anticipated the principle of the intersected pyramid of sight, formulated by Alberti and recommended for practical application by Albrecht Dürer's well-known contraptions. After all, there was no need for geometric construction as long as the painter could look at his subject through a transparent surface or in a mirror. What made central perspective an awe-inspiring miracle was rather that a few geometrical tricks let a draftsman invent and reliably depict lifelike vistas on a flat surface.

## References

1. Edgerton, Samuel Y. *The Renaissance Rediscovery of Linear Perspective*. New York: Harper & Row, 1975.
2. *Antonio Averlino Filaretes Tractat über die Baukunst. . . .* Vienna, 1890.
3. Gioseffi, Decio. *Perspectiva artificialis*. Trieste: Università degli Studi, 1957.
4. Krautheimer, Richard. *Lorenzo Ghiberti*. Princeton, N.J.: Princeton University Press, 1970.
5. Manetti, Antonio. *Vita di Filippo di Ser Brunellesco*. Florence: Rinascimento del Libro, 1927.
6. Panofsky, Erwin. "Once more 'The Friedsam Annunciation and the Problem of the Ghent Altarpiece.'" *Art Bulletin*, vol. 20 (March 1938), pp. 418–42.
7. ———. *Renaissance and Renascences in Western Art*. New York: Harper & Row, 1969.
8. Prager, Frank D., and Gustina Scaglia. *Brunelleschi, His Technologies and Inventions*. Cambridge, Mass.: MIT Press, 1970.
9. Vasari, Giorgio. *Le vite de' più eccellenti pittori, scultori e architettori*. Florence, 1971.
10. White, John. *The Birth and Rebirth of Pictorial Space*. London: Faber, 1957.

# THE PERCEPTION OF MAPS

A MAP is a visual instrument. It transmits information through the eyes, not by sound, smell, or touch. This is obvious enough. What is less obvious is that practically all the knowledge human beings gather from maps has a strong visual component. The same might not be true if a computer were using a map, for example, to read off the distance from Boston to Washington and calculate the price of an airplane ticket on that basis. No spatial image of the relation between the two cities would take form in the machine's brain. But if a human being looks up the location of Washington, he can hardly help noticing that the city perches somewhere near the top of triangular Virginia and pokes into neighboring Maryland. And perusing the map more broadly, our human being will notice that Washington is not placed in the center of our country, as a simple visual logic would demand of a capital, but is shoved prejudicially toward the East Coast.

This sort of enrichment of even a simple piece of geographical information is due to the fact that a map is an iconic image, an analogue, which portrays certain visual features of the objects it represents. Only a subordinate function is given to noniconic, purely conventional signs, such as letters and digits. These, too, can arouse visual images in the mind, but rather than supply the imagery through the picture on paper, they conjure it up from the reservoirs of the viewer's memory. It takes imagination, fed by experience, to generate visual imagery from the reading of the name San Gimignano or from the information that Mt. Rainier is 14,000 feet high.

First published in *American Cartographer*, vol. 3, no. 1 (1976).

Perceptually, map reading can be said to involve three kinds of iconic information. First is the mere "looking up"—the closest to what takes place when somebody consults a dictionary or directory. I may want to know where the Fiji Islands are located in relation to Australia. Here attention is narrowly focused on a specific fact. It is like trying to find a small rabbit in a large painting by Bruegel. But even in such cases the image received by the viewer is never as rigorously restricted as it can be when he looks up a telephone number or the spelling of a word. In an iconic image, such as a map, no detail is ever hermetically closed off from its context. Maps discourage the isolation of single items. They preserve the continuity of the real world. They show things in their surroundings and therefore call for more active discernment on the part of the user, who is offered more than he came for; but the user is also invited to look at things intelligently. One aspect of looking at things intelligently is to look at them in context.

Since mere "looking up" is against the nature of map reading, it blends with a second kind of iconic information, which is the "looking at" things. I may want to look at the Mediterranean: Where is it? What is its size and shape? What countries border on it and in what sequence? I approach the map with an unfocused expectation, the way I approach a painting: "Tell me who you are and what you are like!" This is the attitude teachers of geography and history try to create in their students, and they need much help from maps if they are to be successful. To meet this request, the colors and shapes of maps must spontaneously offer the perceptual qualities that carry the visual answers to the user's explicit and implicit questions. This will be accomplished only if the mapmaker possesses some of the abilities of an artist.

Even more clearly in the realm of the artist is a third kind of iconic information, namely the dynamic expression of colors and shapes. Dynamic expression is not a separate category of inputs, but a property of any percept. Actually it is the most important and primary property of percepts. What meets the eyes first and foremost when one looks at a visual object, such as a map, are not the measurable phenomena corresponding to wavelengths, dimensions, distances, and the geometry of shapes, but the expressive qualities borne by the stimulus data. The smallness of Denmark in comparison to the size of Norway and Sweden, which engulf and protect their smaller partner but are tied by it to the European continent, is not simply quantitative information. The relation between smallness and bigness has a dramatic, animating quality, deriving from the dynamics of the perceived shapes. One sees an interaction of visual forces, which endow the shapes with an immediate liveliness. This direct, primary appeal is the key to any sensory communication, the indispensable opening to the game of learning.

Compare the contours of the United States with those of the British Isles. Ours make for a complacently voluminous, compact shape, like a matronly kettle; theirs are gaunt, nervously tattered by inroads and segmentations. Or look at the peninsulas of Italy and Greece bending almost frantically eastward, especially when seen in comparison with the stern plumbline of Corsica, Sardinia, and Tunisia. Sensitivity to these dynamic qualities is not an idle playing with geographic imagery, a distraction from serious learning. On the contrary, these qualities are the very vehicle of learning, and they provide visual roots for knowledge. Once the student sees the map not as an assembly of shapes but as a configuration of visual forces, the knowledge to be derived is appropriately transformed into a play of corresponding forces in other fields—physical, biological, economical, and political. For example, the contact with the surrounding oceans is felt to be much less immediate for the interior of our own American landmass than it is for Britain, where by comparison you are never truly away from the sea. Similarly, it is essential for an understanding of Italy that its upper provinces are not only more northern but also more western than those of the Mezzogiorno. One can assimilate these facts as static data; but it is difficult to make them come alive unless the student has felt the underlying spatial characteristics as pushes and pulls in his own nervous system.

Whether or not these animating experiences take place depends to a considerable extent on the colors and shapes of the maps. To be sure, the mapmaker is essentially a faithful recorder of given facts. The contours and sizes and directions of lands and oceans cannot be tampered with. And yet, just as in realistic painting, which is constrained by the way human beings or trees look in nature, the range of formative shaping available to a good mapmaker is much greater than might appear possible at first approach. Just as some realistically painted cows are full of life while others are deadly mechanical records, so some faithful maps are alive while others leave us untouched.

The aesthetic or artistic qualities of maps are sometimes thought to be simply matters of so-called good taste, of harmonious color schemes and sensory appeal. In my opinion, those are secondary concerns. The principal task of the artist, be he a painter or a map designer, consists in translating the relevant aspects of the message into the expressive qualities of the medium, in such a way that the information comes across as a direct impact of perceptual forces. This distinguishes the mere transmission of facts from the arousal of meaningful experience. How is such a feat accomplished? In what follows I will discuss a few perceptual phenomena in more concrete detail.

For any map a particular orientation has to be chosen. Although customarily maps are laid out along the cardinal directions of the compass rose, with north on top and south at the bottom, I take it to be the opinion of some cartographers that this convention is of little didactic value. I cannot agree with this view. First of all, visual shapes are sensitive to orientation. Experiments have shown that shapes turned 90° or 180° do not remain the same. They change in character and may not be easily recognized. A square turned 45° becomes a diamond, which is a distinctly different figure; not to mention what happens when one tries to read writing sideways or upside down. There might be occasions at which it is useful to turn the map of Australia upside down in order to make evident to us northerners that Australians receive cold from the south and heat from the north; but one should keep in mind that all shapes and spatial relations are changed by this turnabout and have to be relearned perceptually. Furthermore, the standard orientation of the map ties the geographic layout to the sun and the winds, the prevailing weather, and the difference between morning and evening. Even for most city dwellers, these effects of nature on their living space are vital, and therefore directions are not exchangeable.

The standard orientation of maps is also an effective means of counteracting the isolation that results when parts of a larger whole are shown out of context. If an island or province is presented by itself, but in the same spatial position in which one is accustomed to seeing it when it appears in its broader geographic setting, the correctness of the position helps overcome the disorienting effect of the extirpation.

It is true, of course, in the visual field, as it is projected upon the retinae, the top corresponds to the greatest distance and the median vertical to the direction the viewer faces. Therefore, when a map is oriented the same way, a welcome parallelism is established between what is seen on the map and the actual prospect before the voyager. But this advantage counts only if interest is concentrated narrowly on a particular route; for the parallelism is obtained at a price when the traveler does not happen to move northward. When, for example, a map is intended to show schoolchildren the route traveled by Lewis and Clark, the usual orientation should surely be maintained because the relation to east and west is the essence of the story.

Let me now turn to the representation of the third dimension. The surface of the earth is much more suitably represented by a flat picture than, for example, the human body, whose three-dimensionality shows up very imperfectly, or a building, which requires at least a combination of vertical elevation and horizontal plan. Mountains and valleys are surface features that can be represented tolerably well from a bird's-eye view. When the cartographer creates the impression of spatial relief by the use of highlights and shadows, he follows ancient pictorial techniques and can profit from the traditional tricks of draftsmen and painters. I can confirm here an observation by Arthur H. Robinson, who objects to the use of the spectral sequence of colors for the representation of depth gradients (3). The hues of the spectrum derive, or course, from the different wavelengths of light; but there is no correspondence between this gradual change in the physical medium and the perceptual effect of colors. Perceptually, the scale of hues contains three qualitative turning points in the pure primaries of blue, yellow, and red; and while there are scales of mixtures between each two of these three poles, such as the scale from blue to yellow through the transitional greens, the spectrum as a whole displays no one-dimensional gradient of a single quality that could be made to correspond to the scale leading from depth to height or vice versa. Only a monochromatic brightness scale, for example, the one between black and white, or darkness and light, offers such a gradient. But, of course, values of a brightness scale cannot be as safely distinguished from one another as can a pure blue from a pure red. There seems to be no truly satisfactory solution to the problem.

Cartographers follow in the footsteps of painters when they use line hatchings to make the slope of curvatures explicit at every point of an extended surface that otherwise would be defined only by its outer contour. This graphic technique can be studied in the drawings and woodcuts of an Albrecht Dürer as readily as in the striking illusions obtained by the British painter Bridget Riley (1, p. 161). A special case of the definition of volume by families of lines is the use of isometric contours, known in the arts especially from the grain of wood sculpture. The deformation of a regular pattern of tree rings helps to define the curvatures of the surfaces carved from the wood. When hypsometric lines are used to represent three-dimensional shapes in flat drawings (as by cartographers on their maps), they will serve first of all to provide purely metric information about the slopes of a mountain or valley. In addition, this device can convey the direct perceptual experience of spatial relief, but the effect will come about only where the lines of the drawing create a gradient, for example, when the distances between them increase or decrease gradually.

Maps provide a slightly three-dimensional effect also by figure-and-ground relations and by overlay. Psychologists speak of the figure-ground phenomenon when a shape is perceived as lying in front of its surroundings. On maps the oceans normally appear to recede beneath the land. The land is seen as figure, monopolizing the contour of the coastline, which is seen as belonging to the land, not to the water. This, however, is the case only when the proper perceptual conditions are met. The blue of the water, being a short-wave color, helps make it recede. Texture greatly enhances the substantiality of the land. On sea charts, which give texture to the waters and leave the land empty, the land tends to become ground and to yield the contour of the coastline to the water. When water is surrounded by land rather than surrounding it, it tends to become figure and protrude over the land. This is true for lakes, especially when their shape is convex. The southern half of Lake Michigan lies on the land like a tongue. Conversely, land, too, can profit from convexity. The peninsulas of Florida and Scandinavia are more clearly "figure" than straight coastlines, and Africa dominates the ocean by its bulges to the west and south.

Figure-ground effects can be strongly dynamic. Convexity is experienced as an active invasion of the surrounding space. The continent of Australia pushes northward toward New Guinea, but yields passively to the ocean with its concave southern coast. The interplay of land and water comes alive in these visual attacks and retreats, expressed through the shapes of coastlines.

The third dimension is introduced also by overlay effects. It takes special conditions, however, to make overlays perceivable. Letters seem to lie on a frontal plane as though on a sheet of gelatin, but only if the shapes of the words are sufficiently distinguished from the geographic formations. Names set in straight, horizontal lines create a kind of grid, which detaches itself clearly as foreground from the irregularity of mountains, rivers, and roads, especially when it interrupts them while not being interrupted by anything itself. The more the lettering adapts itself to the orientation and shape of countries, coastlines, rivers, etc., the more it fuses with the landscape and recedes into the background pattern.

The same is true for statelines and roads. When the boundaries of states are geometrically regular, such as those of Kansas, New Mexico, and the Dakotas, they seem to lie on top of the geographic relief, as though the map wanted to denounce the artificiality of modern demarcations, drawn with the ruler rather than acceding to natural landmarks. It is interesting to compare the perceptual effect of such statelines with those indicating landownership on cadastral maps. Since the rectangular grids of the latter are much less reckless in cutting across geometric features, they depict to the eyes a rationalization of the land itself, rather than a network loosely spread over it for political or administrative purposes. Straight highways stick out of the landscape of the map like foreign bodies, whereas country roads following a coast or meandering through valleys like rivers indicate an organic adaptation of human needs to the formation of nature.

One further feature of mapmaking, of interest to the psychology of perception, may be discussed here. It is known to cartographers as the problem of generalization. The term "generalization" is significant because it indicates that an image of reduced size is not obtained simply by leaving out details. Artists as well as cartographers realize that they face the more positive task of creating a new pattern, which serves as an equivalent rather than a mere impoverishment of the natural shape to be represented. Such a newly created pattern is not merely a sandpapered copy of the original. The reduction in size provides the mapmaker with a degree of freedom, which he can use to make his visual images more readable by simplifying them.

A realistic tracing of a fairly complex coastline is, to the eye, an irrational scribble. It can be seen but it cannot be perceived, because perception consists in the grasping of orderly shapes that are found in, and imposed on, the stimulus material. An actual coastline owes its shape to a multitude of physical forces, some of which one can read off the formation of rocks, dunes, and beaches as one drives, say, along the Pacific Ocean. This meaningful interplay of forces vanishes, however, when the coastline is reduced to a contour on paper, and what remains is a disorderly sequence of accidental shapes.

Artists do not make their shapes perceivable simply by smoothing them. They often include a great deal of detail, but a successful draftsman knows how to create hierarchic patterns, that is, how to fit smaller shapes to larger ones in such a way that the whole adds up to a sufficiently simple and orderly configuration. Once shapes can be perceived, they also carry dynamic expression; otherwise they are dead material. Thus the artist, more or less consciously, selects the shapes he wants to convey, be they straight or rounded, flexible or rigid, simple or complex, and to this overall theme he adapts all the rest.

Such generalization occurs spontaneously in all perception. Complex though a map may be, the mind derives from it a simplified pattern. Wanting to understand the spatial relation between Lake Michigan and Lake Superior, one might perceive and learn that the two lakes lie at a right angle to each other, even though there is no strict support for that statement. Simplified images are what is remembered. When one asks students to draw the outlines of the American continent from memory, one typically finds some instances of aligning North America with South America, as though they conformed to a common meridian (2, p. 82). Of course, so radical a simplification is likely to interfere with the usefulness of the information. The cartographer will aim at a suitable compromise between accuracy and the kind of simplification that facilitates perception.

This is particularly crucial in the teaching of geography or history. A map containing a maximum of detail makes it difficult to grasp the essential elements. What are the first things a child should learn about the map of the United States? There is that kettle-shape, surrounded by vast oceans. It is about twice as broad as it is high—a proportion that does not show up very clearly on a large-scale map on which the east and west coasts are squeezed against the margins. Then there are two vertical mountain ranges placed symmetrically on the left and on the right, the Rockies and the Alleghenies (Figure 38). Are they easily discernible on

Figure 38.

the map that hangs in the schoolroom? Another symmetrical feature: the large city of San Francisco lies halfway up on the West Coast, and its counterpart in the east is New York City. Down the middle of the country runs the Mississippi River, terminating in the port city of New Orleans. On the belt line between San Francisco and New York lies Chicago, bordering on a group of lakes, the Great Lakes. These few facts, presented in a visual image so simple that any teacher can improvise it on the blackboard and any child can grasp it at a glance will do its job in grade school much better than the professional map, which can be understood only after the visual skeleton has been acquired.

Every visual image worthy of existing is an interpretation of its subject, not a mechanical copy. This is true regardless of whether the image serves the purposes of art, of science, or, like a good geographical map, of both science and art.

## References

1. Arnheim, Rudolf. *Art and Visual Perception*. New version. Berkeley and Los Angeles: University of California Press, 1974.
2. ———. *Visual Thinking*. Berkeley: University of California Press, 1969.
3. Robinson, Arthur H. *The Look of Maps*. Madison: University of Wisconsin Press, 1952.

# Part V

# THE RATIONALIZATION
# OF COLOR

THE FOLLOWING observations are only a prelude to a complex and complicated subject—a prelude played on a color organ. Color organs have been built from time to time, the first being conceived in the 1730s by the mathematician R. P. Castel, a Jesuit in Paris (2). In an appendix to Castel's book *L'Optique des couleurs* there is a French translation of a letter by a German musician, "le célèbre M. Tellemann," who turns out to be the great Georg Philipp Telemann. During a visit to Paris in 1737 Telemann had occasion to acquaint himself with Castel's project. According to his description, Castel's "Augenorgel" or "Augenclavicimbel" coordinated sounds and colors in such a way that every time the player pressed one of the keys, a corresponding color appeared on a tablet or in a lantern, together with the tone of the pipe. The colors, like the sounds, were produced in succession as well as in simultaneous chords.

Castel's instrument was an early attempt at what I will call the rationalization of colors. It was based on a color system derived from Newton's *Opticks*, which enumerated seven elementary colors, corresponding to the seven tones of the diatonic scale (9, pp. 125ff., 154ff.). Castel used blue as the tonic, and the triad was represented by the three fundamentals, blue, yellow, and red. Newton was convinced that the spaces occupied by his seven colors in the spectrum of sunlight matched the sizes of the intervals between the tones of the musical scale. There were five full tones—blue, green, yellow, red, and violet—interspersed at the proper

First published in *Journal of Aesthetics and Art Criticism*, vol. 33 (Winter 1974).

places by two halftones, orange and indigo or purple. The reference to music is significant since from the days of the Pythagoreans, the musical scale had been the most prestigious example of a rational order in sensory experience, whereas the concepts and names of colors derived rather messily from the organic and inorganic substances constituting the raw material for the manufacture of pigments. Aristotle says in the beginning of his short treatise *De Coloribus* that the simple colors are the ones associated with the prime bodies, fire, air, water, and earth. This is again a definition by indirection, a loan from the cosmic order of the four elements. In Renaissance teaching this germ of a rational order survives, together with the more mundane instructions on how to obtain and employ the various pigments (11, p. 56).

The correspondence between colors and musical sounds envisaged by Newton and Castel was based on a physical similarity of the two media, the alleged quantitative correlation between the musical intervals and the angles of refraction distinguishing the various wavelengths of light. This physical correspondence is only one of four kinds of relation that can be established between colors and sounds. It has never been shown to be convincing. Although writers of the eighteenth and nineteenth centuries had great expectations for the principle of the color organ and even promised that "the sonatas of Rameau and Corelli will give the same pleasure to the eyes when seen upon the philosophical harpsichord as they do to the ear" (4), nothing better than simple analogies between visual and auditory rhythm and fairly stable correspondences between brightness and pitch are perceived as long as similarity of the physical stimuli is used as the *tertium comparationis*. This disappointment has not been overcome by modern technology. Whether we watch the photoelectric sound track of a piece of music or take in the synthetic sounds, colors, and shapes generated by one and the same set of manipulations on the control panel, the resulting relations appear arbitrary to eye and ear.

There are, however, perceptually convincing correspondences between colors and sounds based on shared expressive qualities, such as coldness or warmth, violence or gentleness. They are spontaneously evident in perception, although, as Erhardt-Siebold has shown (3), language had to wait for the Romantic poets to make these intellectually suspect relations acceptable to metaphoric speech.

Such freely perceived correspondences of expression should be distinguished from a third relationship, synesthesia or *audition colorée*, as it is known to psychologists. This phenomenon seems to be a curious blend of physiological interconnections and psychological associations of one kind or another. Some persons see colors when they hear sounds. The sensations are automatic and compelling, but they are not always consistent, nor do they carry the intrinsic validity of isomorphic correspondences. On the contrary, they can be rather disturbing to musical experience.

Finally, a fourth relationship should be mentioned, because it is sometimes confused with the others. It is the combined use of several sense modalities in artistic production or description. A novelist referring to colors and sounds—and perhaps to smell and touch also—achieves a more comprehensive presence of the scene he is depicting. Here the combination is based not on similarities between color and sound but on their belonging to the same situation, and the result is increased concreteness rather than the abstractness created by metaphorical confrontation.

It appears that a rational order of colors cannot be obtained by recourse to a different sense modality. Looking at color theory proper, we note that in our century great progress has been made in the identification and orderly cataloguing of hundreds of color shades; but if by rationalization we mean an understanding of the structural relations between the elements of a perceptual color system, we must confess that we are still in the early stages. It took a true pioneer spirit to foray into the wilderness of color theory. The principal reason for the never-ending puzzlement and frustration in this field is that color is the most capricious dimension of visual imagery. We can tell with the utmost precision which particular shapes a Greek painter used for his vase decorations more than two thousand years ago, whereas our knowledge of color throughout the history of art is based mostly on hearsay and conjecture. Even in works only a few decades old, the original coloring begins to change and fade. Furthermore, if one carries a painting or a scientific model of standardized colors from daylight to tungsten light, the resulting change is not only a transposition, which would leave relations intact, but an often fatal modification of the total compositional scheme. For this reason alone it is not surprising that there is a ratio of perhaps 50:1 between what we can say about shape and what we can say about color in the arts.

Even more significant than their unreliability is the dependence of colors upon one another. Although one can determine the hue and brightness of a color physically by wavelength and luminance, there is no such objective constancy to the perceptual experience.[1] Depending on its neighbors, a color undergoes startling changes in appearance. In a painting by Matisse the deep purple of a robe may owe much of its saturated redness to a green wall or skirt bordering on it, whereas in another area of the painting the same robe loses much of its redness to a pink pillow or even looks quite bluish in response to a bright yellow corner. Depending on what local association one is looking at, one sees a different color.

Attempts to harness the protean medium systematically go back to the eighteenth century, when it was decided that three dimensions—hue, brightness, and saturation—were sufficient in practice to define a color, and that therefore a three-dimensional model could assign a unique place to any possible color. However, the neatly conceived spheres, double cones, and double pyramids of the early years had to give way in our own day to lopsided and more irregular models in order to do justice to the less simple facts. The various color solids, notably those of Munsell and Ostwald, are compromises between platonically idealized three-dimensional systems and various optical, physiological, and technological contingencies (8, 10). For example, since different hues reach their maximum saturation at different levels of brightness, the pleasant symmetry of the sphere or double cone must yield to a body distorted by a tilted equator; and the Munsell model looks like a disheveled tree because it is limited to pigments obtainable with present industrial means.

Although such models serve first of all to identify all colors by a system, they suggest almost automatically certain rules for combining colors. What are such rules intended to accomplish? A sensible theory of musical harmony, for example, cannot limit itself to describing which tones sound nice together and which are jarring. A student of musical harmony learns very little from being taught to avoid, say, the *diabolus in musica*, the tritone. He will rightly wonder why he should do without a certain interval for no better reason than that a thousand years ago Guido d'Arezzo said one should. It is only when he comes to understand the particular character and function of the augmented fourth within the structure of the diatonic scale that he realizes what purposes that particular interval will serve or sabotage. Similarly in color combinations, what was considered offensive a few years ago is eagerly employed today;

---

[1] Psychologists speak of "color constancy," which refers mostly to the influence of colored light on colored objects and is at best only partially effective.

and the problem of which colors are perceived as concordant or discordant is subsidiary to the requirements of compositional structure.

What are colors for? The question becomes genuinely interesting only if one is not satisfied by the answer that colors help identify objects, as indeed they do, and that otherwise they are given to us to increase our *joie de vivre*, generated by stimulation and harmony. If instead one is convinced that visual patterns, whether works of art or not, are made to convey certain cognitive statements about basic facts of human experience, the question of what it is that colors tell us poses itself forcefully.

At the elementary level, particular colors have fixed meanings in every culture. To pick an anthropological example at random: Lévi-Strauss refers to the funeral ceremonies of certain Rhodesian and Australian tribes, during which the members of the matrilineal moiety of the dead person put on a red ocher paint and approach the corpse, whereas those of the other moiety use a white clay paint and remain at a distance (7, p. 87). This sort of social color-keying is related to symbolism, red being associated with either death or life, etc. Art historians are familiar with standardized color codes in religious, monarchic, or cosmological imagery, and even under modern circumstances it makes sense to inquire what the color yellow meant to Vincent van Gogh in 1889 or what blue meant to Picasso in 1903. To some extent such color vocabularies are based on conventions that may differ from culture to culture, but there is likely to be also an inherent expression in color, derived from the responses of the nervous system to light of different wavelengths. About these physiological mechanisms we know next to nothing. Until we find out more we can only describe such responses to color, not explain them.

More fruitful is the study of the relations between colors in compositional patterns. We know that quite generally in perception any similarity between items creates a spontaneous link. Thus when Titian depicts the hunter Actaeon discovering Diana in her bath, he ties the two strong red spots of the composition to the two principal figures, thereby setting them off against the complex accessories of landscape and attendants and connecting them across a large interval of space.

Similarity calls for dissimilarity as its counterprinciple, and here the color medium profits from its ability to present mutual exclusiveness of the most radical kind. Perhaps no two shapes, not even a circle and a triangle, can ever be so completely different from each other as a pure red can be from a pure blue or a pure yellow. Piet Mondrian in his late paintings limited himself to these fundamental hues in order to express total independence, total distinction, and, through the lack of relation, also a total absence of dynamics; he reserved the dynamics of relation to the interplay of his shapes. In certain works of Poussin this same triad of the three fundamental colors serves as a dominant theme of classical repose; composite colors are not excluded but introduce lively interrelations at a subordinate level.

Such exclusiveness can be restricted to a limited realm of the universe of color. Yellow and blue can leave out any reference to red and thereby present mutual exclusion in a particular world of, let us say, luminous coldness. Similarly, a composition of reds and yellows is narrowed to the particular experience of glowing warmth.

When we speak of contrast we generally refer to a relation that combines exclusion with inclusion, by which I mean that it can display the greatest possible difference within a range that includes all three fundamental dimensions of hue. In its elementary form, contrast sets a pure fundamental against a composite of the other two; thus blue against orange, red against green, yellow against purple. At the same time it supplies the satisfaction of completeness by the most economical means. This is what we have in mind when we say that the colors of a contrasting pair of hues are complementary. They call for each other.

There is nothing like this in the realm of shapes. One can try to build the world of bodies in all its complexity from the five regular polyhedra, as Plato suggested in the *Timæus*, but there is no obvious way in which the elements of shape add up to a whole. Circle, triangle, and square resemble one another in some ways and differ in others. The only analogy to the primary colors can be found in the three dimensions of space, which in the "pure" orientations of the Cartesian coordinates exclude one another and add up to the complete spatial system.

The particular nature of color experience can be understood only when one draws a psychological parallel to what Newton taught us about the physical nature of the spectrum, that is, when one conceives of colors as partial experiences, dynamic because of their incompleteness and in constant need of mutual integration. It is this interdependence that makes complementaries demand each other and that puts them constantly at each other's mercy by making them change every time their neighbors change. Goethe, the most wrong-headed but also the wisest of color theorists, saw this and wrote:

Single colors affect us, as it were, pathologically, carrying us away to particular sentiments. At times they elevate us to nobility, at others they lower us to vulgarity, suggesting lively striving or gentle longing. But the need for totality, inherent in our organ, guides us beyond this limitation. It sets itself free by producing the opposites of the particulars forced upon it and thus brings about a satisfying completeness. (5, part VI, sec. 812)

In referring to "our organ," however, Goethe also gave an early example of a confusion that continues to beset the discussion of color contrast. Almost universally, color theorists have derived the nature and effect of contrast as a perceptual experience from the physiologically generated phenomenon of hues creating or modifying each other by simultaneous contrast or afterimages. Similarly colors have been defined as complementary when they produce together a monochromatic gray on a rotating wheel or by some other additive combination of light stimuli. This criterion is false. The physiologically produced color contrasts and complementarities do not correspond to those governing our perceptual experience of color relations in painting and elsewhere. One obvious example will suffice. Blue evokes yellow and yellow evokes blue in simultaneous contrast or afterimage, and blue and yellow together produce a gray or white in additive combinations. But those two colors are neither contrasting nor complementary in the color system that guides the visual order of the painter. In the spontaneous vision to which the practice of the painter conforms, yellow and blue are mutually exclusive, but only within the range of a restricted palette. Instead, yellow is complemented pictorially by purple, and blue contrasts with orange (1, chap. 7).

The cause of this discrepancy between physiological and perceptual color relations is unknown to us. But I believe one can state the reason for the painter's loyalty to the system illustrated by the triangle of the three fundamentals: blue, red, and yellow. In this triangle, first documented by Eugène Delacroix in 1832 in a sketchbook that is now in the Musée Condé in Chantilly, the three fundamentals face the three secondaries, orange, green, and purple, in such a way that each primary is completed by its opponent secondary (Figure 39) (6). The system is governed by a simple order that provides for any combination of two of the three components to be completed by the third.

This simple order recommends itself to the painter as a musical scale recommends itself to the musician: there springs from it a network of kinship relations by which colors exclude or contain each other. There is also contrast, mutual attraction, and completion, there are clashes and there are bridges. Such color patterns do not simply parallel the relations between shapes; they often oppose and counterbalance them. The result is a complex pattern of shape and color relations, by which the artist

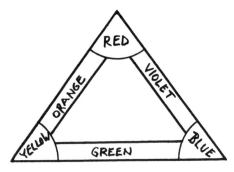

*Figure 39.*

symbolizes through the sense of sight the ways in which the things of the world belong together and stay apart, their ways of building, combining, and separating, of needing and spurning one another. This is what I meant when I suggested that colors help to convey cognitive statements on basic facts of human experience.

Since I began by pointing to the unreasonable behavior of colors, I will end with an answer to the question how so elusive a medium can generate a stable display. If every color is forever changing, depending on the constellation in which it appears, how can one build a valid composition on elements that are so shifty? This problem arises for any whole that is not the sum of its parts, although even a gestalt psychologist like myself may become dizzy when the internal boundaries are as permeable as they are in a manifold of perceived colors. The answer, however, is that even though each element may be modified by every other element, a successful constellation will stabilize the particular character of each element by the concerted interplay of all relevant factors, much as a pole or mast is held upright by the coordinated pull of three guy wires. But whereas the physical forces active in the wires can be invisible to the human eye and therefore can make the delicate balance of the upright pole look like rigid repose, the pulls and pushes regulating color relations occur within the viewer himself; they are field forces of his own nervous system, and hence are felt by a sensitive mind.

The way a green and a red color seek each other is experienced as an active attraction, and this dynamic behavior is a direct quality of the perceptual experience, just as immediately given as hue and brightness are. Or when two colors grate on each other as though in a musical dissonance, this friction is perceived dynamically as a relation between forces inherent in the colors. And the same is true for the way all these relations balance one another in the whole composition. The dynamic interplay of perceptual forces is not just subjectively imposed by the observer upon the patterns he sees, nor does he simply take notice of it intellectually, as a physicist watches a magnet upset a sprinkling of iron filings. Rather, especially for the purpose of the arts, those concerted tensions must actually reverberate in the visual experience if the symbolic messages of colors and shapes are to come alive.

## References

1. Arnheim, Rudolf. *Art and Visual Perception.* New version. Berkeley and Los Angeles: University of California Press, 1974.
2. Castel, R. P. (Louis Bertrand). *L'Optique des Couleurs.* Paris, 1740.
3. Erhardt-Siebold, Erika von. "Harmony of the Senses in English, German, and French Romanticism." *PMLA,* vol. 47 (1932), pp. 577–92.
4. ———. "Some Inventions of the Pre-Romantic Period and Their Influence upon Literature. *Englische Studien,* vol. 66 (1931), pp. 347–63.
5. Goethe, Johann Wolfgang von. *Der Farbenlehre didaktischer Teil.*
6. Guiffrey, Jean, ed. *Le Voyage de Eugène Delacroix au Maroc.* Paris, 1913.
7. Lévi-Strauss, Claude. *La Pensée sauvage.* Paris: Plon, 1962.
8. Munsell, Albert H. *A Grammar of Color.* New York: Van Nostrand, 1969.
9. Newton, Sir Isaac. *Opticks.* London: Bell, 1931.
10. Ostwald, Wilhelm. *The Color Primer.* Ed. Faber Birren. New York: Van Nostrand, 1969.
11. Pedretti, Carlo. *Leonardo da Vinci on Painting.* Berkeley and Los Angeles: University of California Press, 1964.

# PERCEPTUAL DYNAMICS IN MUSICAL EXPRESSION

It is a kind of symbolism for the ear whereby the object, be it in motion or not, is neither imitated nor depicted, but rather produced in the imagination in a wholly particular and incomprehensible manner since there seems to be hardly any relation between the signified and the signifier.

*Goethe in a letter to Zelter, March 6, 1810*

THE FOLLOWING analysis is based on the assumption that what is commonly referred to as the meaning or the expression of music derives from perceptual qualities directly inherent in musical sounds. These qualities can be described as the auditory dynamics of music. While in musical practice the term *dynamics* refers to degrees of loudness in performance, I propose to use it here in the much broader sense I have applied to visual perception (3, 4). In the visual arts, consideration of the "directed tensions" that animate shapes, color relations, and motion has led to a theory of visual expression that has promising analogies in music.

The traditional assumption that the visual world is made up of "objects," at rest or in motion, derives from the common practical use of visual information. For practical handling we deal with the constituents of our world as "things," which are defined by their physical properties, i.e., their shape, size, color, texture, etc. This selective apprehension overshadows our awareness that percepts are prominently dynamic, that is, that objects are perceived as possessed by directed forces. A tree or tower is seen as reaching upward, a wedge-shaped object like an axe advances in the direction of its cutting edge. These dynamic qualities are not mere

First published in *Musical Quarterly*, vol. 70 (Summer 1984). I am much indebted to Steven L. Larson and Michael H. Kurek, whose professional criticism enabled me to improve the text of this essay substantially.

subjective additions to the shapes of things but are primary constituents of percepts; not only are they inseparable from shape, but they often create a more immediate impact than shape itself. In the visual arts in particular, the primary effect of, say, a painting remains unaccounted for as long as images are described simply as agglomerations of objects. A painting speaks only when it is seen as a configuration of directed forces, generated by its various visual components. Accordingly, in aesthetic theory one cannot adequately account for the nature of a visual statement without referring to it as a pattern of forces.

This is all the more true for music because, by the very nature of the auditory medium, tones are perceived not as objects but as activities, generated by some source of energy. Whereas visual objects dwell outside the dimension of time unless they move or are perceived in a context of motion or change, tones are always happenings in time, and this constitutes a primary dynamic vector of music. The persistent presence of a tone is heard not as the continued being of a static entity, but as an event in progress. Sounds therefore lack the principal trait of "objects." They are embodied forces, even though our acquaintance with written music tempts us to think of events in time as objects in space.

Although we often know the physical source that produces a given sound, the source—whether it be a violin or an automobile motor—is not a part of the auditory experience. In the world of hearing, sounds originate from nowhere. They themselves are perceived as being the generators, engaged in constant self-propelling action. A coherent melody presented by an instrument or voice is not primarily an object. It is the path of a motion performed by a single tone in musical space. As this tone rises and falls from pitch to pitch, its behavior is accounted for perceptually by impulses originating in the tone itself or by external forces of attraction or repulsion. (For similar phenomena in mobile visual shapes see Michotte [12].) We watch a tone move along a melodic path the way we watch an insect crawl from place to place. Only secondarily does the melodic action in time add up to a spatial configuration, which is seen by the mind's eye as a simultaneous whole, traversed by a directional arrow. Although written notation has accustomed us to thinking of a succession of musical tones as a chain of beads, auditory perception tells us that the elements of music are happenings. The little generator of a melody moves from one pitch level to another, and even when it stays in place, the sounding is continued action. When one listens to the tones of a triad, played one after the other and followed by the octave, one hears a succession of three leaps, even though physically none of the four tones "moves."[1]

Equally important for our present purpose is the dynamics created by the deviation or divergence from a norm base.[2] Here again, analogous phenomena in vision are illuminating. The structure of visual space relies upon the framework provided by the vertical and horizontal. This framework is the visual "tonic," the zero base at which tension is at a minimum. Every obliqueness is perceived as a deviation from these fundamental directions and derives tension from it. Like all perceptual vectors, such deviation operates in two opposite directions: an obliquely oriented object, for example the leaning tower of Pisa, is seen either as striving away from the norm base or as trying to approach it. Furthermore, both these tendencies can be read as generated either by the deviant object itself or by the norm base; that is, the deviant object is seen either as pushing toward or pulling away from the base by its own active power or as being passively attracted or repelled by the energy center in the base.

The corresponding frame of reference in the music of the Western common-practice era is, of course, the tonal center. In the major mode, the relation of the various pitches to the level of the keynote is thoroughly dynamic and constitutes a principal perceptual source of musical expression. It is not a matter merely of measurable distance from the keynote, but of the tension generated by the attractive power of the base. The configuration of forces that determines the dynamic action of a given tone includes quite prominently the reference to the tonal base. Above the keynote, the melody takes off, overcoming the attraction of the base through its own upward-directed impulse; below it, the melody moves downward against the resistance of the base. Any sound above or below the pitch level of the base represents a small triumph of emancipation from the state of inaction. This is a fundamental phenomenon of all musical perception.[3] Needless to say, the dynamic character of any tone changes whenever the tonal basis shifts to a different key, as is the case

---

[1] Victor Zuckerkandl, whose books contain excellent discussions of musical dynamics (18, 19), refers aptly to an analogous phenomenon in vision, the so-called phi motion, experienced when immobile visual stimuli are presented in rapid succession. Cf. Wertheimer (17).

[2] Leonard B. Meyer deals extensively with the deviation from musical norms in performance (11, chaps. 6, 7).

[3] A similar perceptual situation is known in graphology. Western handwriting is organized around a middle zone as the base for extensions upward and downward. Translating the dynamic features of handwriting into their psychological equivalent, the graphologist

in modulation. So-called atonal music is the limiting case of tonality in which the framework changes so frequently as to be no longer distinguishable in principle from the attractive powers exerted by the single tones upon one another.

Before I attempt to analyze the character of the major and minor modes, one further feature of the perceptual situation that also applies to music must be mentioned. The visual field is dominated by a pervasive dynamic vector, which, by analogy to the physical world, we call the gravitational force. Every visual object is seen as being pulled downward. This creates an asymmetry or anisotropy of visual space, by which an upward motion differs qualitatively from a downward motion. Moving upward involves the overcoming of weight, a liberation from the ground; moving downward is experienced as giving in to the gravitational attraction, a passive letting go. In addition to this overbearing and universal vector, however, each visual object is a dynamic center in its own right. It generates variously oriented forces and asserts its attraction upon neighboring objects. Thus the dynamics of a visual composition, for example in painting, comes about as a complex interaction between the overall vertical pull of the gravitational vector and the power of the various visual objects (5, chap. 2).

A similar complexity prevails in music. The power of any tonal center is overlaid by the downward pull of the gravitational vector. The relation of the tonic to the tones above it and below it would be heard as symmetrical if the tonic were the only base of reference. Rising above the tonic would be the dynamic equivalent of descending below it. This, however, is not the case. Moving upward anywhere on the pitch scale carries the connotation of a victorious liberation from weight, whereas descent is experienced as a passive giving in to weight. In any practical case, the relations to the two centers of attraction either enhance or counteract each other. A downward move toward the tonic is reinforced by the gravitational pull. An ascent toward the upper base of the octave pits the upward pull of the tonic against the downward pull of gravity. More specifically, the leading-tone effect produced by a half step, for example, is directed toward its base of resolution, either upward or downward, but this local dynamics is either strengthened or opposed by the magnetic pulls dominating the structure as a whole.

---

speaks of a tendency to reach beyond the given base or to be satisfied with it. An emphasis on upper extension goes with spirituality, dreaminess, "light weight"; lower extension goes with material concerns, instinctual pressure, "heavy weight." Cf. Roman (14) and Klages (7).

In the musical as well as in the visual realm, the downward-directed tendency may be called the primary one in that it conforms to the condition of the "gravitational" pull that pervades either medium from the outset. Within the anisotropic space of the medium every ascent represents an individual countermove in opposition to the tendency prevailing in the situation as a whole.

If one adds to the effects of the two principal centers of reference the more specific roles played by single tones within the context of the scale, which I will now discuss, one comes to realize the extraordinary complexity of our musical system, revealed when the set of tones is perceived as a pattern of dynamic relations. In fact, Western music could not have attained its high level of sophistication if it were not derived from so intricate a palette of tonal relations. In the following I am relying on a schema of our traditional musical scale that I have presented elsewhere (1, p. 218). The analysis is based on the fact that our modern Western modes, the major and the minor, can be described as having come about through the joining of Greek tetrachords (Figure 40). The tetrachord of ancient music consisted of two whole tones followed by a half tone in a descending direction. Turned upward and combined, two such tetrachords add up to the major scale. In the key of C, for example, the lower tetrachord reaches from C to f, the upper from g to C. When the scale is perceived in this manner, the step from the fourth to the fifth functions as a dead interval between the two substructures—in visual terms, as the "ground" between the two close-up objects, which appear as "figure."

The half step at the end of each ascending tetrachord acts dynamically as a constriction, which greatly enhances the effect of closure, that is, of a happening coming to an end.[4] On the way down, however, the effect obtained in the major mode is almost the opposite: the structure opens from the initial half step to the two whole-tone steps. In this case the motion is stopped only by the bases at the dominant and the tonic.

Each ascending tetrachord arrives at what is perceived as a stable platform, at the level of the fourth and the octave. The interval of the fourth, which embraces the limits of the tetrachord, thereby acquires the character of a wide reach for a base of secure rest. It is true that this tendency toward closure is more pronounced in the upper tetrachord,

---

[4]Visually a similar closure effect is obtained, for example, on the octastyle façades of some Greek temples such as the Parthenon, or the frontal portico of the Toshodaiji Temple in Nara, where the openings between the columns on the two sides are narrower than the others. Such lateral constriction makes the row of columns come to a considered end, whereas otherwise its length might look arbitrary.

which ends with the tonic, than in the lower. The lower owes much of its finality to the fact that it is readily perceived as the upper tetrachord of a related key, e.g., of the key of F in the case of the C scale.

The subdivision of the scale into two tetrachords is overlaid in a paradoxical manner by the triad, which structures the scale quite differently on the skeleton of three steps of unequal length. In the major mode, the first step, a major third, contracts into a minor third, as though gathering its strength, and then stretches for the upward leap to the tonic. The triad creates two new platforms of stable rest at the level of the third and the fifth. It is the most secure way of rising through the space of the scale: on the triadic steps the motion is safely grounded at each stage of the action—think, for example, of the solidly buttressed strides at the beginning of our national anthem.

The superposition of the two structures, the tetrachordal and the triadic, makes for ambiguity at many and perhaps all levels of the scale. For example, the e of the C scale is a stable rest as a stage of the triad, but it is also the tension-laden leading tone of the lower tetrachord. The g marks the weighty second stage of the triad, but it is a mere starting point for the upper tetrachord. A tone will assume either the one or the other function and character, depending on the compositional context; and the paradoxical interrelation between the two enriches the structural resources of the music derived from the scale.

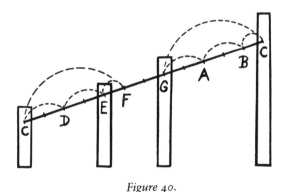

*Figure 40.*

A tone's place and function within the scale determines its dynamics; and since the dynamics is an inherent property of the auditory percept, the listener's awareness of where a tone stands in the scale is not simply a bit of incremental knowledge. Just as a given shade of blue is perceived as a different color depending on whether it appears next to an orange or a purple, a tone of a given musical pitch has a different dynamic character depending on its place in the tonal structure. A single trumpet tone in an otherwise silent world may be centered entirely upon itself, but a keynote will function typically as a base for musical action, and within the scale the nature of each tone is strongly influenced by its orientation toward the tonic. This relationship is complicated by the fact that the tonic exerts its power at the lower as well as the upper end of the scale, so that the ascending pitch, like the hare of the fairy tale in his race against the hedgehog and his wife, has hardly liberated itself from the pull of the lower base when the magnetism of the final state of rest at the top already begins to attract it. Thus every tone of the scale is subject to the spell of the two opposite poles, and the particular ratio of the two attractions is a determinant of the tone's dynamics.

The distinguishing characteristics of the major mode reveal themselves best by comparison with those of the minor. It is well known that these two modes, which came to dominate our musical tradition, developed from the larger group of medieval church modes. In that earlier context, their equivalents are not likely to have been interrelated as they are now in isolation. Therefore, if as I shall suggest the minor mode displays the character it has for us only because it is perceived as a deviation from the major, there is no reason to expect that the corresponding mode in the Middle Ages carried the melancholy quality we hear in the minor. Similarly, the vigor we attribute to our major mode need not have been a property of the corresponding mode in the different context of the Middle Ages.

For obvious dynamic reasons, the decisive structural difference between major and minor resides in the position of the half steps. In its upward climb the major third pushes vigorously toward the completion of the lower tetrachord (Figure 41, left-hand row). In the minor, like a climber carrying a heavy load, the action sags back at the second step, which requires a double effort to reach the level of the fourth (Figure 41, right-hand row). This behavior becomes even more pronounced in the upper tetrachord, where the climber is already lagging behind the brisk advance of the major at the first step, so that an even more excessive effort is required to reach the leading tone.[5]

One need only describe the musical action in dynamic terms to realize

---

[5] I am referring to the harmonic version of the minor mode, in keeping with Schönberg's assertion in the *Harmonielehre*: "The only correct thing to do seems to me to start from the Aeolian mode" (15, p. 114).

the striking analogy between the musical behavior perceived in the major and minor modes and the states of mind described as vigorous and forceful in the one case and as sad and melancholy in the other. Sadness is experienced dynamically as a passive state of letting go, giving in to the pull of weight, a lack of energy in coping with the efforts called for by life. The perceptual coincidence is so compelling and realized so spontaneously that there is no need to assume that the relation between sound and meaning needs to be learned like a foreign language.[6]

It would be equally insufficient to describe this relation as the discovery of analogies between two languages, both of which are known to the listener. Something much more direct takes place: one hears the sadness *in* the minor mode. The music *is* and sounds sad. This has led to endless and, in my opinion, fruitless psychological and philosophical disputation on how it is possible for a state of mind to make its appearance in a pattern of sounds.

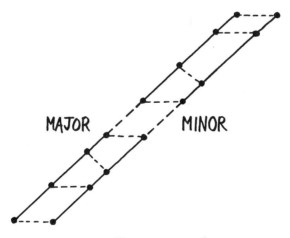

*Figure 41.*

The problem vanishes when one realizes that musical expression is not based on a comparison of two disparate media, namely the world of sound and the world of mental states, but on a single dynamic structure

---

[6] I am not concerned here with the very different controversy over whether the musical tones owe their particular structural characteristics to the physical properties of the harmonics or whether they acquire them by convention. Whatever the cause, the tones of the scale have perceptual properties whose dynamic characteristics are asserted to convey expression and meaning spontaneously.

inherent in both realms of experience.[7] The character of any perceptual event resides in its dynamics and is all but independent of the particular medium in which it happens to embody itself. This interpretation relies on the concept of isomorphism, which was introduced by gestalt psychology to describe similarity of structure in materially disparate media.[8] Thus a dance and a piece of music accompanying it can be experienced as having a similar structure, even though the dance consists of visual shapes in movement and the music of a sequence of sounds. The dancers, in turn, control their performance by patterns of kinesthetic sensations, which they receive within their bodies and which correspond isomorphically to the movement patterns seen by the audience. According to gestalt theory, such structural kinship is so compelling perceptually that it is directly and spontaneously experienced. For example, the visible behavior of the muscles in a human face beset by grief parallels the mental state of a grieving person so directly that any viewer who knows what faces are and what grief feels like perceives the appearance of the person as that of someone in distress.[9]

When in such a case we speak of expression, we mean that a person's or animal's state of mind is reflected in the behavior of that particular individual's body. Expression, however, is not limited to such relations between body and mind. It applies to all perceptual situations that exhibit dynamic patterns. In the field of art, for example, expression is conveyed by music or by the "abstract" or representational shapes, colors, or movements of painting, sculpture, film, etc. In this more general sense, expression is the capacity of a particular perceptual pattern to exemplify through its dynamics the structure of a type of behavior that could manifest itself anywhere in human experience. The expressive "meaning" of such a perceptual pattern reveals itself by a simple principle. As the brief discussion of the major and minor modes will already

---

[7] The spontaneous analogy between sensory percepts and such inner sensations as "emotions" presupposes that not only the former but also the latter are recognized as percepts. Our psychology textooks fail to do this. We are helped by Descartes (6, articles 22–25), who aptly distinguishes three types of percepts, those referring to objects of the outer world, those deriving from our bodies, and those relating to our soul. All three, says Descartes, are really passions, that is, afflictions of the soul. Cf. also Arnheim (2).

[8] For the theory of isomorphism, consult Koffka (8), Köhler (9), and Arnheim (3, chap. 10). Application to music is discussed by Pratt (13) and Langer (10, chap. 8). See also Schopenhauer (16, Book 3).

[9] This is not to deny that a special knowledge of cultural or physical conditions may be necessary to perceive correctly the behavior of a foreign people or of an animal. But the direct impact and comprehensibility of sensory experience is so much more important that we must not let a concern for secondary variations distract our attention from it.

have shown, one need only describe the dynamics of the pattern in question, and its expressive meaning will become apparent in an almost embarrassingly obvious way.[10]

A simple tune may further illustrate the point. The melody of Schumann's *Träumerei* conveys the nature of a reverie, the carefree rising to lofty heights, undertaken with a minimum of effort and risk (Figure 42). How is the character of this behavior expressed? The piece is written in F, and the easy leap that initiates the action accomplishes nothing more daring than a move to the safest level, the platform of the tonic. After an ample rest, our tone creature sinks back by half a step as though even the stable base of the tonic could not quite check its languidness. But this step backward provides at the same time the impulse for a further and much more extensive soar, which leads quickly but easily to the safety of the upper tonic by means of the secure steps of the triad. Throughout this first phrase of the melody, there is a playful and humorous disparity between the amplitude of the adventure undertaken and the smallness of the investment and risk it requires. Soon after the peak has been attained, our tone creature sinks back by means of gliding steps with token attempts to regain height. This passive downslide stops one step short of the base in a half-close announcing a resumption of the dreamy exploit.

*Figure 42.*

Needless to say, this expressive behavior is not obtained by the sequence of pitches alone. It relies equally on the range of durations, from the eighth to the half notes, and on the distribution of the tones on the accented locations of the 4/4 meter. Nor have I mentioned the chords and secondary voices that confirm and enrich the meaning of the principal tune in Schumann's composition. So complete an analysis would go beyond my ambitions here, and it would not alter the basic thesis I am trying to illustrate.

---

[10] Formal analyses of what might be called the architectural design of musical compositions are, of course, common practice. But only when the analysis goes beyond spatial connections and hierarchies and specifies the perceptual dynamics of the musical happening does the structural analogy between the signifier and the signified become concretely evident.

Let me add a reference to a more complex example, the first seven bars of the unaccompanied viola solo at the beginning of Béla Bartók's Sixth String Quartet. (For easier reading, Figure 43 transcribes the passage into the treble clef.) The tempo mark *Mesto* prepares the reader of the score for what awaits the listener: a melancholy, slow performance; and in fact, the melody presents the behavior of somebody or something forced by outer or inner constraints to limit itself mostly to the smallest steps available in our musical system. The holding back by means of half steps, which gives the minor mode its character, is employed here more widely than is foreseen in the diatonic scale. It makes the sequence haltingly chromatic.

*Figure 43.*

The g sharp that begins Bartók's tune reveals itself, if one looks for a tonal base, as the rather stable dominant of the key of C sharp minor, whose keynote will be explicitly presented in the fourth measure. But first, the tone creature probes in cautious half steps the area close to the initial platform; and then, not unlike Schumann's *Träumerei* although less expansively, it rises to the first peak of the b, from which a sequence of heartier whole-tone steps tumbles downward as though the cramp of the beginning had been momentarily dissolved and as though giving in to gravity called for less circumspection. The melody dwells on the tonic of the C sharp for confirmation and recovery of energy. It then rises to the new plateau of the fourth, which is investigated once more with the halting half-tone steps we remember from the exploration of the initial level. And thereafter a hesitant progression, which involves reservations about the adventure of the ascent, winds its way toward the new peak of the C double sharp.

Just as in the earlier example, the kind of behavior expressed in Bartók's melody reveals itself as a matter of course as soon as the sequence of tones is described dynamically. Its perceived nature, however, would seem to depend to some extent on whether or not the listener relates the passage, as a whole or in part, to the key of C sharp minor. If he does, the deviations from that key create considerable tension, but the safety of the tonic base is preserved. In the alternative case, the listener is lured away from that base and surrenders to other centers of reference, suggested here and there through this first section of the melody. This latter way of perceiving the musical structure creates a much less stable situation. The listener has to reestablish his base from moment to moment as he drifts along without anchor. Our example seems to illustrate Schönberg's assertion that there is no difference in principle between tonality and atonality. Earlier in this essay I referred to atonality as the limiting case of tonality. It seems equally appropriate to describe tonality, conversely, as the limiting case in which the safety of a persistent base of reference is maintained at some length. The absence of this safety is of course a decisive feature of the expression conveyed by "atonal" music.

Musicians know that a piece of music is not simply a linear event, in which the various tone creatures, each constantly altering its shape as it takes the form of chords, pursue their paths from start to finish. Even our few sketchy examples remind us that a phrase reveals its structure not before it is known as a whole, when, for example, it rises toward a peak and then descends. The place and function of a single element, e.g., a particular tone in a scale, is defined only by the pattern as a whole. The same is true for any other sequential work of art, be it literary or visual, and I have pointed out elsewhere that the only medium in which a structure can be perceived synoptically is the visual one (3, p. 374). This leads to the puzzling consequence that any conception of a musical structure must be in the nature of a visual image.[11] Let me refer in this connection to the opposite case, namely architecture, in which the visual form is primary in its timeless simultaneity. Architectural structures, however, are typically pervaded also by sequential patterns. As in architecture, the ratio between a musical composition's timeless "architecture" and its character as an event depends on its style. A piano piece by Debussy is more nearly a mere succession in time than a movement of a Corelli sonata. Needless to say, the difference between the stability of a timeless structure and the dramatic happening of a "story" unfolding in time affects the expression of a piece profoundly.

---

[11] As Zuckerkandl puts it (19, p. 22), "Can a gestalt come about anywhere but in space, where it unfolds with all its parts all at once in simultaneity and where it offers itself to the observation without receding immediately?"

It remains for me to comment on the question of what it is that expression expresses. Theoreticians who concede that music has a content generally refer to "emotions." But emotions, as the term is commonly understood, are much too limited a category of mental state to account for musical expression. Bach's *Inventions* suggest neither grief nor joy but are nonetheless powerfully expressive. Many more mental states and much more articulate ones exist than is suggested by the word *emotion*. Even more important seems to me the fact that the meaning of music cannot be limited to mental states. Dynamic structures such as the ones embodied in the aural percepts of music are much more comprehensive. They refer to patterns of behavior that can occur in any realm of reality, be it mental or physical.[12] A particular way of coping with the task of how to move from a beginning to an end can be manifest in a state of mind, a dance, or a watercourse. Although we human beings confess to a particular interest in the stirrings of the soul, music, in principle, does not commit itself to such particular application. It presents the dynamic patterns as such. We thus may find new meaning in Schopenhauer's contention that music represents the Will—the dynamic power inherent in all action of body, mind, and universe.

## References

1. Arnheim, Rudolf. *Visual Thinking*. Berkeley and Los Angeles: University of California Press, 1969.
2. ———. "Emotion and Feeling in Psychology and Art." In *Toward a Psychology of Art*. Berkeley and Los Angeles: University of California Press, 1972.
3. ———. *Art and Visual Perception*. New version. Berkeley and Los Angeles: University of California Press, 1974.
4. ———. *The Dynamics of Architectural Form*. Berkeley and Los Angeles: University of California Press, 1977.
5. ———. *The Power of the Center*. Berkeley and Los Angeles: University of California Press, 1982.
6. Descartes, René. "Les Passions de l'âme." In *Oeuvres et Lettres*. Paris: Gallimard, 1952.
7. Klages, Ludwig. *Handschrift und Charakter*. Leipzig: Barth, 1923.

---

[12]Langer (10) has raised the interesting question of whether the symbolic components of music can be reduced to fixed concepts and therefore be said to yield the elements of a language. Actually the same issue arises in literature as soon as literary statements are recognized as being the images generated by words rather than the words themselves. All works of art are nondiscursive, which does not exclude the possibility of reducing symbolic dynamisms to concepts. In music the tempo marks are an obvious beginning.

8. Koffka, Kurt. *Principles of Gestalt Psychology.* New York: Harcourt Brace, 1935.

9. Köhler, Wolfgang. *Selected Papers.* New York: Liveright, 1971.

10. Langer, Susanne K. *Philosophy in a New Key.* Cambridge, Mass.: Harvard University Press, 1960.

11. Meyer, Leonard B. *Emotion and Meaning in Music.* Chicago: University of Chicago Press, 1956.

12. Michotte, Albert. *La Perception de la causalité.* Louvain: Institut Supérieur de la Philosophie, 1946. Eng.: *The Perception of Causality.* London: Methuen, 1963.

13. Pratt, Carroll C. *The Meaning of Music.* New York: McGraw-Hill, 1931.

14. Roman, Klara G. *Handwriting: A Key to Personality.* New York: Pantheon, 1952.

15. Schönberg, Arnold. *Harmonielehre.* Leipzig: Universal-Edition, 1911.

16. Schopenhauer, Arthur. *Die Welt als Wille und Vorstellung.* 1819.

17. Wertheimer, Max. "Experimentelle Studien über das Sehen von Bewegung." *Zeitschr. f. Psychologie,* vol. 61 (1912), pp. 161–265.

18. Zuckerkandl, Victor. *Die Wirklichkeit der Musik.* Zurich: Rhein, 1963. Eng.: *Music and the External World.* Princeton, N.J.: Princeton University Press, 1969.

19. ———. *Vom musikalischen Denken.* Zurich: Rhein, 1964. Eng.: *Man the Musician.* Princeton, N.J.: Princeton University Press, 1973.

# Part VI

# THE PERCEPTUAL CHALLENGE
# IN ART EDUCATION

SOCIETY has always derived its images of greatness and wretchedness, of joy and suffering, from the imagination of its artists. Today, too, we should welcome the guidance of such images, at a time when there would be such good use for the effective identification of depravity and for the confirmation of the human right to use this earth and enjoy it. It troubles us, therefore, not to be sure whether the arts are still willing and able to illuminate our standards in the accustomed manner.

There are several reasons for this uncertainty. We ask whether the arts still depict for us such basic human conditions as the tragedy of failure or the radiance of fulfillment, the compassion and lucidity of the human mind when it is at its best and its brutal stupidity when it is evil; and we are not sure how many of our artists consider it their task to be concerned with these matters. We also hear it said that to be occupied with the arts in times like ours is an inexcusable frivolity, and that visual form and appearance cannot possibly matter as long as we need all our energy to make the good things come about and the bad ones perish. In a famous poem, Michelangelo admonished viewers not to disturb the sleep of his Night "finchè il danno e la vergogna dura"—as long as harm and shame prevail. Such doubts cannot leave the art educator indifferent; for he must be convinced that art is indispensable if he is to cultivate it in our children.

Based on "Art and Humanism," an address given at the 11th Biennial Conference of the National Art Education Association, April 1971 in Dallas, and published in *Art Education*, vol. 24, no. 7 (October 1971).

Did art cease to represent the humanity of man when for many decades of our century it ceased to depict the human figure? I do not believe that this is the case. In the best of abstract art, the age-old subject matter remained. There was much humanity in the agonizing shapes of an Arshile Gorky or the sensous perfection of Jean Arp's marbles, in the classicist severity of a Mondrian or the romantic exuberance of the early Kandinsky. On the other hand, it is precisely when a recent leading fashion in art returned to the human figure that we were struck by examples of humanism discarded and sterility and vulgarity celebrated.

I doubt that there are times in the history of art that require sterility and vulgarity. But there are situations in which art, in the interest of its own health and perhaps survival, must reduce itself to its barest elements, just as a stomach sometimes needs the blandest diet and a distraught mind must take refuge in the emptiness of the desert. We know from Kasimir Malevich's writing that when in 1913 he exhibited the famous black square on a white ground, he did so in a "desperate attempt to free art from the ballast of objectivity" (3, p. 342). He was forced to this violent act to restore that "pure feeling" which, he thought, had vanished behind a masquerade of dehumanized figures and objects. Today we can look at that black square with respectful compassion and perhaps with envy, as we look at the bare cells of the monks of San Marco; we can also acknowledge its legitimate place in the early history of twentieth-century painting. But sane judgment requires us also to realize that in and of itself that square is next to nothing. It is rather a demonstration, the proof of a sacrifice, a memento of courage like the bloodstains on a tattered flag in the showcase of a history museum. If a work of art is to sustain itself by its own power, more is called for.

Not long ago, artists presented us with two- or three-dimensional objects that baffled or pleased us by their simplicity. Some art educators welcomed these works. They were easy to make, and it was good to know that techniques well within the reach of our youngsters could be considered artistically respectable. The teacher also knew that elementarism is not only unavoidable when the eyes and hands are young, but in fact necessary because all visual orientation and mastery starts with the handling of shapes and colors simple enough to be understood. The art educator, in other words, was right at home with minimal art because he dealt with minimal people—if this expression may be used without disrespect.

Adults, however, who made and appreciated minimal art were not supposed to be minimal people. It became necessary therefore to ask whether the descendants of the black square, in spite of their simplicity, could arouse experiences complex and profound enough to do justice to the human brain. Some of the arguments put forward in their favor are of continuing interest.

It was said, for example, that although the art objects in themselves offered few relations to the eyes, the better sculpture of those days took "relationships out of the work and [made] them a function of space, light, and the viewer's field of vision" (5). The brain of the viewer was invited to supply some of the complexity the objects themselves were lacking. In fact, any cooperative viewer is likely to make such a contribution. If his eyes are imaginative, they will be busy in the outside world seeing the visual miracles of pavements and puddles, reflections, and shadows, ingenious overlaps, and surrealist textures. In an art gallery or museum such a person will watch similar visual attractions with attention and perhaps discover by courtesy of the ceiling lights some cunning play of shape and color on the exhibited cubes. But it is only fair to add that the competition from ordinary daytime sights is considerable, and that unless the art object offers some attractive form of its own, the visitor is likely to do better with the fire extinguisher on the wall or with somebody's overcoat dropped on a chair.

Nor would it be quite cricket to credit the maker of the object for the rich experiences created by the contribution of the setting or the productive imagination of the viewer. Any object or event in this world can strike the human mind most profoundly if the conditions are right. A broken syringe abandoned on the sidewalk can do so, or a daisy in the hand of a child. If the person to whom this happens is a poet or a filmmaker, the experience may be artistic, but it will not be because of a work of art. Or take an obelisk, which by itself, as the word indicates, is only a spit. Place it on the back of Bernini's elephant or in the center of St. Peter's Square, charge it with the memories of the Egyptian temple or tomb from which it was stolen, and it will be a sight of majestic solemnity, not easily equaled anywhere. Even so, in itself the obelisk is little more than a piece of granite, perhaps pleasantly proportioned.

One of my students practices meditation. He tells me that he meditates particularly well in front of a very large American painting consisting of horizontal stripes of varying widths and colors. I can see why. The eyes glide along the stripes through the entire visual field without stopping; they lie at no clearly discernible distance from one another and form no solid picture plane. The viewer loses himself in all three dimensions, and if this is what he wants, there can be no better target. However, when a local museum exhibited the magnificent Japanese treasures of Zen art, this same student found that he could also meditate very well in front of an ink painting by the fifteenth-century Zen priest Kenko Shokei, a larger-than-lifesize portrait of the founder of Zen Buddhism, Bodhidharma (2, #57). The fierce concentration in every muscle of the old man's face, together with the sensitivity of every contour, makes it a most powerful image of spiritual greatness. I suspect that the experiences of my student in front of the two paintings were not the same. If there was a difference it was due to the boundless anonymity of dispersion in one of the pictures and the all-encompassing human concentration in the other; and I suggest that the difference matters.

Speaking of the Bodhidharma, we can carry the argument one step further. Legend has it that when that saintly priest stopped at the Shaolin temple on Mount Sung in China, he sat down in front of a bare wall and gazed at it for nine years in deep meditation. His example is still followed in Buddhist practice today. But it has never occurred to anybody to credit the builder of the wall for the spiritual enlightenment thus achieved.

I am insisting on this point because one of the things an art educator has to teach his students is the ethics of who deserves credit for what. I have always looked with some misgiving at the kindergarten practice of fingerpainting because all too easily the young dauber is credited with the dazzling effects of theatrical shadows and volumes and the magic perspectives produced by accidents of smeared paint and never conceived by their creator. Similarly, when a child produces a simple thing, the inflections in the praise he receives should make it clear that he has done well what he can be expected to do, and that in the mind of the teacher such work is not the end but just a beginning. How else is the child going to find his place in the world?

There is a related issue here, also ethical in part. One of the things a youngster needs to learn is that few efforts are worth his while unless he fully invests his mental and physical powers in them. Only then is he likely to grow as a result of his efforts, and only then will they show human nature at its best. This is particularly important today when, in the marketplace of the arts, we are frequently faced with objects or activities that are not only meager fare for the viewer but also were easy to produce. To dump a grease-smeared bundle of hay on an exhibition floor may be a useful gesture deserving gratitude, but it neither requires the courage needed to, say, burn a draft card nor does it challenge the performer's potential as a worker, thinker, or artist. If we assert that such a performance is not good enough, we are not calling for the puritan virtue of hard work for agony's sake. We do so because we know that a person spending his time on trifles cheats himself of his own humanity. Fortunately, few drives in man are as powerful as that of putting all his resources to work. It takes a strong cultural or personal depression to make him deny himself this basic right.

As I said earlier, we may no longer be sure whether art should be considered necessary for human existence. Of course, there has been art in all civilizations we know. It could be suppressed only temporarily by official decree. But perhaps art is merely pleasurable, not really indispensable. Perhaps we should assume that the paleolithic cave paintings or the bark paintings of the Australian aborigines were the products of luxurious leisure hours during which the "primitive," having satisfied his true needs, discharged his surplus energy by making pictures. It sounds unlikely, and yet there are those who pretend that art is pure luxury. They say that in times of social, economic, and political distress, a concern with form is nothing more than a reactionary diversion. For example, some young architects in an "activist" mood sound like Hannes Meyer, who as director of the Bauhaus began his manifesto on building in 1928 with the statement: "All things in this world are a product of the formula: function times economy. All these things are therefore not works of art. All art is composition and hence opposed to utility. All life is function and therefore inartistic" (4, p. 153). A similar false dichotomy between art and useful purpose can be observed here and there in the practice and theory of painting and sculpture.

I have often wondered what kind of words the tribesmen of so-called primitive cultures use when they talk about the shape of their huts; whether they call it good or bad, right or wrong, correct or incorrect, ugly or beautiful. That they care and talk about it is certain since, far from neglecting shape, they adhere to rather rigid standards. Form is unavoidable; and it is not prescribed by function. Function, as we know by now, determines only the range of admissible shapes, not the actual shape itself. The particular shape has to be invented and selected, and few populations have ever been blind to the language of shape and color.

Granted that if one has to decide whether to spend a million dollars on a hospital or on an art center, there can be no doubt about the priority. But in most cases such a choice is artificial; and it certainly does not prove that art is unnecessary. To pretend that deprived persons have only material needs is to despise them. And to say that good taste is the privilege of a small elite since most people prefer dreadful furniture and bad pictures may be correct, but it implies superficial thinking about the nature of bad taste. Bad taste is not due to the absence of elite breeding; it is rather a symptom of an obstructed mind, in a particular person or an entire culture. The uncorrupted artwork of children or of so-called primitives is never in bad taste. Bad taste, wherever it exists, reflects a deeper deficiency.

In many totalitarian countries the rigidity of ideological oppression manifested itself visually in "socialist realism." The officially preferred style of Soviet painting and sculpture cannot be accounted for simply by the bad taste of uneducated leaders. The attitude of such a regime is quite consistent. It is in no position to tolerate the discord and violence reflected in much modern art or the variety of individual world views. The smoothly idealized, flawless rhetoric of the official party art precisely matches the conformist mentality on which the regime depends. Hitler's objections to "degenerate art" were similarly consistent with the mendacity of the fascist image.

The bad taste of what a majority of our own countrymen enjoy in their living rooms or on television accords with a state of mind that prefers amusement to truth. It likes its passions sweet and titillating and uses tragedy as a mild stimulant to raise the adrenalin level. The cheapened Art Nouveau style of "psychedelic" illustrations matches the noncommittal fantasies of their purchasers; and the immaculate curls and fingernails of comic strip maidens and Hollywood actresses in the rapidly aging products of "pop art" suggest a diagnosis of comfortable alienation. The art reflects the mind, and there can be no good art without humanity.

Artistic form is unavoidable because no object or statement can be made without it. Neglected or despised, it turns up with a vengeance, contradicting and incriminating its own maker. Conversely, it should be equally obvious that there can be no pure form, i.e., form that says nothing. Some years ago there was a large exhibition of Black Art. It was no better and no worse than any group show from which the few great talents of a generation are omitted; but it was noteworthy in its subject matter. An influential art critic wrote—if for the sake of argument I may caricature his position somewhat—that the exhibition abounded in social and political themes related to the Black cause; but since subject matter had nothing to do with art and the handling of color and shape was mediocre, the show was a negligible event. It seems hard to believe that there are still persons in the arts who assert that the message of an art object is irrelevant. The notion that formal relations are all there is to a work and that art is about nothing is hopelessly old-fashioned, whether we read it in the essays of a critic of sixty years ago or in the pronouncements of artists making geometrical ornaments today. Every art teacher knows that there is no way of judging even the simplest arrangement of shapes without some tacit understanding of what the object is meant to tell. And why after all should we cultivate visual language if we have nothing to say?

There were protests against the critic's judgment, one of them by a Black artist asserting that the concern with form was typical of the unthinking White art establishment. He insisted instead that nothing mattered but the activist statement. He was caught as fatally as his opponent in the false dichotomy of content and form.

This last example reminds us that the social determinants of bad taste, discussed a moment ago, are not the only obstacle to artistic achievement. I need not refer here at length to the nature and effects of the disorganized environment in which most of us are condemned to live. Our visual world is dominated by human settlements patched together through the uncoordinated enterprise of innumerable individuals. The resulting chaos is likely to be pernicious because the only defense against it is to suppress one's sense of structure and see the world in unrelated pieces. This would be bad enough if the crippling of vision were limited to our response to the appearance of the external world. But the damage cannot be expected to stop there. Perceptual appearance is the spawning ground of all cognitive understanding. If we see the world in pieces, how likely are we to be alert to relations between neighbors and fellow citizens, connections between political and economic happenings, cause and effect, the I and the Thou? How likely are we to see our own inner self as a whole?

Educators know the problem of coping with children who inhabit a chaotic world. They have begun to realize that a sudden confrontation with the serenity of perfect order may be bewildering to an unprepared child and provoke resistance. But there has also been a worrisome tendency to believe that the best way of initiating their charges to the world they will have to live in is by giving preference to techniques and subjects that convey the violence of disorder, confusion, noise. It is a tempting solution. The teacher feels that he is keeping up with the times, and the student willingly relaxes with disorder rather than submitting himself to the challenges of organized structure.

This brings me to a last observation, on the need to distinguish between sensory stimulation and perceptual challenge. Both are legitimate resources of the human mind, but it pays not to confuse them. Sensory stimulation vitalizes biological functions rather unspecifically. This is true for black coffee or drugs or the electrically vibrating mattresses in motel rooms. In the case of drugs, it is fairly clear what they will and will not do. Under favorable circumstances they will heighten perception, increase sensitivity, loosen connections and conventions; but essentially they provide only a meeting between the individual and himself. One receives what one potentially possesses. This was already quite clear in the days of Charles Baudelaire, one of the early devotees of hashish. He warned against the illusion that drugs introduce superpersonal gifts from the outside. Instead they make a man remain the man he is, only to an increased power. "He is subjugated," wrote Baudelaire in 1860, "but unfortunately only by himself, that is, by that part of himself which is already dominant; he wanted to be an angel, but he became an animal, a temporarily very powerful one, if we can speak of power in the case of an excessive sensitivity without any control to moderate or exploit it" (1, p. 355).

Such stimulation is different in principle from what is accomplished by perceptual challenge, where an outside situation confronts people in such a way as to mobilize their capacities to grasp, to interpret, to unravel, to improve. I am insisting on this difference because there are educational projects in which it seems to be overlooked. There are projects for centers of perceptual stimulation, pleasure domes of capriciously moving shapes and lights, dancing colors, symphonies of noises, textures to touch, and things to sniff. These expensive fantasies have, for me, the quaint aroma of nineteenth-century decadence, those refined *fin-de-siècle* orgies, which as far as I know were not held for educational purposes. They do point to an existing need, but one whose nature may be misunderstood.

How many of our children lack sensory stimulation? One might suspect that most of them receive too much. What is wrong with them may be something quite different, namely, that they are incapable of responding to perceptual challenge. The blunting of their perceptual and cognitive responses may be a defense against incomprehensible, frightening, overwhelming sensations. I am suggesting that what is needed is not more shapeless, mysterious, unrelatable sensations, but instead more perceptual challenge.

To this end, at least two conditions must be met. First, the materials to be used must possess inherent order and permit the creation of such order at a level of comprehension accessible to the child. Children cannot get a grip on what they cannot comprehend, and when they cannot comprehend they can only shut themselves off. But it is precisely this shutting off that we are trying to undo. What is needed is the experience that among visible things, there are some that can be understood after all. Second, sights of sufficient orderliness must refer visibly to something that matters, directly or indirectly, for the way the children conduct their lives. A perverted environment may have failed to teach them that the things they see can reveal facts relevant to their existence, i.e., that there is a functional relationship between what the eyes grasp and what the person must know in order to survive and to enjoy that survival. If we are not careful, we will entertain the senses with pretty displays and exercises confirming the children's suspicion that there is no connection between what there is to see and what there is to know.

A teacher of mine, a psychologist and almost an artist, used to say that the ways a tree's branches intertwine were more intelligent than the minds of most people he knew. Similarly the perceptual challenge of artwork well conceived and well understood is a natural introduction to the tasks of life and to the best ways of going about them.

## References

1. Baudelaire, Charles. "Les Paradis artificiels." In *Oeuvres complètes*. Paris: Gallimard, 1961.
2. Fontein, Jan, and Money L. Hickman. *Zen Painting and Calligraphy*. Boston: Museum of Fine Arts, 1970.
3. Malevich, Kasimir. "The Nonobjective World." In Herschel B. Chipp, ed., *Theories of Modern Art*. Berkeley and Los Angeles: University of California Press, 1968.
4. Meyer, Hannes. "Bauen." In Hans M. Wingler, *The Bauhaus*. Cambridge, Mass.: MIT Press, 1969.
5. Morris, Robert. "Notes on Sculpture, 1966." *Art Forum*, Feb. and Oct. 1966; June 1967.

# VICTOR LOWENFELD
# AND TACTILITY

FOR DECADES now, the late Victor Lowenfeld has had the distinction of being the mentor of American art education. His two books in English, *The Nature of Creative Activity* of 1939 and the textbook *Creative and Mental Growth* of 1947, formulated for American teachers the truly revolutionary principles that distinguish modern art education from that of the past.[1] It was Lowenfeld who declared that the faithful copying of models, far from being the only acceptable yardstick of excellence, hampered the unfolding of what he called "free creative expression." It was Lowenfeld who insisted with the radicalism of the true reformer that "the teacher should on no account force his particular forms of expression on the child"; and it was he who pointed out that the style of any kind of artwork must be understood and respected as the necessary product of its maker's personal disposition and needs.

So thoroughly have these principles been metabolized in educational practice that one tends to be almost unaware of their presence, to leave them unexamined, or to assume lightly that they could be thrown overboard with impunity. It is also inevitable that after Lowenfeld's death, his presence as a person, teacher, artist, and thinker, rooted in his European upbringing and thoroughly devoted to his American mission, was

First published in *Journal of Aesthetic Education*, vol. 17 (Summer 1983).

[1] Lowenfeld's book of 1939 (5) is a translation from the German. I was unable to consult either the German publication of 1960 (6), presumably Lowenfeld's original text, or the one of 1957 (8). Relevant to his and his brother Berthold's work with the blind is an early book, written in collaboration with the Viennese art historian Ludwig Münz (10).

eclipsed by the principles in his books. It seems worthwhile, therefore, to have a look at some aspects of the intellectual setting that formed this remarkable man and at the psychological and aesthetic assumptions of his time, some of which can no longer be ours. In particular, we may want to think about the paradoxical and perhaps ironical fact that our most influential educator in the field of visual art received his decisive impetus from his early work with the blind and near-blind.

Actually, this startling paradox turns out to offer the most revealing access to the ideas that led Victor Lowenfeld along his chosen path. The inability of his early students to use their eyesight in more than the most limited way drew his attention to the perceptual virtues of what he called the haptic or tactile sense. But haptic perception turned out to be more than an expedient for the visually handicapped: it seemed to suggest answers to problems that had begun to puzzle psychologists, philosophers, historians, and educators at that time. The fact is that the problems posed by the new art education must be viewed in the context of the more comprehensive challenge that was presented to Lowenfeld and his generation by the advent of modern art.

The question had arisen of how to cope with styles of art that by no stretch of leniency could be reconciled with the traditional standards of naturalistic representation. That such styles existed and that they demanded a *raison d'être* of their own could no longer be denied, but accounting for them was a puzzle for those who had been made to think of visual perception as a faithful recording of optical projections and of artistic representation as the rendering of those faithful recordings. There seemed to be no room for flagrant deviations from the norm if they could no longer be explained away as due to a lack of skill, mental imbalance, or willful impertinence.

In this precarious situation the sense of touch offered a welcome way out. Touch, an alternative avenue to the world of things, seemed to account perfectly for the qualities of those unorthodox styles of representation. Tactile percepts were devoid of the visual properties of perspective, projection, and superposition. They defined each object as a separate, independent, and complete thing, detached from the next thing, and not united with it in a coherent spatial context. By attributing the deviations from visual projection to the sense of touch, one could salvage the axiom that perception and art are instruments of faithful recording. One could also grant respectability to those unnaturalistic styles by claiming that they were as faithful to the touch experience as traditional art had been to the sense of sight.

In normal human beings haptic perception, although particularly active in the early years of life, operates from birth in union with sight, so that its contribution cannot be evaluated independently. Here, Lowenfeld's visually impaired students in Vienna seemed to offer a welcome test case. Since they could discern visual shapes only at a distance of a few centimeters, their drawings and paintings reflected experiences of the environment that were acquired almost exclusively through the sense of touch and the related kinesthetic sensations in their own bodies.

Recourse to the particular cognitive traits of tactile perception was an innovation in art theory, but it did not originate with Victor Lowenfeld. The influential Viennese art historian Alois Riegl, to whom Lowenfeld refers briefly in his major work, had pointed to the basic duality of the two sensory modes, vision and touch, and he had done so for reasons similar to Lowenfeld's. In a pioneering study that is still unavailable in English, Riegl had taken it upon himself to defend the arts and crafts of the late Roman period against the prevalent view that they were nothing better than the poor creations of the northern barbarians whose invasion had played havoc with the leftovers of antiquity (11; cf. 3, pp. 195ff). Riegl claimed that during the centuries between the reign of Constantine and that of Charlemagne the arts developed a genuine style of their own, which had to be judged by its own standards. Forty years later, Lowenfeld made a similar claim for the artwork of children.

Riegl thought of the period he was concerned with as the last of three art historical stages. In his opinion, the oldest, exemplified by the art of Egypt, had treated form essentially as two-dimensional, perceived by touch but also by vision from a close distance. At the second stage, the classical art of Greece acknowledged spatial relief, perceivable by foreshortening and by light and shadow, and to that end it combined touch experiences with vision from a "normal" viewing distance. The third period conquered full three-dimensionality through the visual conception of what things look like from afar.

For Riegl the development of artistic representation was a gradual shift from tactile to visual perception. He did not base his main argument on a dichotomy between the two sense modalities. He was concerned with a difference in principle between the worldview of antiquity as a whole and what he called the "newer," later art. Ancient man, Riegl asserted, saw his environment as made up of clearly defined and separate individual units, whereas a later style of art was based on the primacy of space, in which all things are embedded and united. He did point, however, to an affinity between exploration by touch and the conception of isolated objects and a corresponding affinity between the overall view provided by the sense of sight and the conception of primary, enveloping space.

This distinction became fundamental for the perceptual theory to which the young art educator Lowenfeld subscribed for his own purposes. Equally decisive for his approach, however, was the polemical character of Riegl's assertions. Riegl felt challenged by the prevailing misinterpretation of Byzantine art, which was commonly judged by classical standards. Even Franz Wickhoff, who with his publication of the *Vienna Genesis* had awakened his contemporaries to the beauties of Byzantine book illustrations, had described deviations from the classical style as symptoms of decay owing to *Barbarisierung*.

In opposition to such parochial imposition of particular aesthetic norms, Riegl declared that different civilizations and periods develop different styles of representation as a necessary consequence of their own worldviews and psychological needs, and that each style has to be understood and valued on its own terms. In retrospect we see how this emancipation from traditional standards reflected the contemporary turning away of modern art from naturalism. It provided an entirely new theoretical basis not only for a less prejudiced evaluation of distant periods and cultures, but also for the acceptance of the unorthodox ways of artmaking that found the public and many critics of those years so thoroughly unprepared. In fact, Wilhelm Worringer's 1908 book *Abstraction and Empathy* (15), in which he defended the geometrical style of "primitive" art as a valid alternative to naturalism and which became a manifesto of then-emerging cubism, was a direct offshoot of what Alois Riegl in his discussion of the reliefs on the Arch of Constantine had called the "crystalline beauty" of Byzantine art. (See 2 and "Wilhelm Worringer on Abstraction and Empathy," above.)

In a similar polemical mood, Victor Lowenfeld fought for the right of the art of children to be judged by its own standards. He showed educators that "it is extremely important not to use naturalistic modes of expression as the criterion of value, but to free oneself of such conceptions" (5, p. 12). What earlier authors had called "childish mistakes" were to be understood as necessary features of an equally valid style of representation, derived from an entirely legitimate way of looking at the world.

Where, however, could one find a perceptual basis for such deviant imagery? I mentioned earlier that Lowenfeld, like Riegl and other influential theorists of the time, was still caught in a narrow conception of visual experience. He could not but identify the visual world with optical images as they are projected by lenses upon the retinae of the eyes or film in a camera. Tactile perception, however, seemed to account for the formal characteristics of the pictures produced by Lowenfeld's visually impaired pupils. There was a problem: the style of representation exhibited by the children who had to rely on their haptic sensations was found in the work of normally sighted children as well—it was a universal trait of all early art. Hence Lowenfeld's conclusion that art begins always and everywhere as a reflection of haptic experience, and that during adolescence there occurs a division between individuals who persist in relying on their sense of touch and others who orient themselves increasingly by vision. From experiments that Lowenfeld published in 1945, he concluded that among his subjects 47 percent were clearly visual, 23 percent clearly haptic.

His assertion that the differences he observed in his work as an art teacher and also in his experiments derived from the dominance of either the one or the other sense modality was based, of course, on little more than hypothetical inference. However, a brilliant group of studies carried out independently by the New York psychologist Herman A. Witkin and his collaborators and published in 1954 confirmed the difference between visual and haptic behavior, although they contradicted Lowenfeld's main developmental thesis. These studies also led to different psychological interpretations of the two types.

Here one must recognize that the term *haptic* applies to two quite different avenues of perception, both of which played a part in Lowenfeld's thinking. Etymologically the term derives from the Greek word for the sense of touch. In this limited sense it referred, for example, to the "haptical apparatus" with which psychophysical experiments were performed in the Leipzig laboratory of Wilhelm Wundt. It is the tactile sense by which receptors at the surface of the body, especially at the finger tips, explore the shape of physical objects. The other sense is kinesthesis, the awareness of tensions inside the body, made possible by neural receptors in the muscles, tendons, and joints. In the arts, sculptors rely strongly on touch, whereas dancers and actors depend on kinesthesis. The Witkin studies were designed to explore how kinesthetic sensations, as opposed to visual orientation, determine people's judgments of spatial verticality. When someone is called upon to decide whether he is standing straight or tilted or whether or not a picture on the wall is hanging upright, one can do so either visually, by referring to the framework of verticals and horizontals in the surrounding space, or kinesthetically, by referring to the tensions of imbalance and balance controlling the body's response to the gravitational pull. Witkin's group discovered that the responses of individuals show a persistent ratio along the scale between extreme reliance on vision and equally extreme reliance on kinesthesis.

The differences observed in experiments in which visual orientation was pitted against kinesthesis turned out to belong in a much broader psychological category, which Witkin defined as the difference between "field-dependent" and "field-independent" persons, i.e., between people who relied on cues deriving from the surrounding field and those who paid little attention to the standards suggested by their environment. Field-dependence corresponded to reliance on vision, which is an outer-directed sensory modality; field-independence went with kinesthesis, which involves concentration on one's own inner self. Individuals who relied on the external framework of their visual surroundings were found to behave similarly in other perceptual tasks as well as in their social relations, whereas those who responded primarily to sensations inside their own bodies were similarly independent of external contexts, social norms, etc. In direct contradiction of Lowenfeld's interpretation, young children were shown statistically to be strongly field-dependent, i.e., visually oriented, and to shift from age eight through adolescence toward "haptic" field-independence. Women were more field-dependent than men.

The important question arose whether the differences derive from an inherent, specific disposition of certain people toward visual rather than haptic perception, which is then generalized to apply to other attitudes of theirs as well, or whether a primary general disposition toward field-dependence versus field-independence takes hold of the corresponding sense modalities wherever they apply. While among psychologists there seems to be no definitive answer to this question even today, Lowenfeld clearly believed in the priority of the perceptual propensities.

How are we to cope with the contradictory findings in this field? First of all, it would seem that the two components of haptic behavior, the tactile and the kinesthetic, although obviously related, should not be united under the same heading, if only because they stand for opposite ways of responding to the environment. The sense of touch is clearly field-dependent. It is extroverted, outer-directed like vision. When psychologists describe sensory-motor behavior as the biologically earliest way of obtaining knowledge, they have in mind the tactile activities of the mouth, limbs, etc. The infant explores things in its environment by touch, in cooperation with sight. Kinesthesis, on the other hand, is essentially inner-directed, introverted, and therefore field-independent. It makes a person withdraw his attention from the environment and concentrate on the signals within. Witkin identified the early field-dependent stage with visual dominance because his experiments did not test the equally relevant contribution of the sense of touch. Lowenfeld called haptic behavior "subjective," i.e., field-independent, because he concentrated on kinesthesis and forgot how many of the characteristics he was describing must be due to tactile perception if they are to be called haptic at all.

The sense of touch is what Lowenfeld must have had in mind when he asserted that haptically inclined persons in their paintings and sculpture tend to start out from the parts of the objects they represent and put them together synthetically. Riegl had suggested a similar approach. He said that the peoples of antiquity conceived of the world as made up of tightly cohering discrete material units. This conception was assumed to stay in opposition to visual appearance. The eye, says Riegl, "shows us things merely as colored surfaces and not as impenetrable material individuals; vision is precisely the mode of perception that presents us the things of the outer world as a chaotic conglomeration" (11, p. 17). This one-sided description arises from the equating of visual experience with optical projection, an equation which led Lowenfeld to believe that whenever drawings or paintings neglected perspective modifications of shape and size and ignored overlap, they necessarily derived from tactile experience.

We can no longer maintain, however, that vision is based on momentary projections. We know that the totality of constantly changing aspects is integrated from the very beginning in the perception of self-contained and fully three-dimensional objects of constant shape and size. This normal conception, every bit as visual as it is tactile, is manifest in early forms of art everywhere. It gives way to naturalistic perspective styles only under special cultural conditions. Therefore, many of the differences in pictorial work that Lowenfeld attributes to haptic versus visual dominance are actually due to early versus later stages of development in the arts of our particular culture.

There is no denying, of course, that haptic sensations can contribute importantly to the character of visual images and to their representation in the arts. Tactile experience does help confirm the objective shape of the things we see. Similarly, the tensions we experience in our bodies when we stretch or bend reverberate in our way of perceiving things that are twisted out of their norm shape or subjected to pressure. Testimony to this effect can be found occasionally in artists' writings. Thus Ernst Ludwig Kirchner writes in a letter to a young painter, Nele van de Velde: "You said you wanted to make drawings of your sister bathing. If you help her with it, if you lather her back, her arms and legs, etc., the feeling of form will directly and instinctively transfer to you. That, you see, is the way one learns" (4, p. 38).

To acknowledge the assistance of haptic perception, however, is not to say that haptically inclined individuals ignore all visual experience, as Lowenfeld insists they do. He forgets that the paintings and drawings of such individuals are after all visual works. While it is true that congenitally blind persons work by touch alone, even his visually impaired pupils had to use what little eyesight they possessed to draw and paint their pictures. This is all the more true of people with normal vision whom Lowenfeld classified as haptic. Nevertheless, he insists, "visually minded persons have a tendency to transform kinesthetic and tactile into visual experiences. Haptically minded individuals are, however, completely content with the tactile or kinesthetic modality itself" (9, p. 107). Yet it seems obvious that even if the perceptual experience determining the work of such persons was indeed entirely haptic, they would still have to cope with the considerable task of translating their nonvisual observations into visual shapes. How can this be done? How is it done?

Here, Lowenfeld lets us down by relying on what he calls "symbols." He says that the geometrical shapes used in early drawings are not depictions, but "mere symbols." Permit me to quote here a passage from my *Art and Visual Perception* (1, p. 164):

> There are explanations that are little more than wordplay, such as the assertion that children's pictures look the way they do because they are not copies but "symbols" of real things. The term "symbol" is used so indiscriminately nowadays that it can be applied whenever one thing stands for another. For this reason it has no explanatory value and should be avoided. There is no way of telling whether such a statement is right, wrong, or no theory at all.

As an example let me cite the so-called baseline used by children and other early artists to represent the floor, the ground, or a table top. Lowenfeld realizes that such a horizontal line is not a direct portrayal of either a visual or a haptic experience. To call it "just a symbol," however, implies that the line merely stands for what it represents but has nothing in common with its perceptual reality. This is far from the truth. Rather, in the medium of two-dimensional drawing, the baseline is the exact equivalent of what surfaces like a floor or a tabletop are in three-dimensional space. The line in such a drawing supports the human figures, trees, and houses in the second dimension just as the horizontal ground plane does in the third. The perceived world and the picture are connected by what gestalt psychologists call isomorphism; i.e., the two different spatial realms have analogous structural properties. Similarly, features such as the "folding-over" of upright shapes and the "x-ray" pictures of what is inside bodies or houses can be accounted for only if they are treated as two-dimensional equivalents of physical objects rather than as mishandled nature.

I am insisting on this point because I am convinced that we are dealing here with a paradigmatic shift that has still to be accomplished, a shift that will change our thinking about artistic representation as fundamentally as did the realization in Lowenfeld's time that art need not be a rendering of visual projections. We must realize now that the counterthesis, defended by Riegl, Worringer, Lowenfeld, and others, can be made plausible only if we understand that non-naturalistic artworks, such as those of children, early cultures, or the "modern" styles of our twentieth century, come about not as more or less faithful copies of visual or haptic experiences, but as structural equivalents of those experiences, executed with the means of some particular medium. A landscape painted by a child is not a real group of houses and trees distorted and bent into flatness, but a translation of the landscape's relevant features into the language of the second dimension. (See "Inverted Perspective and the Axiom of Realism," above.)

One further aspect of Lowenfeld's teachings should be mentioned in this connection, namely, his insistence on the subjectivity of art. Subjectivity was the quality he cherished most in non-naturalistic art, and he identified it with haptic perception and with expression. To be sure, the assertion that art, as distinguished from science, is strongly subjective has been a commonplace of aesthetic thinking since the Romantics. A closer look, however, reveals that the concept of subjectivity is hardly limited to a single meaning. Moreover, there is no simple relation between subjectivity, haptic perception, and expression. In fact, Riegl, for example, identified tactile perception with objectivity because the sense of touch reveals the physical shape of things as it "really" is, whereas visual projections convey highly subjective images, in need of much interpretation.

Lowenfeld believed that aesthetic expression was the privileged contribution of haptic experience. It was subjective in the sense of the theory of empathy, which held that observers project their kinesthetic experiences upon the objects they perceive.[2] We must keep in mind, however, that empathic projection, although subjective in its reliance upon the resources of the self, is entirely objective in focusing its attention upon the character of the observed objects or actions. In Lowenfeld's thinking, this aspect of empathic projection was overshadowed by a differently oriented subjectivity, which he described as "ego-linkage." In this view, deviations from what he called "the pure schema" of children's drawings are caused by the child's personal needs. The features of the model objects that children select and emphasize were supposed to derive their importance not simply from what the children consider relevant to the things depicted but from what matters to the children about those things. Attention is geared not so much to the nature of the object as to the needs of the subject.

This sort of interpretation was in the air in the days of expressionist art. It was then a favorite way of talking about expression. For example, Peter Selz writes at the beginning of his book on German expressionist painting, "Emphasis has shifted from the outer world of empirical experience to the inner world that a man can test only against himself" (12, p. 3). He asserts that the subjective personality of the artist had assumed control. It is true that the artists of that period insisted on their right to represent things as they saw them. But here again such subjectivity did not imply that the artists had withdrawn their attention from the human beings and landscapes and cities they depicted. We know from what they said and wrote how passionately they cared about their subject matter. And in fact, had they confined their attention to their own broodings and stirrings, the validity of their work would have been severely limited.

A similar consideration must hold for art education. Pioneers like Victor Lowenfeld have taught art teachers once and for all that every child should be free to represent the things of his world in his own way. It is also true that children's imagery is influenced by what happens to capture their imagination. This, however, is quite different from trying to steer them toward an egocentric approach that would distort their conception of the world by a continuous emphasis on what matters to the child's own self.

---

[2] The theory of empathy, developed by Theodor Lipps, strongly influenced the thinking of Wölfflin, Worringer, and others. See (15) and the essay "Wilhelm Worringer on Abstraction and Empathy," above.

As we look back at the story of Victor Lowenfeld's formation and influence, we realize that he arrived in America at the right time. An emphasis on creative learning had reached educators through the teachings of John Dewey; but art classes were still largely dominated by the traditional techniques of "correct" drawing. Furthermore, art teaching in schools was just beginning to emerge as a professional specialty and needed principles that would enable the work to be conducted in accord with the creed of progressive education. Here Lowenfeld entered the scene with the enthusiasm of the young artist and teacher, eager to apply to the "country of unlimited possibilities" the ideas and experiences he had nurtured in the narrow intensity of his Viennese practice. His individualism, his insistence on freedom and spontaneity, and even the subjectivistic cast of his version of self-expression appealed to similarly attuned American educators. I have tried to show how some of the more theoretical aspects of his approach derived from the philosophical and psychological ideas active in the prewar Europe that had shaped him. Absorbed, transformed, amended, and partly forgotten, these ideas continue to reverberate in present theory and practice.

## References

1. Arnheim, Rudolf. *Art and Visual Perception*. New version. Berkeley and Los Angeles: University of California Press, 1974.
2. ———. "Wilhelm Worringer and Modern Art." *Michigan Quarterly Review*, vol. 20 (Spring 1980), pp. 67–71.
3. Gombrich, E. H. *The Sense of Order*. Ithaca, N.Y.: Cornell University Press, 1979.
4. Kirchner, Ernst Ludwig. *Briefe an Nele*. Munich: Piper, 1961.
5. Lowenfeld, Victor. *The Nature of Creative Activity*. New York: Harcourt Brace, 1939.
6. ———. *Vom Wesen des schöpferischen Gestaltens*. Frankfurt: Europäische Verlagsanstalt, 1960.
7. ———. *Creative and Mental Growth*. New York: Macmillan, 1947.
8. ———. *Die Kunst des Kindes*. Frankfurt, 1957.
9. ———. "Tests for Visual and Haptical Attitudes." *American Journal of Psychology*, vol. 58 (1945), pp. 100–111.
10. Münz, Ludwig, and Victor Lowenfeld. *Plastische Arbeiten Blinder*. Brünn, 1934.
11. Riegl, Alois. *Die spätrömische Kunstindustrie*. Vienna: Staatsdruckerei, 1901.
12. Selz, Peter. *German Expressionist Painting*. Berkeley and Los Angeles: University of California Press, 1957.

13. Witkin, Herman A., et al. *Personality through Perception*. New York: Harper, 1954.
14. Witkin, Herman A. "The Perception of the Upright." *Scientific American* (Feb. 1959).
15. Worringer, Wilhelm. *Abstraktion und Einfühlung*. Munich: Piper, 1911. Eng.: *Abstraction and Empathy*. New York: International Universities Press, 1953.

# ART AS THERAPY

THE PRACTICAL approach of the therapist does not take off from art but starts with the needs of patients, with human beings in trouble. Any means that promises success a healer will welcome: medication, the exercise and repair of the body, clinical conversation, hypnosis—why not art? Received with hesitation and some suspicion, the practitioner of the arts enters the scene. He must prove his worth not only by practical success, but also by persuasive theoretical argument. He is expected to describe the principles by which art claims to be beneficial.

To meet this demand we must consider the nature of the arts and be on the lookout for properties that might serve or hamper the purposes of therapy. Such a look at the nature of the arts and their present status reveals two influential features relevant to therapy, namely the democratization of the arts and the hedonistic tradition in Western aesthetics.

In our particular culture, art has an aristocratic past. It used to be produced for an elite of princes and churchmen by expert craftsmen, who acquired during the Renaissance the additional accreditation of being gifted geniuses. Art was mostly for the happy few. It is hardly more than a century since the development of democracy led to the claim that the arts exist for everybody, and this not only in the sense that they should be made accessible to every citizen's eyes and ears. More important was the growing conviction that everybody is indeed qualified to profit from the arts and possesses the inherent ability to produce artwork. This rev-

Based on a lecture presented at the annual conference of the American Art Therapy Association, held in November 1980 in Kansas City, and published in *The Arts in Psychotherapy*, vol. 7 (1980).

olutionary belief furnished a new basis for art education. It also paved the way for the appreciation of folk art and so-called primitive art; and, a few decades ago, it fostered the idea that artistic activity can inspire and revitalize the average person in need of mental help in ways that had been considered the privilege of artists.

This new belief in the usefulness of the arts had to contend with a recent European tradition which held that art distinguishes itself precisely by being useless. When the arts lost their function of conveying religious and monarchic ideas, a new middle-class mentality reduced them to means of enjoyable decoration. The corresponding philosophy asserted that art exists for nothing but pleasure's sake. Any psychologist should have responded to this hedonistic approach right away by pointing out that pleasure in itself affords no explanation, for pleasure is nothing but a signal that some need of the organism is being fulfilled. One must then ask: What are those needs? Sigmund Freud made the principal first attempts to answer the question for the individual person. Other psychologists and sociologists followed.

My own bias has it that the arts fulfill, first of all, a cognitive function. All knowledge we acquire about our environment comes to us through the senses; but the images we receive through our eyes and ears and through our sense of touch are far from easily readable diagrams of the nature and function of things. A tree is a confusing sight, and so is a bicycle, or a crowd of people in motion. Sensory perception, therefore, cannot limit itself to simply recording the images that hit the receptor organs. Perception must look for structure. In fact, perception *is* the discovery of structure. Structure tells us what the components of things are and by what sort of order they interact. A painting or sculpture is the result of such an inquiry into structure. It is a clarified, intensified, expressive counterpart of the artist's perception.

Even more important for our present purpose is the fact that all perception is symbolic. Since all structural qualities are generalities, we perceive individual appearances as *kinds* of things, *kinds* of behavior. The individual percept stands symbolically for a whole category of things. Thus when poets or painters or the art therapist's clients perceive and represent a tree as struggling to reach the light or a volcano as a fearful aggressor, they rely on the normal capacity of perception to descry generality of wide significance in any specific case.

We remember further that the significant features perceived in our environment are embodied in such expressive qualities as shape, color, texture, movement. Therefore, even when the physical objects of the environment are left behind and only the shapes, colors, etc., are retained, these "abstract" appearances can by themselves interpret relevant behavior symbolically. This makes it possible for the therapist to find basic attitudes of his clients reflected not only in the recognizable objects presented in their artwork, but also in abstract patterns. For the same reason, of course, the abstract shapes of music are received as statements on ways of being and acting.

All perception, then, is symbolic. Strictly speaking, one never deals with unique individuality. One deals with a particular thing or person as a kind of being, in accordance with the general qualities conveyed. This basic human way of handling experience is supplemented by another ability, namely that of trying out and replacing reality situations with stand-ins. Somewhat like the scientists who in their experiments test the responses of factors relevant to a class of situations, we all enact fictional replicas of situations that concern us. These trial runs may be mere "thought experiments," in which one enacts in imagination the answer to the question: "What would happen if . . . ?" Such fictions can also take tangible shape, as in the theatrical improvisations of the psychodrama, in story telling, and in the paintings and sculptures done in art therapy. And it is well known that the creators of such images are not obliged to respect the objective facts, as scientists must in their experiments, but can shape them to accord with their own needs.

To a remarkable extent such enactments are accepted as substitutes for the real thing. The performances and creations in the therapist's art room are so much more than mere fantasies, so much more also than mere manifestations of a personal attitude. It is indeed remarkable that when a patient confronts the image of a fearsome father or dares in imagination to possess a desired love object, the performance often has some of the effect of having been actually carried out. The patient really *has* braved the tyrant father and possessed the beautiful woman or man. I believe we still tend to treat such so-called substitute behavior with an undeserved contempt; we think of the people who practice it as letting themselves be fooled by the cheaply obtained figments of their corrupt imagination. We tend to consider physical reality the only kind of reality that counts. Actually, human beings are essentially mental rather than physical. Physical things affect us as mental experiences. After all, a physical victory or defeat counts in the last analysis only by what it does to the minds of the persons concerned. The loss of liberty, the loss of property, even physical injuries, come to people as mental sensations.

Since we do respect the visions of artists or mystics as valid facts of reality, we should go further and acknowledge that when we try to orient a person toward the so-called reality principle, we are not drawing him away from "mere" mental reality to the "true" facts of physical reality, but are making him adapt his mental images to conditions likely to be confirmed by what future experience has in store for him. The validity of such imagery should be tested with the utmost seriousness, not only because it is symptomatic but also because its consequences are as tangible as those of events occurring in the so-called real world.

This has a bearing on a related subject, namely the importance of quality, that is, artistic excellence, in the work produced by patients. Several art therapists have insisted that the artwork should be as good as possible. Such insistence derives not from a dogmatic demand for high aesthetic achievement for its own sake, but from the well-grounded conviction that a person's best work bears therapeutic fruit not obtainable from lesser efforts. First of all, quality is directly related to the reality value of art. Good works of art tell the truth. To be sure, this is the very opposite of what Freud asserted in his references to art. He thought of good form as a mere sugar coating, intended to make the receiver accept the fulfillment of instinctual wishes, which is provided by the content of the work. This theory has always seemed to me entirely unconvincing. I see no need for such sugar coating. We have no aversion to wish fulfillment as such. We are perfectly willing to accept the ideal hero, the victory of virtue, and the defeat of evil when they are offered in good works of art. We do so not because we are bribed by pretty shape and pleasant outcome to accept wish dreams but because the good artist proves to us that those desirable outcomes can be quite true to life. Under circumstances that show the human condition "in its pure state," virtue is in fact rewarded and evil punished, for the reason that virtue is nothing else but what enhances well-being and evil is what disturbs it. Mediocre works are rejected when they obtain wish fulfillment at the price of distorting the truth. When the good are cheaply virtuous and improbably successful, when the evilness of the villain is unrelieved and the seductiveness of the love object a mere figment of lustful fantasy, we object because we cannot afford to have reality betrayed.

Similarly, in the judgment of the art therapist the quality of a patient's work is directly related to whether or not it presents a credible reality. This is true even for the weird artwork of some gifted psychotics, as we know from the publications of Prinzhorn (2) and Bader and Navratil (1).

The destructive power of psychosis can liberate the patient's imagination from traditional standards; and some crazily stylized visions illuminate human experience with brutal starkness.

The reality status of artwork depends neither on its particular style nor on its level of sophistication. I referred earlier to our "democratic" appreciation of early forms of art. This approach allows us to see that the requirements of good quality can be fulfilled even in very simple products. We look for presentations shaped by the impact of direct experience, not fossilized by mechanically applied schemata. What counts is that experiences be made visible by shapes and colors or whatever other medium in such a way that they appear with the greatest strength and clarity. Form is not a hedonistic pacifier, but the necessary means to the end of conveying effective statements.

To be sure, a majority of patients in art therapy are handicapped by the sad state of much art education. Lack of training, lack of confidence, dependence on inferior standards, prevent the average citizen from developing his natural gift for artistic expression. It seems to me that art therapists cannot afford to ignore this sorry state of affairs. They must not believe that for their particular purposes the quality of the patient's work is irrelevant. Aesthetic quality is nothing but the means by which artistic statements attain their goal. Not only should the conception be genuine, it should also be carried to the best possible realization, because through its clarity and strength the work of art exerts its power, even on its own maker.

In this respect, we make no distinction between the great art of the happy few and the modest products of the therapist's art room; for when we distinguish great art from its opposite, we must point in two different directions. On the one hand, a scale of decreasing originality, complexity, wisdom, and strength leads from the great works to the simplest ones; but even folk songs or young children's paintings have their own level of integrity and perfection and serve the well-being of the human mind. On the other hand, great art stands in opposition to the devastation of artistic value wrought by the commercialism of the entertainment industry and the mass media. This pollution prevents the minds of viewers from making contact with their own genuine experience and from developing their own productive abilities. It is therefore the most dangerous obstacle to the art therapist's endeavors.

When art is kept free of such pernicious coercion, it exerts an uncompromising logic by which it compels its maker to shape the facts according to their intrinsic nature, regardless of what his personal desires and fears might prefer. Art can present the facts so unmistakably that they often state their demands with more power than they do in daily experience. I remember among my college students a dancer, a gifted and intelligent young woman, who at the time was struggling with contradictions between the religious beliefs in which she had been brought up and certain practices of the religious authorities to which she objected. In the midst of this conflict, whose resolution required much courage, she decided to do a piece of solo choreography to be called "The Dance of the Grand Inquisitor." In this dance, forced by the character of the figure that shaped itself in her imagination and quite against her conscious intention and her traditional standards, she portrayed a harsh, demonic dogmatism, which made it inevitable for her to face some of the facts she had been reluctant to touch outside the dance. There can be little doubt that her integrity as a dancer helped her to mature as a person.

Let me conclude with the suggestion that art therapy, far from deserving to be treated as a stepchild of the arts, can be considered a model that might help lead the arts back to a more productive approach. It seems to me undeniable that lately the general practice of our painters, sculptors, and other artists has suffered from a lack of genuine impulse. Playing around with purely formal sensations and indulging in the superficial attractions of violence and eroticism have reduced the average quality of what we are being shown in galleries and museums. There seems to be talent but little purpose, little commitment.

Under such conditions the applied arts should take the lead, and art therapy is an applied art. They should show by their example that the arts, to sustain their vigor, must serve substantial human needs. Those needs are often more conspicuous among the sick, and more conspicuous also are the benefits sick people receive from the arts. By demonstrating what it can do for the distressed, art reminds us what it is meant to do for everybody.

## References

1. Bader, Alfred, and Leo Navratil. *Zwischen Wahn und Wirklichkeit*. Lucerne: Bucher, 1976.
2. Prinzhorn, Hans. *Artistry of the Mentally Ill*. New York: Springer, 1972.

# Part VII

---

# STYLE AS A GESTALT
# PROBLEM

As LONG as a culture conducts its affairs in a reasonably uncontested way, questions on the nature of its style will hardly arise. Constant factors of the situation may go unnoticed and will therefore pose no problems. Only when alternative behaviors invite comparison and when instead of consistent uniformity reigning a variety of tendencies struggle for supremacy are thinkers driven to ask about the kind of base needed for optimal functioning and the conditions that support or threaten it. Our own culture seems to have entered such a critical phase. The music historian Friedrich Blume, for example, calls the nineteenth century "the deeply torn century," characterized by "the abundance of contradictions that constitute it—an image that is all the more shocking because it follows a classical age of music, distinguished by a clearly articulated uniformity of its aesthetic intentions" (9, p. 226). And the twentieth century has overwhelmed us with an ever more accelerated succession of radically different ways of producing visual art. This perturbing spectacle has raised questions about the necessary conditions for a productive style.

## Styles as Modes

The questions are urgent because they have come to involve not only the quality of art products but also the quality of the producing agents themselves; and this aspect of the problem is new. In many cultures, choices of the best way to handle a particular artistic task were known and quite

First published in *Journal of Aesthetics and Art Criticism*, vol. 39 (Spring 1981).

acceptable, but those choices operated well within an established tradition. In classical antiquity, Vitruvius demanded that as a matter of propriety the choice between the Doric, Ionian, and Corinthian orders should depend on the character of the divinity for whom a temple was intended. Jan Bialostocki mentions in his influential book *Style and Iconography* that in classical rhetoric, the grand style of discourse was distinguished from the intermediate and the simple style (6, p. 13). Somewhat similarly in Chinese and Japanese calligraphy, different purposes were served by the block-letter-like simplicity of the *kaisho* style, the more softly rounded *gyosho*, and the fluid and spontaneous cursive of the *sosho* (13). Closer to our own past, Nicolas Poussin in a letter to one of his patrons, the Chevalier de Chantelou, pointed to the modes of Greek music and asserted that paintings, too, had to be composed in different modes, in keeping with the particular character of their subject. With reference to Poussin's letter, Bialostocki has asserted that in many instances differences attributed to style are actually differences in mode, i.e., explainable by the particular character of the subject matter as well as by the social setting and patron for which they were intended (6, p. 18; see also 4, pp. 306–10). He pointed out that in the nineteenth century, for example, certain styles of the past, such as the Classicist or the Gothic, became modal precedents, suitably invoked for particular purposes, and that for this reason even the various forms of Romantic expression might best be described in terms of modal rather than stylistic differences.

Modes of representation, dictated by their purpose, were thought to be independent of the character of their makers. Poussin's point was that the particular manner he selected for a painting should not be attributed to his own attitude. He needed this defense because by his time it was becoming evident that art was not only a craftsman's technique for making pictures and statues correctly, but also a manifestation of the artist's personality. It had been obvious already in Michelangelo's work that the changes in his style over time were due not to variations in subject matter or his patrons' tastes, but to the ripening of his own thinking and feeling. This became increasingly true for later artists; and when in our own time a Picasso could switch from manner to manner without effort, the feat could no longer be accounted for simply as a craftsman's skillful juggling act. Style as manifestation of its creator's personality and social setting became a syndrome by which to judge the nature and quality of the entire culture. A generation worried by its "identity crisis" was driven to inquire about the conditions that influence styles and make them prevail or recede. In the narrower precinct of the arts, style became one of the prerequisites of good quality. No wonder, then, that we have statements on the nature of style by major art historians as well as by philosophers and psychologists.

## Problems with Current Views of Style

There were also more specifically professional reasons for worrying about style. Art historians became increasingly dissatisfied with the traditional model of art history as a linear sequence of self-contained periods, each characterized by a persistent set of traits and having a datable beginning and end. As more became known about the actual complexity of the historical facts, it became necessary to make allowance for all sorts of overlaps, exceptions, mavericks, subdivisions, and displacements in time. The neat boundaries between one style and the next became muddy and controversial. Erwin Panofsky opened his book on the Renaissance and renascences in Western art with the sentence: "Modern scholarship has become increasingly sceptical of periodization" (14). But despite the messy appearance of the picture emerging from research, the underlying paradigm stood and stands unchanged. The practice of using styles as rubrics to identify a certain period of time as Romanesque or a certain individual as Cubist continues to this day.

It occurs to me that the fundamental problems raised by this state of affairs might be approached with the principles of gestalt theory. The problems of style concern structure, and gestalt theory, together with various attempts at structuralism, has discussed structure with much theoretical and empirical precision. I shall rely in part on principles already formulated in the gestalt literature; but I shall also propose certain extensions of the theory, which might find their place eventually in that literature. Before I do so, however, some further aspects of the problems awaiting such treatment should be spelled out here.

## The Constancy of Styles

First of all, style is an intellectual concept derived from myriad perceptual observations. This is true for style in general as well as for any particular style. It is well, therefore, to make clear whether one is talking about the concept or its perceptual source. As a mental construct, a style, like all concepts, is constant "until further notice." Someone's concept of, say, Mannerism may be modified from time to time, but at each point it must have a constant meaning for it to be usable as an instrument of discourse. Thus when Meyer Schapiro defines style as "the constant form—and sometimes the constant elements, qualities, and expression— in the art of an individual or a group," his statement is unassailable as long as it refers to style as an intellectual construct (15, p. 287). Controversy arises when constancy is attributed to the referent of the concept, that is, its factual counterpart. In the traditional model of art history to which I referred, constancy is considered a necessary condition of style. Skeptics might ask: In what ways can styles be described as constant?

What are the criteria of constancy? If one were to insist that to be called "constant" a style had to remain unchanged in all its properties, we would have to concede that no constant style has ever been known to exist. One can loosen the requirement by determining which properties are essential and then finding out whether or not these essentials remain constant. Similarly, if one thinks of a style not as a sum of attributes but as a structure, one can find out whether that structure, rather than the sum of the parts, remains unchanged. Even then, however, there are problems. Are we prepared to limit the style of an artist to what remains constant as his early works give way to his middle and late ones? And if we allow for the distinction between early and late style, how much change can we allow and still speak of "a" style?

Remember here that concepts of style can be arrived at in two ways, namely deductively or inductively. Arnold Hauser asks whether Wölfflin's well-known principles should be considered a priori categories (10, p. 140). He answers in the negative, and with good reason, because otherwise Wölfflin's principles would be raised to the status of generative agents, whose power would have to derive from some general condition inherent in the nature of man or the nature of art. For example, Tzvetan Todorov, as quoted by Ann Banfield, distinguishes between historical and theoretical genres in literature. The latter are deduced from a theoretical order, which describes the number of possible genres as chemistry's periodic table describes the number of possible elements (11, p. 184). Again, J. A. Schmoll gen. Eisenwerth suggests that once the principle of stylistic pluralism is accepted, one could do justice to it by describing a historical period as a "polygonal tension field," in which each individual phenomenon would be characterized by a particular configuration of certain constitutive categories (9, p. 18).

This might sound unduly scholastic unless the "a priori" categories can be shown to derive from constant properties of the instrument and the human agent. Half a century ago I tried to derive the possibilities of the new media of film, radio, and television—media then in their infancy or not yet in existence—from an analysis of their technical characteristics (1, 2). In principle, such a deductive procedure might indeed predict the kinds of style a medium could develop.

## Historical Definitions

More commonly, concepts of styles are derived from inductive observation. But here we run into a peculiar problem. Aesthetic style is the only means we possess for classifying art objects as *art* objects. Now generally when we characterize objects by their properties, we identify those properties independently. We can describe cherries by their redness if we know what red is. But if in the same breath we define redness by what cherries are, we are in trouble. The threat of such circular reasoning is precisely what confronts us in the arts. We call the aesthetic qualities of certain historical groups of works Surrealistic, and then use this cluster of traits to decide who and what belongs under the heading Surrealism. Of course, one can standardize a style's constituents by fiat, as in the manifestos of a Breton or a Marinetti, but such programs are themselves products of style rather than concepts usable for scholarly classification.

In search of independent identification, art historians often define styles by the political or cultural periods in which they flourished. The art of the Sung dynasty is described as a style. But there is no *a priori* reason why all artwork of a 300-year period should conform to a particular style. To investigate whether there was such a style, one cannot, without begging the question, define the Sung style as the kind of art done under the Sung emperors. The same is true for geographically oriented style categories, such as Venetian or Florentine art. Least promising is the identification of style by calendar years. Whereas there are reasons to expect a kinship among manifestations of social, cultural, and aesthetic tendencies, no such relation can be expected from the contents of the shells of chronological time. Time, by itself, is no causal agent. In fact, when we speak of the fifteenth century in Italy as the Quattrocento, we are smuggling aesthetic connotations into a purportedly temporal concept.[1]

---

[1] In an early paper, the psychologist Kurt Lewin discussed the relation between "types" of phenomena and their embodiments in empirical practice and observed that in art history there were attempts, e.g., by Paul Frankl, to distinguish the concept "Baroque" as a historically and geographically confined group of objects from "Baroque" as a timeless type of style (12).

## Hopeless Complexity

The predicament would not be serious if styles were compact, unitary entities. It is true that the great styles looked that way when viewed at low magnification. The disturbing chaos seemed to be limited to the most recent two centuries. The more closely art historians examined the past, however, the more clearly those old monoliths were revealed as complex combinations of strata, whose presence was not simply related to particular times and places. Examples accumulate everywhere. Hauser speaks of the "open question which of the various tendencies manifested in Italy at the time of Raphael's death is to be considered the most typical and the most relevant. The classical, the mannerist, and the early baroque styles persisted and flourished side by side; none of them could be called antiquated, none premature" (10, p. 158). And Panofsky concludes that, paradoxically, "the acme of medieval classicism was reached within the general framework of the Gothic style, much as the acme of seventeenth-century classicism, as represented by Poussin, was reached within the general framework of the Baroque, and that of late eighteenth- and early nineteenth-century classicism, as represented by Flaxman, David, or Asmus Carstens, within the general framework of 'Romantic sensibility'" (14, p. 68). It also became evident that the greater the artist, the less readily the personal style of his work could be identified with a general style of his time. In fact, it was not easy to find any artist at all whose work could be summarized satisfactorily as that of, say, an Impressionist or a Cubist.

The complications caused by the now prevailing approach remind one of the epicycles of the Ptolemaic solar system. Clinging to the traditional model means putting up with intolerable complications. At a symposium on the concept of style recently edited by Berel Lang, the art historians sounded defeatist. Since most of the trouble with style arises in the time dimension, George Kubler proposed to limit style to an extension in space, i.e., to "a description of nondurational, synchronous situations composed of related events"—which, it seems to me, would be like trying to analyze a piece of music solely by a few vertical sections through the staves of the score (11, p. 127). Svetlana Alpers has suggested a hardly less radical solution. She wants to avoid speaking of style altogether and therefore insists, for example, "on teaching Dutch art of the seventeenth century rather than northern baroque" (11, p. 95). But the categories available for the description of paintings as art are nothing but the categories of style, and unless one wishes to present Dutch art as a jumble of unrelated pictures, the problem of characterizing it remains.

## Objects versus Fields of Forces

Rather than abandon ship, it would seem sensible to look for a different paradigm, and one is in fact available. Perhaps the most radical change that has occurred in the history of theoretical thinking is the switch from the atomistic conception of the world as an assembly of circumscribed things to that of a world of forces acting in the dimension of time. Best known from the theories of modern physics, these forces are found to organize themselves in fields, interacting, grouping, competing, fusing, and separating. Compact solids no longer constitute the primary medium; they become the secondary result of special conditions that set up boundaries in the flow of space-time events and create stably encased things. In such a world, the simultaneous occurrence of a variety of events is the rule rather than the exception. Change is more normal than constancy, and a linear sequence of firm entities is unlikely to occur. At the same time, this new model lends itself to theoretical analysis just as much as the one it replaces.

Gestalt theory can provide the methodology for such a dynamic approach to structure. It developed early in our century as an outgrowth of the dynamic conception just mentioned. A gestalt is not an array of self-contained elements, but a configuration of forces interacting in a field. Since this approach deals with structure, it eliminates a number of pseudodichotomies, some of which are pertinent here. Constancy and change, for example, are incompatible only as long as the whole is defined as the sum of the parts; whereas gestalt theory can study the conditions that make a structure remain constant although the vehicle for it undergoes changes. The theory can also predict the conditions under which a change of context will alter the structure of a given set of elements. It suggests, for example, that there is no necessary contradiction between the way an artist views his own work and the different style his work displays when considered in the context of the whole period. Nor is it unexpected that a given work will reveal a different style when seen as a part of an artist's entire *oeuvre*. Changes in range often change the appropriate way of viewing a given structure, and such different views can all be equally and objectively correct.

Gestalt theory also shows that the methodological distinction between individuality and the character of a group is false. Individuality is perceivable only as a structure, and a structure is independent of the number of cases to which it refers. To interpret an individual work means to deal with the structure of its style—a procedure no different from dealing with the style of a whole group of works or artists.

Before I proceed I must mention a pair of concepts that offers immediate application to the new model I am recommending, namely the distinction between phenotypes and genotypes in biology. In keeping with what I said earlier about the history of theoretical thinking, the classification of plants and animals began historically with the phenotypical description of species as independent entities, distinguished by certain external properties such as shape and color. The decisive turn to the genotypical approach amounts to conceiving of the various organisms as the confluences of underlying structural properties or groups of properties, so that the taxonomic system must now be based on the underlying strands rather than on external appearance.

Apply this approach to art history and you are compelled to abandon the notion that styles are labels, to be attached to such entities as single works, the *oeuvre* of individual artists, or periods of art. Instead, history appears as a primary flow of events, which is revealed upon analysis to be an interweaving of trends or strands coming and going in varying combinations and ratios of dominance. As a result, the cross section of the flow as a whole changes from moment to moment. The components are dependent or independent of one another to varying degrees. A style rubric like Classicism or Fauvism is not a sorting box for a group of works or artists thought to belong in this container rather than another. It is the name for a way of making art, defined by a particular use of the medium, the subject matter, etc. Such a style can be traced and isolated as a component in the work of one artist or several, in one period or place or several, and it can show up as dominant or secondary, persistent or temporary. Cézanne is neither an Impressionist nor a Cubist; but the individual nature of his work can be described as a unique gestalt structure composed of these and other stylistic constituents. The diagram of Figure 44a shows the traditional conception of art history as a sequence of beads or boxes, each labeled as a style. Figure 44b tries to remedy the

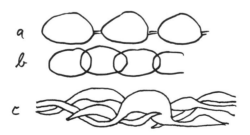

*Figure 44.*

static character of this notion by showing the traditionally self-contained units as blending into one another. The chain of elements is replaced with a kind of continuous flow. But this refinement is not good enough; it changes nothing in principle. Figure 44c is meant to illustrate the new paradigm advocated here. The units depicted in 44c are not individual art objects or collections of them, but the components of such objects—qualities rather than things.

One might think of the categories described by Heinrich Wölfflin in his *Principles of Art History*: linear versus painterly, closed form versus open form, etc. (16). If qualities such as these are used not as mere subsidiary traits of concepts such as Classicism or Baroque but as the primary constituents of the flow of history, one arrives at the paradigm proposed here.

It will be evident that, seen in this new light, a particular style can no longer be defined primarily by the dates at which it makes its entrance and exit. Rather, each style represents a particular quality, strong in the art of one time and place, weak or nonexistent in another, and perhaps reappearing centuries later in a different place, modified by a different context. A plurality of styles will be recognized as the rule rather than a bothersome obstacle to conceptualization, and homogeneity or constancy will be shown as what it is, namely a rare exception.

## Determinism and the Individual

Among the problems that a gestalt approach lets us see more clearly is that of the relation between historical causality and the unique structure of each individual case. Hauser observes that "although in the course of history, individual and social factors are ever-present, one finds in historical thought and writing a continual shifting of sympathies from individualism to determinism and vice versa" (10, p. 203). It seems to me that the one cannot be handled without the other. Every individual derives entirely from its genetic tributaries and environmental influences; and the determining agents generate nothing but individual structures, be they persons or groups of people or objects such as works of art. The problem arises because causality can be conceptualized only as the behavior of linear chains of events. Such causal chains, however, lose their linear identity as soon as they enter a gestalt context. The causality governing the formation of a gestalt is a structural organization that cannot be described as the sum of the inputs. Hence the notion that causality stops where individuality starts. According to that notion, history is acknowledged to be governed by causality, but its individual products are seen as floating in the river of determined events like unaccountable foreign bodies. That is an absurd situation.

An individual is created solely by such determining causes as those of heredity, the environment, and others. The gestalt context neither introduces additional ingredients nor suppresses any of those that constitute it. One cannot separate, therefore, the artist as a person and citizen from the artist as a creator—as, for example, Kurt Badt has done, subtracting the historical conditions of place and time as "negative determinants" (5, pp. 47, 106). The only reason why the individual is not equal to the sum of its ingredients is that the process of gestalt formation organizes those ingredients in an entirely new structure. As far as the intellectual constructs of linear causality are concerned, the gestalt is a limiting case that can be approached, although never matched, by a judicious tracing of the components and their interrelations in the gestalt process. If this procedure falls short of the determinist's ambitions, it also saves him from the nihilism of the uncompromising individualist. And furthermore he may be comforted by the realization that he shares this limitation with every science, social or natural, whenever it faces any kind of holistic structure. In the meantime we have gained a unitary view of genetic and historical processes, one in which cause and effect account without break for all their individual components.

The rules that govern the formation of gestalt structures can be developed to explain why the organization of certain sets of components works out better than that of others, i.e., why the resulting structure may be harmonious rather than discordant, powerful and articulate rather than weak and bland. Granted, this leaves us a long way from accounting for the emergence of either geniuses or imbeciles, good art or bad art; but at least the road to understanding is no longer blocked in principle.

## Zeitgeist and Gestalt Formation

Related to questions of causality is the problem that some sociologists and historians have tackled by invoking a *Zeitgeist*, supposedly responsible for the shared characteristics of a given period's thought and art products. There have been strong objections to such a model. It is a problem that faced gestalt psychology from the outset, when Christian von Ehrenfels in his pioneer essay "On Gestalt Qualities" proposed that gestalten differed from mere sums of elements by special additional qualities (7). It took time until men such as Max Wertheimer and Wolfgang

Köhler were able to state that a gestalt owes its structure to nothing but its own components and context; but to this day, formulations that describe the relation between "the whole" and its parts risk promoting the notion that the whole is a generative entity of its own, acting and being acted upon by the parts.

Hauser asserts that the group mind "is just a collective concept, which as such must never be supposed to be 'prior' but only 'posterior' to the components that it unites" (10, p. 135). Surely this view is essentially correct. Hauser seems to overlook, however, the possibility of distinguishing two basic types of gestalt formation. One kind of gestalt comes about by the meeting and structural integration of originally separate components, such as takes place in the marriage of two persons and the subsequent generation of children issuing from that marriage. Examples from art would be the encounter of an Impressionist and a Cubist strand in a Seurat or a Cézanne, or the merger of traditional Mexican art with the Spanish Baroque of the invaders. Under such conditions, the striving toward a unified structure may be successful or counterproductive, and the structure may be made up of several more or less equally strong elements. It may also be ruled by one or several dominant factors, which impose their influence on the whole.

But there is also gestalt formation of a second kind, where the structure derives from an "organizer" in the biological sense of the term, that is, from a structural governor that determines the character of the ensuing whole. An egg or germ is the most obvious example, or the theme from which a musical composition develops. When Picasso undertook to give visual shape to the subject of *Guernica*, the resulting mural derived its pervasive spirit from the artist's conception of the theme (3). To be sure, the theme develops and operates during the generation of the work as one of its structural components, but it can also be said to have originated the work as a causal agent existing "prior" to it.

## The Ideal of Consistent Structure

As a final point, I would like to suggest what the gestalt approach can contribute to a question that has been asked by historians about the form of the course of history as a whole. Is there any understandable logic to the story of mankind and its creations, or is that story a mere *divertimento* of separate episodes that have so little to do with one another their order could be changed at random? To be sure, history, like any other kind of macroscopic event, is subject to straight determinism. But we need to know to what extent and by what means the sequences are fitted to an overarching structure. Gestalt theory deals with the fourth dimension of time in the way it deals with the three dimensions of space and asks: Under what conditions do the temporal changes in a structure add up to a highly unified whole?

Time, like space, is infinite, and therefore any analysis of temporal structure depends on the range to which it is applied. In the arts one can extend that range to the entire history of man, from the paleolithic caves to the latest discoveries of American art dealers; or one can limit it to the creation of a single work, from its first conception to its completion. One can maintain that there is order in a single person's *oeuvre* but none beyond it on the larger scene, or one can impose a theme on a chosen period at a given place, as did Vasari when he described the rebirth of Italian art from Giotto to Michelangelo as the three ages of infancy, adolescence, and maturity.

A consistent structure is most likely to come about when a simple configuration of impulses controls it with little opposition. A ballistic curve, controlled by the forces of propulsion and attraction, may serve as an example. Compare this with two versions of an old-fashioned pinball machine. If the board of the machine is slanted, the consistent action upon the ball by the force of gravity provides a strong theme that may or may not be perceived as more dominant in the structure of the event than the obstacles deflecting the ball from a straight-line course. But if the board is horizontal and the action is provided by various springs, then everything depends on whether the vectors add up to a concerted action or to chaos. In both cases, determinism rules uncontested, and the ball runs its course and reaches its goal.

The intellectually simplest and most pleasing conception of history is that of a progression from lowly beginnings to the accomplishments of the present. In the arts, such visions have been offered from time to time. Meyer Schapiro calls Alois Riegl "the most constructive and imaginative of the historians who have tried to embrace the whole of artistic development as a single continuous process" (15, p. 301). A recent fancy-free attempt is Suzi Gablik's application of Jean Piaget's stages of cognitive development to the progress from early Mediterranean art to the abstract minimalists of our time (8). The chances for such comprehensive schemes depend mainly on the relative strength of constant impulses. Basic features of the human mind are good candidates, especially when they are broad enough to be grounded in biology. A favorite is the law of differentiation, which leads from simple structure to high complexity. Cognitively, this law accounts for more and more complex actions and creations in response to more and more complex aspects of the environment.

Within the process of a single work's coming into being we can often observe a fairly surveyable approach to the solution of a given problem. But as soon as the range of the observation is extended to the entire lifework of an artist, the consistent maturing of his competence may go with changes in outlook and goal that add up to a style of far from simple structure. By the time we encompass a whole period, let alone the total history of art, our desire to keep the structure of our models simple is increasingly handicapped by the multiplicity of the forces that challenge our desire to understand.

## References

1. Arnheim, Rudolf. *Film as Art*. Berkeley and Los Angeles: University of California Press, 1957.
2. ———. *Radio, An Art of Sound*. New York: Da Capo, 1972.
3. ———. *The Genesis of a Painting: Picasso's Guernica*. Berkeley and Los Angeles: University of California Press, 1962.
4. Badt, Kurt. *Die Kunst des Nicola Poussin*. Cologne: Dumont, 1969.
5. ———. *Eine Wissenschaftslehre der Kunstgeschichte*. Cologne: Dumont, 1971.
6. Bialostocki, Jan. *Stil und Ikonographie*. Dresden: VEB Verlag der Kunst, 1966.
7. Ehrenfels, Christian von. "Ueber 'Gestaltqualitäten.'" In Ferdinand Weinhandl, ed., *Gestalthaftes Sehen*. Darmstadt: Wissenschaftliche Buchgesellschaft, 1960.
8. Gablik, Suzi. *Progress in Art*. London: Thames & Hudson, 1976.
9. Hager, W., and N. Knopp, eds. *Beiträge zum Problem des Stilpluralismus*. Munich: Prestel, 1977.
10. Hauser, Arnold. *The Philosophy of Art History*. New York: Knopf, 1959.
11. Lang, Berel, ed. *The Concept of Style*. Philadelphia: University of Pennsylvania Press, 1979.
12. Lewin, Kurt. *Gesetz und Experiment in der Psychologie*. Berlin-Schlachtensee: Weltkreis, 1927.
13. Nakata, Yujiro. *The Art of Japanese Calligraphy*. New York, 1973.
14. Panofsky, Erwin. *Renaissance and Renascences in Western Art*. New York: Harper, 1969.
15. Schapiro, Meyer. "Style." In A. Kroeber, ed., *Anthropology Today*. Chicago: University of Chicago Press, 1953.
16. Wölfflin, Heinrich. *Kunstgeschichtliche Grundbegriffe*. Munich: Bruckmann, 1920. Eng.: *Principles of Art History*. New York: Holt, 1932.

# ON DUPLICATION

He tells me that he had an ornithology professor from the Museum listen to recordings of bird songs and that the good man could identify with assurance only imitations produced by a music hall whistler. The authentic songs, which had been obtained in nature with much trouble, he thought were fuzzy, hardly characteristic,
and, in other words, total failures.

MICHEL TOURNIER (10, p. 86)

WE ARE afflicted not only with too many forgeries but also perhaps with
too many disquisitions about forgery—too many because the same arguments keep turning up and the same examples cited. The subject is
beginning to look like one of those scenic spots where too many vaca-
tioners have had a picnic. Is yet another attempt at interpretation really
justified?

Fakery has attracted legitimate attention because it offers a welcome
symbol of what is seen as the absence of sterling qualities in modern
man. The title theme of André Gide's *Les Faux-Monnayeurs* is represented by the coin that has a surface of gold but is glass inside. The false
coin sounds almost like the real thing, but it lacks weight. It stands for
an absence of probity, the virtue that the novel's central figure, Bernard,
considers the finest. "I wish," confesses Bernard, "that all my life I would
respond with a pure, honest, authentic sound to the slightest impact.
Almost everybody I have known sounds false. One should appear exactly
what one is worth and not try to seem more than one is. . . . One wants
to cheat oneself, and one is so much concerned with appearance that in
the end one no longer knows who one is" (4, p. 245).

Forgery is also used as a demonstrative challenge. A shoddy society
deserves to be paid in false currency. Thus youngsters who distribute fake

---

First published in *The Forger's Art*, ed. Denis Dutton (Berkeley and Los Angeles: University of California Press, 1983).

coins are not only intent on monetary gain, but also dignify their fraud as a gesture of rebellious defiance. Gide clipped from a Rouen newspaper of 1906 the report of a court trial in which the judge asked one of the accused adolescent counterfeiters whether he belonged to the Luxembourg "gang." "Please call it symposium, Your Honor," replied the young man. "Our group may have been producing fake money, I don't deny that, but we were mostly concerned with questions of politics and literature." Gide noted in his journal that he would like to use this quotation as an epigraph for his book (5, p. 21).

The facts of forgery are welcome also for a different although related purpose, namely, as proof of a contention that has been popular in some recent social psychology and philosophy. The inability of the public and indeed of trained experts to tell the genuine product from a fake showed to the satisfaction of certain scientists and thinkers that a person's values are not derived from true insight, but simply from the prestige imposed by influential authority (2). Tell the average person that he is confronted with the work or utterance of an esteemed author or artist, and he will accord it reverence. More broadly, fakes are cited to show that facts do not exist objectively and that their evaluation is not based on understanding. Facts are nothing but products of convention, they vary with the setting, and they therefore possess no absolute validity. In support of such a thesis, the psychological factors involved in the perception of fakes are often misinterpreted. I propose to discuss some of these factors in what follows.

For my purpose I shall exclude the motivational and ethical aspects specific to forgery and deal with the neutral phenomenon of duplication. By duplication I shall mean, in the broadest sense, the various ways in which one thing can be like another. This will provide a context for the more particular character of forgery.

All things in this world resemble one another in some ways and differ in others. In the development of human cognition, knowledge begins with generalities, which are subjected to differentiation as needed. One comes to know "trees" before one learns to tell oaks from maples. To be sure, understanding is gained also by the converse procedure, namely by generalization; but the overall strategy of wisdom proceeds most successfully from the general to the specific. This is so because, for most purposes, things are more relevantly defined by the *genus major* than by the *differentia specifica*. (It would be useful some time to investigate the particular social conditions under which the differences between things are considered more important than the characteristics they share. The competitive spirit of private enterprise, for example, generates an unhealthy emphasis on difference.)

In philosophical aesthetics, tedious pseudoproblems have been introduced by dichotomous thinking. In looking, for example, at the various stages of an artistic creation, one may be tempted to ask: Which of them is *the* work of art? Are we to opt for the original concept formed in the artist's mind before it is given shape in some particular medium? Or is the work of art delivered only by the perceivable object, the completed painting or the written poem? Is the purity of the creation defiled when it adopts material shape, or does it become truly existent only when it can be seen or heard? When an artist makes a drawing in preparation for an etching or woodcut that will be executed by himself or by some other craftsman, is the drawing the work of art or does only the executed print deserve that distinction? Is the description of a work in a different medium—a film script or dance notation, the instructions for a painting transmitted by telephone, or the written score of a piece of music—to be considered the work of art, or does such a description merely supply the information needed for the production of the work? Do poems exist on paper or only in audition? None of these questions can be answered by an either/or decision.

If instead one starts from the realization that properties of the work of art reside in all its various embodiments, one arrives at an interesting and manageable problem. One can ask: In what ways do the various manifestations partake in the work, each in its own manner? Rather than try to decree that a copy or reproduction, forged or honest, is or is not the work of art, one asks: Which qualities of the work are found in such a duplication? Which are lost?

It is rarely possible to separate the mental conception of a work from its realization in the perceivable medium. This is less obvious in poetry since words in the poet's mind have already most of the qualities they have on paper. Even so, a glance at the worksheets of poets reminds us how much of the work requires that the words be surveyable in their spatial context (1). They reveal their interaction when they can be seen as a coherent pattern on paper. This is all the more true in the visual arts, where the actual perceptual effect of shapes, colors, or movement can be judged only when the painting, sculpture, dance, or film is examined by the artist's eyes. The creation of such a work consists in a dialogue between the conceiver and the conception that gradually takes shape in the medium. By no means can the work be described as a mere executor of the artist's preconceived vision. The medium offers constant surprises and suggestions. Therefore the work is not so much a replica of the mental *concetto* as a continuation of the shaping and inventing that began in the artist's mind.

It would be equally inappropriate to describe a work of representational art as a mere replica of its model. Such a work is elicited by "nature," that is, by the things and actions observed in the surrounding world, and equally by the many solutions and inventions contributed by the artist's contemporaries and forerunners. In the arts of the Renaissance, for example, there is no way of distinguishing with precision the imitation of Classical sculpture from the renewed observation of nature. In developing his own conception, the artist takes from both sources, and his attitude toward them tends to be similar. This is true for art in general. The attitude ranges all the way from slavish imitation to the most carefree playing with the offerings of nature and art. When a forger endeavors to imitate someone else's work, his anxious, puny concern with detail after detail resembles the mechanical copying of nature in mindless realism. The result can be quite similar. Examined in detail, both imitations exhibit what may be called an "ugly facture." In a genuine Van Gogh, the tissue of harmonious strokes shows that the artist's eyes and hands were controlled by an unhampered and integrated sense of form. Every stroke of the brush swings with the flow of the total movement. In a typical forgery, on the contrary, each stroke is separately controlled by the comparison with some detail of a particular original work or the artist's style in general. In consequence, the pattern as a whole looks incoherent. A similar ugliness of facture is found in the products of artists who "forge nature," that is, who imitate what they see piece by piece. They are "di natura buona scimia," as the forger Capocchio calls himself in the *Divine Comedy*—that is, nature's good ape.

The most successful forgers tend not to suffer from this defect. Instead of duplicating by mechanical imitation, they rely on fairly free invention in the spirit of the original's style. They produce analogies or equivalents, which makes for better aesthetic quality. This accounts in part for the appreciation received by the sculpture of a Bastianini or Dossena or some of Van Meegeren's paintings. The forger who is somewhat gifted himself can take chances and thereby obtain an additional resemblance to the work of the great. Being an artist oneself helps when one tries to match the work of others.

It is not sensible to accept only original works as art and dismiss all reproductions as nonart. Even the cheapest of the small copies of Michelangelo's *David* retains some of the original's powerful audacity, and the chalky plaster casts of Greek sculpture standing forlorn in the corners of art schools are capable of inducing the shock of greatness. This happens even though at the same time one may be quite aware of the copy's short-comings.

Besides, the distinction between original and reproduction is anything but obvious. The sacred Ise shrine of Japan has been razed and totally rebuilt every twenty years since 478. The faithful maintain that every one of these embodiments is *the* Ise shrine, thereby reminding us that no individual entity is under obligation to exist only once. As long as the carpenters use the same *hinoki* wood, the same tools, and the same techniques, the shrine meets all the requirements of the original. The use of power tools and nails, however, would call the authenticity of the building into question, regardless of whether or not the average visitor could tell the difference. It is of the ancient building's essence that it be made by hand in the old manner and fitted together without the barbarous coercion of nailing or gluing.

Or take the problem of bronze casting. Many of the original plasters from which Henry Moore's sculptures were cast are now on view in the Ontario Museum of Art in Toronto. Those pieces convey the immediacy of the artist's presence by surface qualities that are absent from the cast. The incisions of carving tools and the pressures and squeezes of an artist's hands make for qualities that differ qualitatively from the shapes one obtains by pouring liquid metal into a mold. Not only is there a disturbing contradiction between the visible manifestations of carving or modeling and the metal that yields no such effect; the poured liquid also smoothes all shapes and makes them noncommittally vague. One is reminded of the insipid smoothness of a dancer's body sheathed in a leotard.

In many important ways the cast exhibits less of the original work than did the sculptor's handiwork, even if the artist enlivens the cast by retouching. But it would be foolish to deny that every cast of the work is *the* work created by the artist. The cast is a reproduction, and a reproduction should be treated as the work to the extent that it conveys the work's essential qualities. This is true also of etchings and woodcuts made by the artist or someone else from a drawing. When the artist himself handles the burin or knife, an essential quality of his style is preserved in the print. But when one of Hogarth's pictures is translated by a professional engraver into insipidly anonymous contours and shadings, there is no denying that the authenticity of the work is much reduced. We see Hogarth's unique quality only through a glass darkly, which still leaves enough of the artist's conception to let us say "This is a Hogarth."

On the other hand, one could maintain that the drawings of an Utamaro or even a Sharaku for the *ukiyo-e* prints acquire their intended steely precision only through the technique of the professional woodcutter. Similarly, the electric amplification of music or song produces a crudeness of timbre and impact that offers an appropriate complement to the barbarism of popular music but is out of place in traditional opera. The same process of duplication that is needed to create the authentic rock song is damaging to classical music.

The usefulness of photographic reproductions depends on how much of the original essence they preserve. A black-and-white slide of a painting by Poussin retains much of the pattern of shapes on which the composition is based, whereas the kind of work conceived primarily in terms of color relations, for example, Josef Albers's *Homage to the Square,* becomes a pointless ornament or, in the work of some other colorists, a meaningless conglomeration of patches. Reduction, therefore, leads to falsification when indispensable aspects of the work are suppressed. Otherwise, the abstracted image may even help clarify aspects that are less noticeable in the undiminished original. Some art historians prefer black-and-white reproductions, not only because the photographic rendering of colors is often so poor, but also because they like to concentrate on aspects of shape and subject matter. They are well served by selective duplication.

A similar problem arises in preparatory duplication. A drawing intended as a model for a painting or sculpture may contain enough of the intended composition to serve as an indispensable guide. More often than not, however, the addition of color or of sculptural volume requires modifications in the pattern of the drawing because every added component tends to affect the others. In this respect, an artist's sketches differ in principle from musical scores. The written score is, of course, not the music but an expedient, introduced when oral transmission was no longer a satisfactory means of preserving music. At the other end of history, sound recording has made available a more complete duplication, which supplements and sometimes replaces the written score. The written score is a preparatory duplicate, but unlike the artist's sketches it is generally not to be overridden by further elaboration. Rather it is to be filled in. It is but a set of instructions for the production of a piece of music, limited essentially to pitch and duration. It neither preserves the further qualities that the piece had in the mind of the composer nor prescribes all the aspects that have to be supplied in performance. The musical score, like the written play or choreography in dance notation, presents us with the startling fact that works of art created for performance are considered adequately defined by a distinctly partial version.

The question arises how much of a description is needed to define such a work. Which of its aspects can be left to the varieties of execution introduced by the performers? And which aspects should be left unspecified if the work is to remain accessible to the changing styles of performance?

Obviously, if someone banged out the rhythm of a Beethoven symphony on the table, the information would be too limited to serve as a score. An actual performance, on the other hand, may provide too much of a score, i.e., too many constraints. As long as music has to be reconstructed in order to come into being, one must keep in mind that musicians of today cannot really play in the style of yesterday without losing genuine identification. The same holds for choreography and playwriting. In the performing arts the very absence of a complete score, i.e., of a complete duplicate, enables music, dances, and plays to survive. The tension created by the adaptation of a work of yesterday to the style of today is an essential part of the history of the art in progress.

Once we abandon the kind of dichotomous thinking that decrees that a certain entity either is or is not a given work of art, we recognize that works of art are events occurring in time. They change appearance as they survive in the minds of successive generations. At the same time they can retain enough of their essential nature to preserve their identity. Monteverdi's *Orfeo* is still Monteverdi's *Orfeo*, even though what we hear today is not what was heard in the seventeenth century, and even though we make it sound different from the work as it was performed in Monteverdi's day.

A work of art is not an immutable entity, even when we possess a physical object that serves as its enduring carrier. Right now Michelangelo's paintings on the ceiling of the Sistine Chapel are being thoroughly cleaned for the first time. For over five hundred years, the grime of pollution and the zeal of restorers have transformed the paintings into variations of themselves, and it would take courage to assert that none of these modifications have touched the works' core. Is it not more honest to admit that nobody has known the originals since the days when they began to be contaminated? It remains to be seen whether after the restoration we can say with some assurance that we know them now. Still, we must be grateful for knowing Michelangelo's paintings at least by approximation, just as we are grateful to glean an idea of lost Greek sculptures through Roman copies.

Equally effective and more interesting are the changes that occur because new generations see things with new eyes. One might ask how this is possible since the work remains what it is and therefore should convey the same images to whoever looks at it. Perception, however, is not a mechanical absorption of stimuli. It is always a search for structure because only structured form can be perceived. A good work of art is highly structured. It therefore reveals itself to correct perception and resists misinterpretation. However, an inappropriate attitude on the part of the viewer may be strong enough to override the resistance put up by the work. Furthermore, within the range of an acceptable interpretation there is room for much variety. By a shifting of emphasis one can see Seurat mainly as an Impressionist or mainly as a Cubist. Order can be discovered in works that looked chaotic to an earlier generation; and what was perceived negatively as primitive rigidity may be recognized by others as powerful stylization.

Whoever undertakes to duplicate an image is likely to reflect in his renditions his particular "reading" of the model. It has often been remarked that forgeries which looked entirely convincing when they were made reveal an obvious deficiency to the eyes of a later generation. This is so because the forger unintentionally endows the works of the past with the qualities he and his peers see in them. In consequence, a nineteenth-century version of a work of the Quattrocento may have looked more convincing and more enjoyable than the original as long as a particular stylistic slant prevailed.

Such a stylistic bias, like all constant factors, tends to drop out of consciousness. It is automatically deducted from any object of experience, but at the same time it helps to make the object palatable. I remember seeing in Japanese newspapers photographs of myself in which my eyes had been given an oriental slant by retouching. I shared this treatment with Commodore Perry, whose American features became those of a samurai in his portraits of around 1850 (3, p. 6). The adaptations are unlikely to have been made on purpose, nor did my Japanese friends notice my acculturation.

"The forgery is a kind of short-cut," writes Otto Kurz. "It translates the ancient work of art into present-day language and serves the same purpose as translations and modernizations in literature" (8, p. 320). The great works of literature are in need of retranslation every few generations because the earlier translators' period style begins to overpower the character of the original. Similarly, Van Gogh's paintings after motifs of Millet or Delacroix look to us today like typical Van Goghs, in which the themes of the earlier artists reverberate only distantly. Ironically, then, the better forgers, against their intentions, share with their fellow artists the compulsion to impose their own conceptions upon the sights they try to reproduce.

Art experts who have been taken in by forgeries have been easy targets for derision. Such criticism, although justified in some cases, tends to go by the mistaken assumption that connoisseurship in the arts should amount to total knowledge. But whereas in art history, as in other sciences, there are facts that can be stated with certainty, the more interesting problems are not generally of that nature. Scientific truth is typically tentative. It holds until new facts call for a revised interpretation. (Ernst Mach has written: "The natural scientist does not search for a completed view of the world; he realizes that all his work can only broaden and deepen understanding. There exists for him no problem whose solution is not in need of further deepening, but also none that he must consider absolutely insoluble" [9, p. 280].) Similarly in the arts, practical indications can make it quite certain that a particular painting was done by Rembrandt; but when such a proof is based on documentation it may not require any knowledge of Rembrandt's art whatever. It can be obtained by a detective or lawyer. The art historian's true challenge consists in coming to know the characteristics of Rembrandt's art to such an extent that he can distinguish it with certainty from the work of others. This task, however, is necessarily endless; and by no means does the endlessness of the search imply that the final truth does not exist.

I stated earlier that perception is not a mechanical absorption of stimuli but a search for structure, and that, as a rule, a given compositional pattern admits a range of readings that reach all the way from what is compatible with the work to flagrant misinterpretations. What, then, determines the particular structure a given observer finds in a work? Remember that no percept comes about in isolation. It is received as part of a context, and the context strongly affects it. When a painting is seen as a genuine Rubens, the properties that conform to the stylistic traits of Rubens come to the fore perceptually. The same painting, considered a product of Rubens's workshop or a forgery, is not only judged differently but actually seen as a different painting. Nelson Goodman has pointed out that this is particularly true when the forger's style has become known and provides an alternative context in which to see the work (7, pp. 103ff). Van Meegeren's *Supper at Emmaus*, for example, was so successful not only because it was a good painting, but because it fitted the context of Vermeer's known work perfectly. "Every art historian had learned at school that Vermeer's style derived ultimately from Caravaggio. Now a lucky discovery provided the final proof. The new painting was based on Caravaggio's 'Disciples at Emmaus'" (8, p. 333). What matters here is that to consider an object in its context is not an uncritical surrender of independent judgment, but a legitimate and indeed essential procedure. To be sure, the context must be trustworthy; but that is another problem.

Once a work is suspected of being a fake, it becomes a different perceptual object. Under such conditions, even a bona fide original may exhibit suspicious features. When in Jean Giraudoux's play *Amphitryon 38*, Queen Alcmène is no longer sure whether she is facing her husband or a forgery perpetrated by Jupiter, she discovers unfamiliar traits in his appearance and behavior. Amphitryon advises her: "Il ne faut pas se regarder trop en face, entre époux, si l'on veut s'éviter des découvertes" (6, Act II, scene 7).

I have tried to show that one cannot hope to understand the nature of forgeries and of responses to forgeries as long as one operates with either/or distinctions between what is art and what is not and as long as one insists that certain qualities can only be either present or absent. Instead, I suggest that art be viewed in the context of a world in which human beings and other species of creatures and things are more alike than different from one another. Correspondingly, art is a world of pervasive similarities and dependencies, imitations, remembrances, approximations, and reinterpretations—a collective effort to give shape to the common human experience. In such a world copies, reproductions, borrowings, and forgeries are to be considered not only, nor even primarily, by what distinguishes them from their models or prototypes, but by how much of a given aesthetic substance they share. We are so used to basing social value on distinctiveness that we easily forget all those cultures that consider good things worthy of duplication, with changes made only when they are needed.

If this is the case, however, are we justified in attributing so much importance to verifying "originals" and distinguishing them from duplicates that are much like them and that for many practical purposes fulfill the same functions? I believe we are. Just as it is in the interest of the human potential to extend knowledge of the truth beyond the limits already attained, there is merit in pursuing aesthetic achievement to its peaks. We know from much evidence that art comes at all levels, from the poorest to the highest, and that therefore we need to distinguish all these levels from one another by their objective characteristics. Precisely because all works of art are basically duplicates of one another in that they are all engaged in the same task, it is possible and necessary to compare their levels of excellence. Those distinctions, however, are not readily apparent to everybody. A cheap popular song, novel, or picture may provide a full aesthetic experience within the narrow horizons of poorly prepared recipients, and it takes the persistent best efforts of the best experts to come ever closer to recognition of the highest achievements.

To this end, we are in need of uncontaminated facts. It is difficult enough to probe the secrets of things when the evidence is authentic. We cannot afford to be misled by falsification.

## References

1. Abbott, Charles D., ed. *Poets at Work*. New York: Harcourt Brace, 1948.
2. Asch, Solomon E. "The Doctrine of Suggestion, Prestige, and Imitation in Social Psychology." *Psychological Review*, vol. 55 (Sept. 1948), pp. 250–76.
3. Bemmelen, J. M. van, et al., eds. *Aspects of Art Forgery*. The Hague: Nijhoff, 1962.
4. Gide, André. *Les Faux-Monnayeurs*. Paris: Gallimard, 1925.
5. ———. *Le Journal des Faux-Monnayeurs*. Paris: Gallimard, 1926.
6. Giraudoux, Jean. *Amphitryon 38*. Paris: Grasset, 1929.
7. Goodman, Nelson. *Languages of Art*. Indianapolis: Bobbs-Merrill, 1968.
8. Kurz, Otto. *Fakes*. New York: Dover, 1967.
9. Mach, Ernst. *Die Analyse der Empfindungen*. Jena: Fischer, 1903. Eng.: *The Analysis of Sensations*. New York: Dover, 1959.
10. Tournier, Michel. *Le Roi des Aulnes*. Paris: Gallimard, 1970.

# ON THE LATE STYLE

OUR WAY of looking at the seasons of human life is determined by two conceptions, which I have tried to symbolize in a diagram (Figure 45). One of these conceptions is biological. It describes an arch rising from the weakness of the child to the unfolded powers of the mature person and then descending toward the infirmity of old age. In this view, the late style of life is that of the old man leaning on his cane—the three-legged creature, as the riddle of the sphinx describes him. It is the season of the "winter of pale misfeature," as Keats has it in his sonnet.

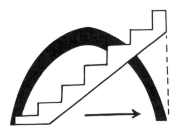

*Figure 45.*

The biological view considers not only the decline of physical strength, but also the weakening of what one may call the practical powers of the mind. The acuity of vision and the range of hearing decline, short-term memory begins to fail, reaction time lengthens, and the flexi-

Derived from "On the Late Style of Life and Art," *Michigan Quarterly Review* (Spring 1978).

bility of intelligence gives way to a channeled concentration on particular established interests, knowledge, and connections. When these biological aspects determine the view of advanced age, people are afraid of getting old and look upon their capacity for further productive achievement with doubt and irony. *Sins of My Old Age* is the title given by Rossini to a group of late piano pieces; and the unorthodox and uncompromising qualities of late styles in the arts have been attributed often and conveniently to the failing powers of their makers. The Renaissance biographer Vasari observed that Titian, although able to command high prices for his late works, would have done better if in his last years he had painted only as a pastime, in order not to diminish, by weaker works, the reputation of his better years. Most of us nowadays, however, admire Titian's late works as his most original, most beautiful, and most profound. Correspondingly, there is another way of looking at the accomplishments of the aging mind.

This second conception complements the first by finding in the passing of the years an ever-continuing increase in wisdom. In my diagram, the symmetry of the biological arch is overlaid by a flight of steps leading from the limitations of the child to the high worldview of those who have lived long and have seen it all. It is a conception that expresses itself socially and historically in reverence for ancient counselors, prophets, and rulers and respect for the older members of the traditional family. It accounts also for the attention paid to the late works of artists and thinkers. The curiosity of our modern theorists and historians about the particular character of late works is often coupled with the expectation of finding the highest achievements, the purest examples, the deepest insights in the final products of a life of search and labor.

Although reverence for the old probably exists in every mature culture, the theoretical interest in the motives, attitudes, and stylistic characteristics of late styles presumably is limited to periods that have reached a late phase of their own development. This is so not only because history and psychology are favorite occupations of late civilizations, but also because generations discovering in their own conduct the symptoms of a declining age are naturally interested in the great examples of the corresponding stage of individual development. In fact, we may not be able to go very far in a study of late styles without finding parallels to them in certain features of our present aesthetic and intellectual climate and perhaps also in our personal way of life.

Inevitably we begin by looking at works created at the end of long careers. Longevity is one of our indispensable assistants, and only with hesitation do we also consider the late products of short careers. We dwell on the late works of a Michelangelo, Titian, Rembrandt, Cézanne, Goethe, or Beethoven, who all lived long lives; but it takes a special dispensation to include artists like Mozart, Van Gogh, or Kafka, who died young. These short-lived geniuses can concern us only if we assume that death did not strike them blindly in the midst of a career that was structured for a longer duration. Biologists tell us that small, short-lived mammals live at a correspondingly faster pace than large, long-lived ones. I read recently that small creatures breathe faster and have faster-beating hearts, so that all mammals do roughly the same amount of breathing and heartbeating during a normal lifespan. One is tempted to suspect that something similar happens in some of those short but spectacularly rich human careers, in which a maturity of a particular kind distinguishes the last efforts.

Be this as it may, we are not merely concerned with chronological age when we refer to the late works of artists. What we are interested in is a particular style, the expression of an attitude that is found often, but neither necessarily nor exclusively, in the end products of long careers. On the other hand, there are people, and there are artists among them, who live to "a ripe old age" without ever receiving the blessings of maturity.

Much of what is observed about the qualities of the typical aged mind concerns the relation of the person to his or her world. In this respect we may distinguish three phases of human development. An early attitude, found in young children and surviving in certain aspects of cultural and individual behavior, perceives and understands the world only in broad generalities. The various facts of experience are not clearly articulated. In particular, there is little differentiation between the self and the other, the individual and his world. It is a state of mind in which the outer world is not yet segregated from the self, a state that Freud described as the origin of the "oceanic feeling."

This primary lack of differentiation is followed by the second phase, a gradual conquest of reality. The self as an active and observant subject distinguishes itself from the objective world of people and things. This is the most important outcome of an increasing capacity for discrimination. The child learns to distinguish categories of things and to identify individual objects, places, and persons. An adult attitude develops, to which our Western culture offers a historical parallel in a new interest in the facts of outer reality, a curiosity that awoke first in the thirteenth century and created during the Renaissance the age of natural science, scientific exploration, and the cultivation of individual persons, places, and events. It is a state of mind expressed in chronicles, in treatises on geography, botany, astronomy, anatomy, as well as in naturalistic painting and portraiture. This second phase of the human attitude toward reality is distinguished by a hearty worldliness that scrutinizes the environment in order to interact with it.

Perhaps that germinal age of the Renaissance already contained some features of the third phase, in which we recognize the symptoms of aging. But it is in more recent times that the characteristic late attitude has manifested itself clearly. I will mention some of the symptoms.

First, interest in the nature and appearance of the world is no longer motivated primarily by a desire to interact with it. The paintings of the Impressionists, for example, are the products of a detached contemplation. The images depicting the natural and the man-made setting abandon the properties of texture, contour, and local color that report on the material particularity of the objects. The character and practical value of those material characteristics is not considered relevant. A similar attitude can be observed in certain aspects of pure science, especially as it develops in Europe.

Such a detachment of contemplation from practical application is not simply negative. It goes with a worldview that transcends outer appearance to search out the underlying essentials, the basic laws that control the observable manifestations. This tendency is evident in the physical sciences, and it has also expressed itself recently in the exploration of deep-seated structure in anthropology, psychology, and linguistics.

Another symptom of what may be called the late phase of the human attitude is the shift from hierarchy to coordination. Instrumental here is the conviction that similarities are more important than differences, and that organization should derive from consensus among equals rather than from obedience to superordinate principles or powers. Socially, of course, this calls for democracy, the most mature and sophisticated form of human community, which presupposes the greatest wisdom even though in practice, more often than not, it makes do with much less. In the arts it involves, for example, the renunciation of governing compositional schemes, such as the triangular groupings of the Renaissance, in favor of the spread of coordinated units. These units, in turn, forgo the uniqueness that gives each element of a composition an individual character of its own and identifies its equally unique place and function in the composition or plot of the whole. Instead, in works of a late style the viewer or listener meets the same kind of thing or event in every area of the spatial pattern and in every phase of what in earlier styles is narration or development in time. The sense of eventful action gives way in all dimensions to a state or situation of pervasive aliveness. This structural uniformity in the late phase cannot but remind us of the earliest one, in which, as I suggested, discrimination between things as well as between the self and the world is still weak. However, a lifetime of difference separates a state of mind that cannot yet discriminate from one that no longer cares to.

In describing the three phases of the human attitude I have already anticipated much of what can be said about the characteristics of works of art in a late style. Let me dwell for another moment on the tendency to homogenize the structure of a work as a whole. In painting, the various objects and parts of objects lose their distinctive textures, which once defined them as individual characters in the picture story. In earlier portraits, the smoothness of a woman's hair contrasted with the heavy flow of the brocade, and the skin differed from the fabric as in landscapes the foliage of trees differed from granite and marble. In a late work, all these subjects have become creatures of the same kind, characterized by the community of their fate and mission. Similarly, in late musical works, e.g., in Beethoven's last string quartets, timbres of the various instruments blend into the rich sounds of a kind of superorgan, and the antagonism of phrase and counterphrase gives way to an articulate flow.

Such evenness of texture goes with a lack of interest in causal relations. The dynamics of cause and effect presupposes agents and targets distinguished from each other by differences in character and different places in the whole. For example, in classical French tragedy it is the profound difference between, say, Queen Phèdre and Prince Hippolyte and between their positions in the constellation of human relations that generates the propulsive energy of the drama. Compare this, say, with the late mood of the novelist Flaubert, in whose stories characters of ambiguous motivation and muted impulse drift toward, and away from, one another.

The assimilation and fusion of elements, indicating a worldview in which the resemblances outweigh the differences, are accompanied in late works of art by a looseness of the work's fabric, a diffuse-looking kind of order creating an illusion of the various components' floating in a medium of high entropy with interchangeable spatial locations. The second part of Goethe's play *Faust* as well as that of his novel *Wilhelm Meister* gives the impression of loosely strung episodes, united by a common theme. Or compare an early version of Rembrandt's *Return of the*

*Prodigal Son*, in which father and son have rushed toward each other and are hooked together like tongue and groove, with the very late version, in which five human apparitions, each reposing within itself, interact mainly by their common immersion in darkness. Or notice how much coordination rather than hierarchy there is in the late-style compositions of Rodin's *Gate of Hell* and *Burghers of Calais*. There again, causal interaction is replaced by common fate.

This brings to mind a related feature of comparison between styles, which I can best describe by saying that in typical works of what I called the second phase, the phase of biological vigor, the dynamics of the total action originates in separate motivational centers. This is most easily seen in a figural work, where, let us say, the brutal aggression of a Sextus Tarquinius copes with a Lucretia vigorously defending her virtue. The same kind of dynamics activates the components of a musical conception typical of that active outlook on life, for example, in the interplay of the peasants' dance and the thunderstorm in Beethoven's *Pastoral* Symphony. One might say that the artist, from whose initiative all activity in the work ultimately springs, has delegated his energy resources to the agents of his composition. And these agents behave as though they were acting on their own inherent impulses.

In late works, on the contrary, the dynamics moving the various characters is not of their own making. Rather they are subjected to a power that affects them all equally. As always, the artist has delegated his initiative to his creation, but this initiative no longer animates the individual motors of his characters. It is now manifest as the power of a fate pervading the work's entire world. The living and the dead, the corpse of Christ and his mourning mother, they all are now beings in the same state, equally active and inactive, aware and unaware, enduring and resisting.

This changed mechanism for generating and distributing energy in the late works manifests itself in a different handling of the formal means of expression, for example, in the role of light in painting. In an earlier style, light is produced by a well-defined source, which, as a distinctive agent of its own, casts illumination upon the recipients, upon human figures or architecture, and they in turn display their individual reactions to it. But in a late Titian or Rembrandt, the entire scene is aglow. The state of being inflamed is possessed and shared by all. One might describe this phenomenon more generally by saying that the imports from the world of reality, in which discrete forces act upon one another, have been metabolized by the aging mind so fully as to be transformed into characteristics of the presentation as a whole. They have become attributes of what we call style. The late style fuses the contributions of the objectively given in a unitary worldview, the outcome of long and deep contemplation.

A single example from the visual arts may serve to illustrate some of these properties of the late style. Titian's *Christ Crowned With Thorns* (Figure 46), painted six years before his death as the reworking of an earlier composition, all but hides the central figure of the flagellated Christ in a pattern of coordinated figures. They are knit together by a weave of sticks that makes us look in vain for a dominant hierarchy— the kind of structure that would focus on the principal theme in its cause-and-effect relations with the subordinate elements. The torturers and the victim are not clearly distinguished. They are intertwined in a pervasive but not excessive action, an action that fills much of the pictorial space as an overall property of the represented world as a whole. A loose network of connections leaves each figure somewhat detached from the others, and a diffuse glow of golden light seems to emanate from each head and limb rather than strike the scene from some external source.

The differences between late and earlier styles point to a worrisome consequence in teaching for the relation between master and disciple. If the differences in outlook and procedure are so great, how are teaching and learning possible? Pedagogy is at its most powerful when the truly wise serve as teachers to the truly youthful. But how can there be any give and take if there is no common base? Indeed, the conflict between what the master has attained and what the disciple is striving for can be observed in all productive instruction. But this conflict is only one aspect of the relation. The art historian Kurt Badt, whose observations on our subject are reflected in much of what I have said here, has maintained that the late works of artists do not influence the style of their successors. It is rather the works created by the great men in their middle years that act as examples and guiding images to posterity and thereby make history. But "the late works of the great masters, which come about at the same time as the period style of a subsequent generation, tower above the flow of history as solitudes [*Einsamkeiten*] inaccessible to the context of time" (1, p. 6).

Such an outcome would follow logically from the differences between young and old that we have observed. But what actually happens may be more complex. One can think of examples in which the late works, although indigestible to the immediately following generation, powerfully affect a later one. This is true for the poetry of Hölderlin, the music

*Figure 46.* Titian, *Christ Crowned with Thorns.* 1570. Alte Pinakothek, Munich.

of Wagner, and the late paintings of Cézanne. In such instances a new generation assimilates from a late style those aspects it can accommodate to its own outlook. As a relatively recent example we may recall the influence of the late works of Claude Monet on the American abstract expressionists. In Monet's last landscapes we see the final outcome of a lifelong development, during which the subject matter was gradually absorbed by an ever more conspicuous texture, fully realized in his water lilies, his footbridge paintings, and other late works. Essential to our appreciation of these works, however, is the fact that, despite the radical transformation of the subject matter, all the fullness and wealth of experienced reality remains present. The greatest possible range of artistic content reaches from the concreteness of the individual things of nature to the uniformity of the artist's all-encompassing view. This we might describe as the final achievement of the human mind when it matures at an advanced age. It is only natural that in the case of Monet, the influence he exerted on the painters of a later and younger generation could not reach the depths he had attained himself.

I can think of no better way to conclude these observations than by quoting a statement written by an artist, Hans Richter, in his mid eighties, when he thought back to an exhibition of the late paintings of Lyonel Feininger (2, chap. 8). Richter was struck by the spiritualization that had occurred in the work of the painter of landscapes, seascapes, and towns:

Hardly were there any "subjects" left. In the transparency of the picture plane it no longer mattered whether there was a sky, an ocean, a sail, or a human figure. Here spoke the wisdom of an aged artist for whom the world of objects had shed its disguise. Visible beyond that world, inherent in it and above it, was the unity of Nirvana, the creative nowhere to which the artist had entrusted himself. That was what spoke in those images. A ringing voice without sound, on the border between being and not-being, a man capable of giving utterance in this sphere of the almost divine.

## References

1. Badt, Kurt. *Das Spätwerk Cézannes*. Constance: Universitätsverlag, 1971.
2. Richter, Hans. *Begegnungen von Dada bis heute*. Cologne: Dumont, 1973.

# Part VIII

# OBJECTIVE PERCEPTS,
# OBJECTIVE VALUES

When I went to see the cathedral of Strasbourg for the first time, I had my head full of general ideas about good taste. From hearsay I honored the harmony of masses, the purity of shapes, and I was a decided enemy of the confused arbitrariness of Gothic ornamentation. Under the heading *Gothic*, as though in the entry of a dictionary, I heaped all the synonymous misunderstandings that had ever crossed my mind as to the indistinct, the disorderly, the unnatural, the overloaded, the patchwork. . . . How unexpected was the sensation that surprised me when I faced the building. My soul was filled with one whole, great expression, which consisted of a thousand harmonious details and therefore could be savored and enjoyed although in no way recognized and explained.

GOETHE, *On German Architecture,* 1773

Is SENSORY perception trustworthy? The question arises when we want to know how reliably we are being informed about the nature and behavior of the physical world of which we are a part and on which our well-being depends. If we bump into an invisible thing or if a thing we see turns out not to be there, we are faced with a disturbing contradiction between the reports conveyed by our different senses. Vision tells us one thing, the senses of touch and kinesthesia another, and it may be vitally important for us to know on which perceptual facts we should rely.

## Are Percepts Reliable?

What we ask in such cases is when and to what extent perception is veridical. In the arts this question is of secondary importance because it refers only to the physical carrier of the work of art, not to the work itself. Granted, it is necessary that the walls of a building not only look

Derived from Part II of "Dynamics and Invariants," in *Perceiving Artworks,* ed. John Fisher (Philadelphia: Temple University Press, 1980), and "The Dimensions of Disagreement," *Journal of Aesthetics and Art Criticism,* vol. 38 (Fall 1979).

upright but be upright, and that a sculpture not topple even though it looks balanced. The pigment on a canvas may look dry, but is it? To make sure, we often buttress our sensory judgment with measurements by instrument. But obviously these are technicalities.

Aesthetically, the work of art does not serve to inform us about the nature of the physical object that is its conveyor. A painting can be used to tell about properties of pigment and canvas, but it does not do so aesthetically. The depth effect created by perspective in a painting is no less acceptable than an awareness of the flatness of the canvas, although only the latter reports veridically about the physical state of affairs. When the size, shape, or spatial orientation of a visually perceived object deviates from its physical measurements, only the former matters. In the visual arts, a square *is* a square when it looks like a square, even though by geometric measurement it may not be one; and the brightness and hue of a color are what they look like in a particular context, regardless of what the light meter and the colorimeter say.

Since aesthetically the perceived image is the final fact, the question of its relation to its physical carrier does not arise. But the image's objective validity is relevant in another sense of the term, which concerns us here. We ask: Do all people see the same image when they look at the same thing? In fact, does one person see the same image every time he looks at a thing under the same external conditions? Obviously, the answers are of fundamental importance. If there were unbridgeable differences between people's perceptions, no social communication could exist, and if the images of the same object a person receives at different moments were incompatible, that person would end up insane. This is true not only for the practical use of our senses but equally in the arts.[1]

In practice, we operate quite successfully on the assumption that where one person sees a red light, the next fellow will see the same, unless his eyes are blind or otherwise impaired. This amounts to saying that, for all practical purposes, percepts are objective facts. The natural sciences make the same assumption when they rely on the readings taken from their instruments, and the experimental psychology of perception is dedicated to finding out what "people" see when they look at a given stimulus constellation. (Here and in what follows I am limiting the discussion to visual perception, although the same questions and answers come up for the other sense modalities.)

---

[1] I am not investigating here the ways a work of art can be objectively truthful to the human experiences it represents. This is an additional, large problem, not unrelated to the discussion in the present essay.

Even so, the situation becomes less simple as soon as the stimulus pattern becomes more complex and the mental resources on which perceivers draw go beyond the basic mechanisms of vision. Different people do see different things. The arts offer convincing examples. Think of the many attempts, in books and lectures on art theory, to describe the composition of a picture by means of geometrical figures. Certain portions of the work are shown to be held together in a triangle or circle and separated from the rest. Diagonals are made to sweep across the picture space and thereby to indicate relations between elements that are quite distant from one another. Often the demonstration leaves the onlooker unconvinced. He does not see what he is asked to see. To him, the picture organizes itself in some other way. This is not just a difference in "interpretation" that would leave the perceived image the same for all viewers. It amounts to perceiving a different picture.[2]

The history of art offers impressive examples of competent observers who were incapable of seeing works that offered no difficulty to the average person a few generations later. We find it hard to believe nowadays that when the young Kandinsky visited an exhibition of French Impressionists in Moscow in the 1880s, he did not recognize the subject matter represented in a painting of Monet's: "The catalogue told me that this was a haystack. But I could not recognize it, which I thought embarrassing. I also felt that the painter had no right to paint so unrecognizably."[3] And as late as 1904, the art critic of the *Petit Parisien* compared Cézanne's method of spreading pigment "with a comb or toothbrush" to the pictures produced by schoolboys who squash the heads of flies in a folded piece of paper (15, p. 198).

## The Tolerance of the Image

How are such perceptual discrepancies possible since the retinal images, from which all visual perception derives, are and remain the same for all viewers? They occur because perception is not a mechanical assimilation of the retinal data but the creation of a structured image. Perceiving consists in finding a structural pattern that fits the configuration of shapes and colors transmitted from the retina. When that configuration is

---

[2] This is not meant to deny that the structural patterns on which works of art are organized exist objectively and can be verified. I myself have suggested that one such pattern can be shown to underlie all successful works of visual design (4).

[3] See Kandinsky (11, p. 15). Significantly, however, Kandinsky was profoundly impressed by the painting whose subject he did not recognize.

simple and clear-cut, there is not much room for variety. Not even a willful effort will enable a person to see the line drawing of a square as anything but a square. When only the four corner dots are given, the square shape will still be the spontaneous choice of most observers, although other patterns can also be accommodated to the four dots (Figure 47). This sort of ambiguity can decrease when the given configuration is made more explicit, for example, when one of the alternative structures is spelled out. When the four edges of the square connect the four dots, they override other connections. But increasing complexity can also increase perceptual ambiguity, mainly because artists freely exploit the "tolerance" of structural features. By its tolerance, defined in the dictionary as "leeway for variation from a standard," a structural feature can accommodate quite a range of deviations. For example, we may see a composition as triangular although the triangle is not given by explicit lines. The shapes seen as conforming to it do so only approximately. Colors, too, have a range of tolerance, by which, under the pressure exerted by some neighbor, a red may also be seen as an orange, etc. This creates twilight zones, in which the same configuration may submit, more or less willingly, to more than one structural "template."

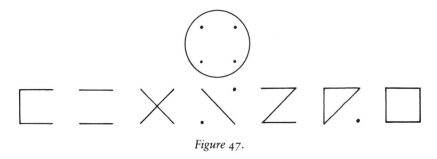

*Figure 47.*

Genuine ambiguity is aimed at by few artists. It is more often the unintentional effect of poor composition. If the work is successful, a careful weighing of all its features leads to the correct perception. The structure of the whole indicates which readings of a particular component are compatible with the composition, although an inspection limited to the part may not afford such a decision. This unequivocal character of a successful composition does not exclude a range of tolerance. Whereas the drawings of geometry must offer the clearest and simplest embodiment of concepts, works of art can play out the full range of empirical variations that can fit under a visual concept. The criterion for what can be included in this manner is not mathematical precision but a visual resemblance of a more topological nature.

The extent to which the shapes and colors of a work of art conform to the underlying compositional pattern is a matter of style. In some styles the adherence is of almost geometrical exactness. Others flirt with a variety of interpretations, and the very complexity of their adherence determines their particular character. Such styles are not ambiguous in the sense of offering more than one reading that can claim exclusive dominance. They are simultaneous variations on a theme.

## The Range of Interpretations

This sort of complex pattern, however, is often perceived in a one-sided way. Different analysts single out different structural versions, and the resulting multiplicity of contradictory descriptions seems to confirm the assertion that works of art are not objective percepts but victims of subjective interpretation. As a test case, I will refer to a survey made by Leo Steinberg of the principal structural patterns that have been attributed by various distinguished art historians to the ground plan of Borromini's Church of San Carlo alle Quattro Fontane in Rome.[4] It would be difficult to find another instance in which a complexity of shape has led to so many different readings. If one can show that even here it is possible to speak convincingly of an objective percept, our thesis will be considerably strengthened.

San Carlino, as it is familiarly called because of its smallness, is one of the most ingenious and most beautiful churches of the Baroque. At a first glance one is likely to see an oval interior—an impression confirmed by a look at the cupola, which is in fact a perfect oval. The interior beneath the cupola, however, weaves in and out of the oval shape in a subtle rhythmical undulation whose richness and balance cannot but enchant the viewer (Figure 48). A closer look reveals that the outline of the interior is composed of a number of smaller units, punctuated by sixteen columns (Figure 49). There are, first of all, four chapels (C), one at the entrance and one at the opposite end, at the apse that holds the main altar. Halfway down, on left and right, there are two additional, smaller chapels. The diagonals are marked by the only elements having a straight outline (P) in the entablature that encloses the entire interior above the

---

[4] See Steinberg (13). I am indebted to Professor Steinberg for permission to use his diagrams.

*Figure 48.* Church of San Carlo alle Quattro Fontane, Rome. 1638.
(Alinari photo).

columns. All other elements are variously curved. Connecting the chapels
and the four straight elements at the diagonals are six niched bays (B),
which are slightly concave and which, by their position, are given a two-
fold allegiance. In pairs they flank three of the chapels, but they do the
same for the four straight elements. This ambiguity adds to the elusive-
ness of the interior's boundary.

For the purpose of his analysis, Steinberg reduced the interpretations

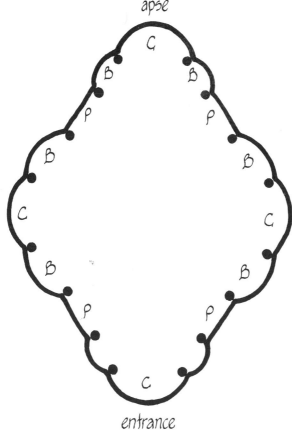

*Figure 49.*

of earlier authors to diagrams, some of which are cited below. As I mentioned, the first overall impression conveyed by the interior is of an oval. Consequently several authors have asserted that Borromini derived his conception from an oval, subjecting it to some modification. A first reading (Figure 50) provides for the four chapels by pushing four bulges outward from an internal oval. The bulges hint at a cruciform shape, which overlays the oval with vertical and horizontal axes. A second reading (Figure 51) also stresses the cruciform pattern but acknowledges the dominance of the two chapels in the long axis by deriving them from a stretching of the oval, whereas the lateral chapels are only secondary excrescences. Here the straight wall sections (P) are barely visible as secondary links.

In Figure 52, by contrast, the modification of the oval is obtained by

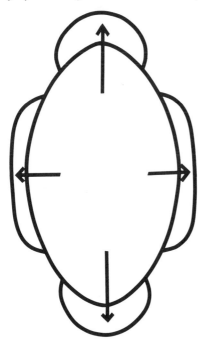

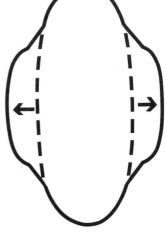

*Figure 50.* (after Steinberg).          *Figure 51.* (after Steinberg).

four indentations, which in this case push inward diagonally from a per-imetric oval. An inversion of figure and ground transforms the four chapels into mere leftover spaces between the four prominent straight elements (Figure 49, P). These elements, although inconspicuous in the ground plan, justify the importance given them in this interpretation by belonging, in the elevation, to the four piers that carry the pendentives and thereby support the cupola. They are said to have been derived from the similar piers by which Michelangelo supported the dome of St. Peter's; those, too, are placed diagonally, although as corners of a square, not a rectangle.

Even more explicit is this interpretation in Figure 53, where the theme of the diagonal piers is no mere modification of the basic oval but an intrusion into it by alien shapes, four chamfered corners, which straighten the niched bays into inseparable parts of the piers. In this version, too, the floor space left open between the corners reveals a positive strengthening of the cruciform shape, which is invested in the four chapels.

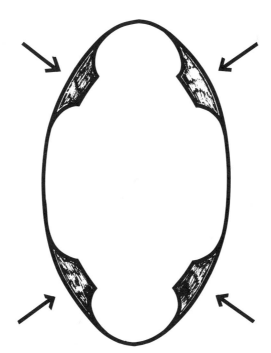

*Figure* 52. (after Steinberg).

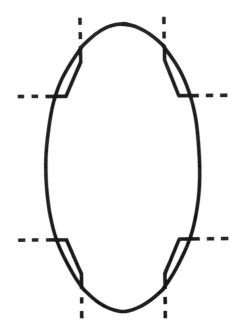

*Figure* 53. (after Steinberg).

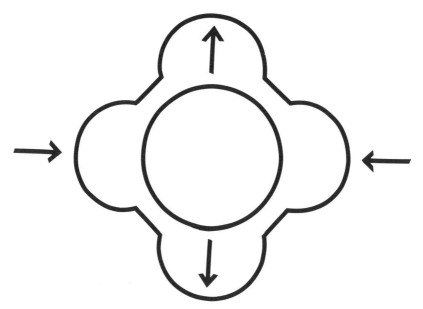

*Figure 54.* (after Steinberg).

The reduction of the ground plan of San Carlino to an oval and particularly the reference to Michelangelo's plan for St. Peter's point to an ultimate simplification, namely a centrically symmetrical shape organized around a circular dome (Figure 54). In this case, the cruciform pattern and the diagonal pattern balance each other. From this simple quatrefoil, Borromini's Baroque complication would be derived by a stretching of the longitudinal axis and a flattening of the lateral bulges.

(In passing, let me draw attention to the visual dynamics implied in these interpretations. A basic shape, e.g., an oval, is assumed to be the primary conception, from which the complexity of the solution is derived not by mere addition or subtraction, but by a dynamic pulling, pushing, and stretching, as though the envisioned structure were elastic. This implied interpretation of the creative process as action within a field of forces accords with a conviction I have supported elsewhere, namely that sensory images in general are perceived as fields of forces [2, chap. 9].)

The tendency to reduce oval shapes to circular ones is evident in another of the readings cited by Steinberg (Figure 55). Here the curves of the chapels, with the help of the concave niches, are adapted to three circles. Modification by stretching or compression is replaced by the mere overlay of three rigid, concentric shapes. This interpretation sacri-

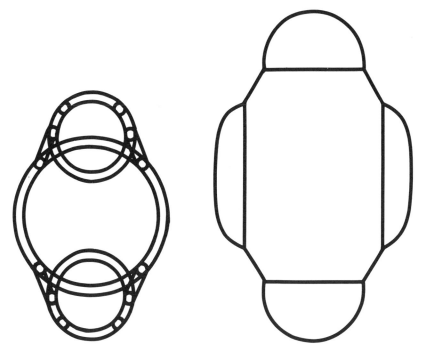

*Figure 55.* (after Steinberg).               *Figure 56.* (after Steinberg).

fices the dynamics of the Baroque conception by referring it back to a more Classicist immobility.

Finally I will mention two readings that abandon the prototypical oval entirely. Figure 56 is based on a rectangle whose corners are chamfered to account for the piers and treats the chapels as secondary attachments. Here again the swinging rhythm that dominates the overall character of Borromini's conception so decisively is sacrificed in favor of a static patching and trimming of pieces.

Similarly rigid is Figure 57, which comes about when the plan of San Carlo is derived from a lozenge. This reading takes its cue from the four straight-edged piers and accounts for the concavities of the chapels by making two small ovals and two circles intrude into the basic shape. Here again the lively expression of the architectural invention is missed because a mere overlay of geometric shapes replaces modification by dynamic stretching and pushing.[5]

---

[5] Observe here the fundamental difference between schematic representations of a work's perceptual structure and the purely technical devices used to construct complex

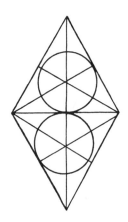

*Figure 57.* (after Steinberg).          *Figure 58.* (after Steinberg).

One can call these various readings mutually exclusive, in the sense of giving different descriptions of the same thing. Actually, however, they are one-sided rather than incompatible. Each of them focuses on a particular structural feature and gives it exclusive authority. The correct interpretation, as Steinberg has convincingly shown, reveals the plan of San Carlo to be a "multiple form," in which three basic shapes are coordinated in one integrated, complex whole: the oval, which combines the curves of the four chapels in one unified oblong; the cross, which uses the chapels as anchoring points for a vertical/horizontal framework; and the octagon, which relies on the four piers. In his book, Steinberg documents his conviction that the visual triad of Borromini's design, which was commissioned by the Trinitarian Order, symbolizes the Trinity.

The various interpretations indicate that each observer noted some aspect of what I call the objective percept of the little church. Each reading, however, was inadequate because it left other aspects of the structure unaccounted for. If Steinberg's own interpretation seems to approach the objective percept most closely, this is so not because he had the last word but because his scheme covers the given pattern most completely. In his

patterns. One of Borromini's own drawings, known as Albertina #173 (13, pp. 85ff.), indicates that he derived the basic proportions of his plan from a combination of two equilateral triangles in which he inscribed two circles (schematically indicated in Figure 58). While this diagram with its further elaborations stabilized some of the spatial relations of the ground plan, it does not depict the compositional scheme of the completed design. See also Naredi-Rainer (12, p. 211).

view, the pervasive tension of the Baroque design can be said to derive from the perceptual effort needed to integrate the three underlying figures in one complex shape.

## Misplaced Specificity

One-sided percepts of a complex structure are not the only kind of misinterpretation to cause the false impression that a work of art is nothing but a multitude of incompatible views without objective validity. I will mention another kind, which I will call the fallacy of misplaced specificity.[6] The decisive fact, neglected in this sort of misinterpretation, is that every work of art is conceived at a particular level of abstraction and its various features have to be interpreted accordingly. Below that appropriate level interpretations become arbitrary, so that contradictions between them cannot be blamed on the work. If, let us say, a nonobjective painting consists of nothing but a striped triangle, we may be dipping below what one may call its abstraction floor by describing it as a pyramid, a mountain, or a church. Although all these contradictory interpretations may accord the triangular shape, no one of them is demanded by the work, and none is therefore admissible to the exclusion of the others. A rule of economy valid for all semantic statements prescribes that nothing must be specified *praeter necessitatem*; in other words, everything must maintain the highest level of abstractness compatible with its function in the statement. Misplaced specificity of interpretation is not merely redundant; it is misleading. The appropriate level of the abstraction floor derives from the nature of the work, and to determine this level is one of the more delicate tasks of the interpreter.

Suppose we are concerned with the Rembrandt painting that goes under the name *Aristotle Contemplating a Bust of Homer* (Figure 59). The fancifully dressed philosopher is actually not looking at the bust, but his gesture indicates that he has it somehow on his mind, and to question what precisely he is thinking about seems natural enough. Although none of us is likely to consider a work of art an "illusion," we are tempted to treat it as information about a potentially or actually "real" situation, expecting it to be as complete as real situations are. Since the painted

---

[6]This section is derived from an earlier paper of mine (5). I gather that what A. N. Whitehead called "the fallacy of misplaced concreteness" (16, pp. 75ff.) refers to the opposite mistake, namely that of attributing characteristics of abstractions to more concrete instances.

*Figure 59.* Rembrandt, *Aristotle Contemplating a Bust of Homer.* 1653.
Metropolitan Museum of Art, New York.

Aristotle is a man, he must be thinking about something. Is he returning in his memory to what he wrote about Homer in his *Poetics*? Is he pondering the wisdom of blind men? Or is he comparing the glory of poets with that of philosophers? The painting does not give us the answer, which may suggest that it is hopelessly ambiguous, that it has no character of its own, and that one interpretation is as good as the next.

This erroneous conclusion derives from misplaced specificity. The level of undifferentiated abstractness at which Rembrandt kept his description must be respected. In fact, its generality raises the work above the particular episode and gives it a universal meaning that could not be more precise. Wherever the painter cares to be more specific he succeeds without difficulty. This is true, for example, for Aristotle's mood. The sadness of resignation expressed in the face is indisputable. We can therefore legitimately ask: Why was sadness put into the picture? The search for an answer sends us to the outer layers of knowledge, beyond direct visual evidence. We may recall Rembrandt's own moody personality. Or we may adopt Julius S. Held's suggestion that the notion of the melancholy sage was derived from Aristotle's own observation (*Problemata* XXX) that "all those who have become eminent in philosophy or politics or poetry or the arts are clearly melancholy" (8, p. 29). This bit of historical erudition might help us enrich the aesthetic orchestration of Rembrandt's portrait.

The benefit of the information, however, would be too dearly paid for if it persuaded us that the painting is to be understood as an illustration of Aristotle's theories on the temperament of creative people. The mere suggestion shrinks the aesthetic substance of the picture. This reinforces our conclusion that for aesthetic purposes every work of art has a particular level of abstractness, which must be respected if one is to deal with it adequately.

## Levels of Abstraction

It is, however, in the nature of abstraction that there exists a qualitative difference between responding to a work of art at too low a level of generality and at too high a level. I have shown that misplaced specificity leads to arbitrary interpretations, which create the false impression that a work of art has no objective meaning of its own. What happens in the opposite case, when the level of perception is pitched too high, that is, when the viewer gains too generic an image? Here again a multiplicity of views results, but they include rather than contradict one another, and they cannot be said to create misinterpretations. They can only be accused of using too wide a net to catch the work's meaning.

Actually, within certain limits, each level of excessive abstraction is an illuminating version of the whole. The first and most immediate impression of, say, a painting may exclude much detail and all awareness of the subject matter, if such there is. But that first impression often reveals the style of the work, its grade of originality, its balance or imbalance, and the basic configuration of forces on which its composition is built. In that first approach, the work may already be present in its essentials, although more careful scrutiny enriches the image with details carrying out the principal theme or rendering it more complex through counterthemes. Often there seems to be no limit to the depth to which one's understanding can penetrate.

Even so, the work is available at the various levels, and they all can be legitimate layers of the work's objective percept. It is as though one were looking at a flower while approaching it from some distance. The flower is already present in all its splendor while one is still fairly far away. A closer look reveals qualities of texture, shades of color, and the overlapping of delicately curved shapes, which "spell out" the image. Whether one prefers to say that the percept is a unitary image consisting of layers or to call it a composite of several images is a secondary problem that does not touch the objectivity of the complex experience.

The need for further specificity does not stop with the elements actually delivered by the retinal image. All percepts are enriched by facts of memory and knowledge, and resemblances and explanations not only add to what is seen but modify what is seen. As an illustration I will refer to one of Michelangelo's paintings on the ceiling of the Sistine Chapel; it represents God separating the earth from the waters (Figure 60). No human being with unimpaired vision will see the picture without applying

*Figure 60.* Michelangelo, *God Separating the Waters from the Earth.* Sistine Chapel, Rome. 1508. (D. Anderson photo).

his knowledge of the human figure. For argument's sake, however, we might imagine a viewer who has never seen a human body and therefore perceives the picture purely as an arrangement of abstract shapes. He might see something like an oval container floating in space and crowded with voluminous shapes, one of which breaks through the enclosure and reaches with spreading and grasping tentacles into the empty outside. At this high level of abstraction the percept may be said to carry the compositional theme of the work, a theme capable of referring symbolically in the manner of a nonfigurative painting to a wide range of biological, psychological, philosophical, and even social connotations.

At the next level of recognition, a viewer acquainted with human beings but totally ignorant of the story illustrated by Michelangelo might see a powerful old man, accompanied by children, pushing beyond the boundary established by the vehicle of his robe and reaching with his arm into the world at large. At this lower level of abstraction, the range of symbolical connotations is now more limited, but the statement may have gained in intensity by its greater concreteness. An even better-prepared viewer will apply to the picture all the associations of the Book of Genesis; and beyond intellectual erudition, only a viewer who devoutly believes in the miracle of the Creation can receive the full impact of Michelangelo's religious vision.

Further enrichment may come from knowing how this particular painting relates to the artist's work as a whole, to the arts and philosophy of Italy in the sixteenth century, and to what is known about Michelangelo's conception of his task. Complete knowledge is, of course, unattainable, and in this sense it may be said that every apprehension of a work of art remains imperfect. What matters for our present purpose is that above the appropriate level of abstraction, many perceptions yield images of a work that, although they may be only approximations, can reveal aspects of the whole that are easily overlooked in more focused observations.

## The Viewer and the Target

Let me return to the relation between the objective percept of the work of art and the ways particular viewers perceive it. To account for the outcome of any such meeting between work and viewer, one needs to know, first of all, which psychological, social, and philosophical factors determine the viewer's way of looking and what previous experiences are called up by the present one. These personal or cultural determinants of the viewer's experience are receiving much attention nowadays. They are particularly important when differences are great, e.g., when one tries to understand why different generations in different periods or cultures saw the same objects differently. In an atomized civilization like our own, the overwhelming variety of approaches leads easily to the extreme doctrine that nothing exists beyond the variety of views and that there can be no sharing of the next person's experience. Among the many statements of this doctrine, let me quote one by Carl Gustav Jung, from the conclusion to his book *Psychological Types*: "In my practice I am overwhelmed again and again by the fact that human beings are nearly incapable of understanding a point of view other than their own and to concede its validity" (10, p. 353). Jung believed that the mind is "collective" only at the very depths of the unconscious, although surely for his own successful dealing with his patients he must have been able to communicate on other levels of shared experience.

Such a defeatist view, although today more fashionable than ever, is surely one-sided. It must be complemented by other approaches. In the natural sciences, for example, the "objective" status of careful observations is generally accepted without question. Granted that even in the exact sciences the selection of research problems and an approach to solving them are influenced by the philosophy and practical needs of a particular period. But nobody questions the objective validity of Newton's laws of planetary motion on the grounds that they were nothing but subjective outgrowths of seventeenth-century England. To account for a response to a reality situation, we need to know more than the determinants in the viewer. My example from architecture will have shown that there is no way of understanding a response unless one knows what was responded to; and what was responded to is the "objective percept."

The situation may be clarified by a diagram I have used elsewhere (Figure 61), in which T stands for the target of the cognitive process and A, B, C, and D for a sampling of different respondents or groups of respondents (3, p. 6). Each response is a gestalt context constituted by T and the particular observer's intrinsic determinants. The extreme relativists to whom I referred ignore the input of T and derive an almost sadistic satisfaction from heaping ridicule on the innocents who naively believe in T's existence. At the other extreme there is the kind of investigation that studies the nature of T with the implied assumption that nothing else matters.

Radical relativism, although cherished by some philosophers, is almost entirely ignored in concrete application. In practice everybody operates on the assumption that he is dealing with objective facts, even though it often takes some doing to ascertain them. It is worth recalling here that the principal goal of Albert Einstein, the standard-bearer of relativity, was not to prove that "everything is relative," but on the contrary that the laws of nature hold absolutely in spite of the relativity introduced by individual frameworks of observation. Gerald Holton reminds us that Einstein in his early years "preferred to call his theory not 'relativity theory' but exactly the opposite: *Invariantentheorie*. It is unfortunate that this splendid, accurate term did not come into current usage, for it might well have prevented the abuse of relativity theory in many fields." Our modern Sophists might do worse than meditate on the little pocket compass that Einstein received as a boy from his father. That compass impressed him so enduringly because it retained its direction regardless of how one handled it (9, pp. 359, 362).

What is true for physics is true for psychology. Why is it indispensable to know the objective properties of the target object? An example from clinical psychology may illustrate the point. The inkblots used in the Rorschach test are deliberately selected to be as multireferential as possible because they are intended to offer the largest range for differences in response. Even so, the diagnostic interpretation of the test results remained limited as long as no one had considered which aspects were due to properties of the inkblots themselves rather than to the personal idiosyncrasies of the respondents. It was pointed out, for example, that in being symmetrical and resembling organic shapes, the standardized perceptual targets favored certain kinds of attribution and discouraged others (1, pp. 90–101).

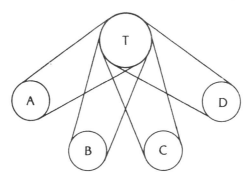

*Figure 61.*

## The Percept in Context

The need to ascertain the objective properties of the target raises, however, a delicate methodological problem. Since T is a percept, it comes into existence only by the good graces of observers; but every observer's view is beclouded by the particular conditions determining his outlook. This amounts to saying that nobody has ever seen *the* objective percept— a dilemma from which we can extricate ourselves only by extrapolation. Such a procedure is common practice, for example, in experimental psychology. For the study of elementary mechanisms, which are particularly important because the more complex responses are built upon them, the experimenter uses a random sample of observers. The differences in their responses are considered incidental to the phenomenon under observation. They are "noise," which can be eliminated by averaging the responses of a sufficiently large number of randomly chosen observers. Cleansed of accidental features, the percept emerges in its purity.

This procedure, however, is sufficient only for the study of elementary phenomena which are so basic to organic functioning that they are all but unaffected by the individual attitudes of the observers. Certainly in the arts, particular responses are of considerable interest. Suppose we are puzzled by Van Gogh's statement that he wanted the painting of his bedroom in Arles to be suggestive of rest and sleep. "Looking at the picture ought to rest the brain, or rather the imagination" (7, vol. 3, #554, p. 86). The painter's response is important, but it can be evaluated only if we know the properties his painting possesses as an objective percept. We must ask: Is the picture "really" that way?

To this end, it might be useful but would not be sufficient to record the responses to it of a number of randomly selected viewers. The pertinent parameters of their personalities cannot be expected to be randomly distributed in such a way that they would average out by summation. More nearly appropriate would be the technique of the public opinion pollsters, who select the groups of persons they interview on the basis of what they suppose to be relevant characteristics. But instead of putting together a sample of people representative of the total population to be tested, we might try to establish the inclinations of selected observers and weigh their responses accordingly. For an investigation of the Van Gogh painting, it would be essential to know whether the person interviewed is an American art historian, a French psychiatrist of 1890, a modern interior decorator, a Japanese housewife, or the painter himself. A person accustomed to the violent colors of twentieth-century Fauvism and expressionism, for example, might have a different response to Van Gogh's colors than someone nurtured on the gentle landscapes of Pissarro. By comparing and integrating the weighted results, one could arrive at the desired approximation of what the picture is in and of itself.[7]

Once this is achieved, one could attempt to understand and explain why a given person, e.g., the painter himself, responded the way he did. The procedure may seem cumbersome, but informally this is exactly what art historians do when they try to abstract from their own bias and see a given style of art with the eyes of observers belonging to other eras. They are particularly interested in discovering why certain works looked the way they did to the people of the period that generated them. But any such investigation would float in the void unless it presupposed, tacitly or explicitly, that there exists the work "as such," lurking behind all those particular readings. And where would art historians find the courage to present analyses of a work's composition if they were not convinced that there is an objectively adequate way of describing what they see?

There is no need to be alarmed by the fact that the work as such, the objective percept, will never be seen by anybody. This is a liability, if one wishes to call it that, of all gestalt contexts, that is, of all physical or psychological situations in which the nature of each component is determined by its position and role in the whole. No such component is available in isolation, but this does not prevent it from exerting in each context a predictable effect, caused by the properties of the element as such and in itself. Just as a given temperature feels warm to someone who comes in from the cold but cool to another person who just escaped from the heat, the same color will look different depending on its neighbors, and the same tone sounds different depending on its place in the melody or chord.

Our target objects T are available only in gestalt contexts and therefore cannot be perceived "as such." It might be permissible to say that the objective percept is the percept that would be generated in the nervous system if the modifying internal factors, which make for the differences, did not exist. In some cases the objectivity of percepts can be referred to indirectly by analogy to their physical equivalents. The water that feels cold or warm has a measurable temperature. But, of course, the physical stimulus is not the percept.

---

[7] For a simple version of this procedure, see the concept of "personal equation" in the studies on reaction time (17, p. 300).

This distinction is often neglected in the arts. The measured brightness or wavelength of a color is not a property of the percept but only its physical correlate, and only percepts are available to human experience. One can measure the width of a street, but when one wishes to determine why that street looks oppressively narrow to the prince but comfortably broad to the pauper, it is not physical measurements that provide the answer.

It might seem absurd to include the artist himself among the persons whose particular bias makes them see a work in a way that differs from the objective percept. Yet this is surely necessary even though the artist's own view of his work is of particular importance. An extreme case in point is offered by Balzac's painter Frenhofer, who saw a beautiful woman where his colleagues saw nothing but meaningless scribbles (6). More generally artists are quite commonly not aware of the particular style that characterizes their work—the quality that strikes the outside observer first. Surely, style is one of the principal components of the objective percept, but to the style's possessors it is one of the invariant conditions of their existence, of which they are no more aware than of the air they breathe.

The analyses of the Church of San Carlo I cited earlier will have proved that a disagreement of views is not the final stop in the search for truth. If every contender simply rested his case with a shrug of the shoulders, the most satisfying phase of the debate would be missed. Views are subject to modification, and corrections are pertinent when they point out by reference to the given facts that an error has been committed. There is no finer experience than having one's eyes opened to the revelation of something one had seen falsely or not at all. It is not simply the experience of "Now I see it differently!" but "Now I see the truth!"

Most useful in this connection is the realization that not all templates work; that is, certain ways of seeing a visual object arouse the object's resistance. One senses that one is doing violence to the facts. The object does not conform to the proposed structure or exhibits properties not allowed for by that structure. To become sensitized to the ways works of art respond to one's approach is essential to education in the arts.

## Valuable for What?

Once the objective validity of percepts is investigated, one is likely to ask further in what ways the value of objects, and particularly of works of art, can also be considered an objective property of those objects. Obviously the question can only be raised after the perceptual objectivity of the work has been ascertained because if percepts possessed no validity beyond the particular experiences of viewers or groups of viewers, any objective verification of the percepts' value would be excluded *a fortiori*.

We are facing a strange situation. In practice, everybody in the arts proceeds on the implied assumption that some works of art are objectively better than others. Titian is better than Norman Rockwell, although a popular referendum would assert the opposite. The medieval palazzo on the Piazza Venezia in Rome is more beautiful than the "wedding cake," the marble monument to King Victor Emmanuel II, even though the average tourist might opt otherwise.

Unless such objective values exist, all teaching that attempts to distinguish the good from the bad and to lead from the inferior to the better would be a farce. If, however, one asks these same practitioners of the arts in a general theoretical way whether the value of particular works rests on an objective basis, quite a few of them, under the influence of fashionable doctrines, will respond "No, of course not." Value, they will say, depends entirely on the particular taste and preferences generated by cultural and individual conditions.

Objects, situations, or actions can be said to have "value" only when they fulfill certain functions. The practical value of an automobile consists in its capacity to move passengers safely and efficiently at a certain speed. Nobody would confuse this evaluation with the different question of whether a particular car pleases a particular customer or whether it can serve some other purpose as well. Given a particular purpose and a particular tool, one can objectively inquire how well they suit each other.

The same is generally conceded for architecture, as long as its physical functions are at issue. One can objectively determine whether the elevators of an office building are large and fast enough for their purpose or whether a basement is watertight. At the same time one assumes that these inherent values are shared by the client. Indeed, they are so generally accepted that we neglect to consider the different values of persons who maintain that elevators deprive the human body of exercise or that wet basements are romantic.

When it comes to the more clearly psychological properties of buildings, the situation changes. The responses to proportion, color schemes, the degree of openness or closedness are considered matters of nothing but subjective taste. One fails to remember that each of these perceptual properties, exactly like the physical functions of tools, creates certain definable effects and therefore possesses an inherent, objective value for

320 / OBJECTIVE PERCEPTS, OBJECTIVE VALUES

the obtaining of those effects. One also fails to consider that unless these inherent values are recognized, their value for a given consumer cannot be understood.

The same is true for aesthetic excellence. There is no such thing as value in and of itself; value exists only in relation to the functions and needs that are to be fulfilled. Just as in ethics, we cannot ask in the arts whether a thing is good, but only whether it is good for this or that purpose. Aesthetic excellence may be defined by a number of categories: Is the artistic statement profound or shallow, unified or fragmented, impressive or bland, true or false, original or trite? Each of these properties fulfills certain functions, which can be defined objectively. Th extent to which they apply to particular works can also be investigated—not by exact measurement perhaps, but that does not keep the facts from having an objective existence. Once the values inherent in the work are known, their value for particular recipients can be understood.

## Dimensions of Value

It appears that we must ask, Valuable for what? before we can ask, Valuable for whom? And furthermore, in order to answer either question, we need categories for the properties that carry value. To illustrate this need, I will refer to Bruno Zevi's book on the modern language of architecture (19). Zevi complains that no serious attempts have been made to define the characteristics of modern architecture with sufficient generality. He asserts that what John Summerson in his 1964 radio lectures did for "the classical language of architecture" needs to be done for its modern counterpart. Zevi proceeds to formulate the "invariants" of modern architecture by the simple device of turning some of the properties of classicism into their opposites. Actually Summerson offered no formal list of such properties in his lectures. He maintained that a building can be called classical only if it displays the trappings of classical architecture, meaning essentially the five traditional orders. At the end of his survey he also stated that, in a most general sense, the "rational procedure" controlling and inspiring invention is a legacy of classicism to the architecture of our own time (14). Similarly, Zevi wishes his own principles to be understood as a reinterpretation of architecture in general, past as well as present.

Zevi's criteria are given more systematically than are Summerson's descriptions, from which they are extracted. He presents his readers with a set of neat propositions. For example, since symmetry dominated the classical approach, he decrees that symmetry must be avoided in the anticlassical code. Whereas in a classical building all functions are integrated in a compact cube, anticlassical buildings should be decomposed into several independent units.

I am not asking here whether Zevi's program, obtained by the simple negation of a traditional approach, offers an acceptable description of "modern" architecture or whether it can serve as a suitable manifesto for the directions in which architects should proceed in the future. I am referring to his program only as a means of pointing to some of the categories that are used for evaluation in practice.

Zevi speaks as a polemicist, not as a detached observer. Therefore he thinks in mutually exclusive alternatives: a building is either this or that. But since in each of his pairs of opposites one approach is the negation of the other, one can describe every pair of opposites as the poles of a continuous scale. It is my contention that such gliding scales constitute the dimensions on which the perceptual and aesthetic judgment of works of art, and therefore of buildings, is based.

Instead of calling buildings either symmetrical or asymmetrical, we can acknowledge that there are degrees of symmetry. A sphere has an infinite number of symmetry axes. For a cylindrical tower—a Romanesque campanile, say—the same is true only in the horizontal sections; and the ornamentation of a medieval wheel window limits the symmetry axes to the number of times the radial design is repeated. Symmetry is even more limited when it is not centric but axial. A typical façade repeats its design to the left and right of the central vertical, and this same pattern is sometimes carried through the inner space of the building. Like the body of an animal, such a building is symmetrical in relation to its sagittal plane. When it comes to asymmetry, the deviation from symmetry may be slight or total. The Palazzo Venezia in Rome is symmetrical except for the displacement of the tower and the axis through the main entrance, whereas Le Corbusier's chapel at Ronchamp avoids all symmetry in its overall design.

Symmetry/asymmetry is one of the dimensional scales by which the character or style of a building can be described. Every building can be assigned a place on such a scale. An enumeration of the building's placement or score on the various scales can serve to describe the relevant perceptual properties of the individual work of architecture.

The dimensions are not independent of one another. For example, symmetry may be said to be a special case of the scale leading from simplicity to complexity, and the same is true for other form or color relations. The simplicity/complexity scale is one of the most fundamental and comprehensive ones. It can also serve to show that the perceptual categories are not neutral, but carry connotations that directly influence evaluation. Simplicity is the state toward which all configurations of physical and psychological forces tend. This being the "natural" tendency, a preference for simplicity differs in principle from the striving for its opposite, complexity. Symmetry requires a less specific explanation than any deviation from it. Correspondingly, a taste for symmetry is based on a more elementary propensity of the mind than its opposite. When Zevi, for ideological purposes of his own, asserts that the geometrical simplicity of the classical style of architecture stands for dictatorship and coercive bureaucracy whereas the anticlassical style offers "free forms, congenial to life and the people," he overrides the primacy of simplicity in the service of a more particular inclination. On the other hand, it would also be pertinent to inquire about the needs that make a classical style resist the temptation to deviate from simplicity.

Other categories are equally weighted with relevant connotations. For example, buildings are characterized by their location on the scale of upward-directedness vs. downward-directedness. Every building contains both tendencies, but some buildings give the overall effect of rising whereas others weigh heavily upon the ground. Since we live in a gravitational field, the two directions of up and down are not symmetrical or equivalent. Being downward-directed means giving in, being inert, striving toward safety, whereas upward-directedness means overcoming, making an effort, being proud and adventurous. These general connotations affect the buildings to which they are applied.

The same is true for the degrees of weightiness and lightness, darkness and brightness, openness and closedness, low and high tension, and all the other dimensions. In each case, the physical and psychological characteristics that distinguish the two extremes of the scale are heavily imbued with human implications and therefore assign a special quality to the location on the scale at which a building is placed. Given these objective characteristics, one can begin to understand why certain buildings are valued by certain people.

A systematic investigation of the dimensional scales by which works of art are perceived would be most helpful. Here I can only enumerate a few more of them at random: homogeneity/heterogeneity, dominance of the whole/dominance of the parts, endlessness/finiteness, consonance/dissonance, hierarchy/coordination. The categories used by Heinrich Wölfflin (18) to distinguish Renaissance art from Baroque art should be included here.

## Differences in Degree

It is my contention that the ways viewers perceive and evaluate works of art differ essentially in degree; that is, they differ by the placements assigned an object on the various dimensional scales. The ease with which we can change an object's position on those scales accounts for the astonishing ability to appreciate works of very different styles—an ability particularly characteristic of art viewers in our time. Ironically, while some theoreticians expound the doctrine that the absence of common ground prevents human beings from sharing one another's percepts and values, a widespread catholicity of taste demonstrates the opposite in art galleries and museums. During a two-hour visit, the typical visitor moves from Impressionist paintings to African sculpture and from Rubens to Paul Klee—and appreciates them all. If this meant leaping constantly from one qualitative principle to another, the feat would be astonishing. The shifting of adaptation level, however, is a common biological and psychological ability. Humans and animals adapt to considerable changes in temperature or barometric pressure. They adapt to changing intensities of light and sound and to variations in perceived size when things are seen at different distances. The same is true for responses to less elementary stimuli.

The dimensions or categories of human experience are shared by all because they derive from the general conditions of our existence. If differences of style are essentially differences of degree, flexibility of response seems natural enough. What needs to be explained, rather, are the inhibitions that prevent people under various circumstances from appreciating styles deviating from the one to which they are geared. Strong personal and cultural commitments and a fear of what the qualities of an unfamiliar style may stand for interfere with flexible adaptation. Powerful factors of this kind must have been responsible for the ancient Greeks' rejection of any style but their own as barbarous. In our own time, broad strata of our population continue to accept only realistic art. Popular fashions in architecture exert a similar tyranny.

When our typical museum-goer faces the proportions of an Etruscan bronze figurine, twenty times as tall as it is wide, or those of a pudgy paleolithic "Venus," he may be momentarily startled. But the shift in degree on familiar dimensional scales demands relatively little effort. It is an act of transposition. (When differences in principle do occur, communication is indeed threatened; consider the change from representational to abstract art, from visual to "conceptual" imagery, or from diatonic to atonal music. But such qualitative differences are of secondary aesthetic importance. They act like works written in a foreign language. Once the new language is learned, the properties applying to the works are seen to lie along the familiar universal dimensions.)

To be exposed to works that reflect the human condition by dimensional placements different from those that accord with a viewer's own standards involves a stretching that may only be temporary but is one of the most cherished fruits of aesthetic perception. It makes the recipient try for experience levels at which he does not commonly operate. Such stretching is a much more productive event than a mere exchange of one experience for another.

The valued qualities offered by the various perceptual dimensions are of a strongly dynamic nature, and they are modified by the equally dynamic tendencies inherent in the needs of viewers. In architecture, for example, massive walls pierced by small windows may be seen as very low on the openness scale by a person who cherishes free intercourse between people. It is essential to remember here that visual percepts are not limited to the features physically recorded on the retinae; they are affected also by any other features that, by way of symbolic analogy, apply to them visually. In the present example the walls with the small windows will be seen as subjected from the inside to a pressure trying to burst the coercive shell. Conversely, a viewer with a strong need for protection and privacy might see the same building as a reassuringly safe refuge. Its degree of openness will look just right. In his view the walls will not be seen as resisting internal pressure, but on the contrary will contract gently inward with a hugging gesture to which the inside willingly conforms. In both instances, a personal need of the viewer translates itself into a dynamic vector, which modifies the perceived image.

A similar example comes from the impetuous attack on symmetry launched by Bruno Zevi in his aforementioned book. He sees any kind of strongly unified and regular shape as an expression of authoritarianism and bureaucracy. In his view any geometrically simple exterior is a Procrustean bed, which mutilates everything inside it into uniformity. A geometrical façade does violence to the different functions of the rooms within. Zevi also objects to uniform floor levels, which impose the same ceiling height on every space regardless of its functions. One of the dimensional scales of evaluation that apply here concerns the relation between the whole and its parts. At one extreme of the scale the whole dominates the parts; at the other extreme the independence of parts all but destroys the unifying whole. Zevi, for whom the liberation from authority is the guiding theme of anticlassical architecture, sees any regular shape as a corset squeezing the functions and the users of the building into uniformity. His particular bias makes him forget that rooms of varying shapes coerce one another every bit as badly as regularly shaped rooms. He is also unwilling to see that in the classical style subordination does not necessarily stand for despotic suppression. After all, the bed of Procrustes tortures only those it does not fit. The subordination of the parts to the whole in a building's design can be seen socially as the happy reflection of a well-functioning hierarchical organization. Viewed in this fashion, the regular shape of an architectural whole stands for the harmonious fitting of the functions of parts to an overarching unity.

## Values Lawfully Determined

I have tried to show that the values attributed to objects, situations, or actions, far from being an unassessable free-for-all, can be understood, within the limits of human knowledge, as deriving lawfully from the conditions prevailing in the target and in the recipient. This position differs from that of destructive relativism by asserting that the objective properties of the target to be perceived and evaluated are an indispensable component of any such encounter.

Suppose now we grant that the question Valuable for what? can be answered in an objective manner, quite independent of who is doing the evaluating. The fact remains, however, that the needs of any one recipient can be expected to differ from those of the next. This suggests that the answers to the further question Valuable for whom? will vary all over the place. Where does this leave the conviction to which I referred earlier, namely, that in the practice of the arts we assign an objective quality of excellence to art objects? We assert of a great work of art not only that it fulfills its functions extremely well but also that it meets our own objective needs particularly well. What could be the criterion for such an evaluation?

The answer, it seems to me, must be that we harbor ineluctably an image of what is in the best interest of mankind. It is by this general criterion that we do not hesitate to attribute more value to truth than to falsehood, to peace than to war, to life than to death, to profundity than to triteness, even though this or that individual may judge otherwise. By such standards we conclude, to the best of our wisdom, that the values exhibited in the works of great artists serve the needs of mankind so exceptionally well that we willingly confirm the exalted place society has reserved for them.

## References

1. Arnheim, Rudolf. *Toward a Psychology of Art*. Berkeley and Los Angeles: University of California Press, 1966.
2. ———. *Art and Visual Perception*. New Version. Berkeley and Los Angeles: University of California Press, 1974.
3. ———. *The Dynamics of Architectural Form*. Berkeley and Los Angeles: University of California Press, 1977.
4. ———. *The Power of the Center*. Berkeley and Los Angeles: University of California Press, 1982.
5. ———. "What Is an Aesthetic Fact?" *Studies in Art History*, vol. 2, pp. 43–51. College Park: University of Maryland, 1976.
6. Balzac, Honoré de. Le chef-d'oeuvre inconnu.
7. Gogh, Vincent van. *The Complete Letters*. Greenwich, Conn.: New York Graphic Society, 1959.
8. Held, Julius S. *Rembrandt's Aristotle and Other Rembrandt Studies*. Princeton, N.J.: Princeton University Press, 1969.
9. Holton, Gerald. *Thematic Origins of Scientific Thought*. Cambridge, Mass.: Harvard University Press, 1973.
10. Jung, Carl Gustav. *Psychologische Typen*. Zurich: Rascher, 1921. Eng.: *Psychological Types*. New York: Pantheon, 1962.
11. Kandinsky, Wassily. *Rückblick*. Baden-Baden: Klein, 1955.
12. Naredi-Rainer, Paul v. *Architektur und Harmonie*. Cologne: Dumont, 1982.
13. Steinberg, Leo. *Borromini's San Carlo alle Quattro Fontane*. New York: Garland, 1977.
14. Summerson, John. *The Classical Language of Architecture*. London: Methuen, 1964.
15. Vollard, Ambroise. *Paul Cézanne*. Paris: Crès, 1924.
16. Whitehead, A. N. *Science and the Modern World*. New York: Macmillan, 1926.
17. Woodworth, Robert S. *Experimental Psychology*. New York: Holt, 1938.
18. Wölfflin, Heinrich. *Kunstgeschichtliche Grundbegriffe*. Munich: Bruckmann, 1920. Eng.: *Principles of Art History*. New York: Holt, 1932.
19. Zevi, Bruno. *Il linguaggio moderno dell'architettura*. Turin: Einaudi, 1973. Eng.: *The Modern Language of Architecture*. Seattle: University of Washington Press, 1977.

# INDEX

Designer:    *Jim Mennick*
Compositor:  *Graphic Composition, Inc.*
Text:        *10/13 Sabon*
Display:     *Bembo*
Printer:     *Murray Printing*
Binder:      *Murray Printing*